Caro Llewellyn is
self-employment c
about the idea after a year in a secretarial job from hell. Deciding that life is too short for 40-hours' misery a week, she put her own and her son's welfare on the line and left the wage-earning world. She joined her friend Frankie Lee, in Hip Operations, a publicity and management agency for the music industry. Then she started her own desk-top publishing and design business, Ripe, and somewhere in between she also ran a ticketing agency called Hip Tix. She lives in Sydney with her six-year-old son Jack, and is trying to concentrate on one business at a time and to maintain a more manageable schedule.

Skye Rogers, 30, is a freelance illustrator and homewares designer. She is trained in graphic art and design but believes that she has learned much of what she knows about her artwork through observing life and by being armed with a keen curiosity. Skye has never really been interested in working full-time in a company; the one time she tried it she was fired! The nature of her work allows her to be self-employed, and as a consequence she has become interested in the issues associated with self-employment and the various ideas about work that are generated by our society. Skye lives in Sydney and is currently working on further publishing projects.

# Jobs for the Girls

## Women talk about running a business of their own

Caro Llewellyn and
Skye Rogers

Random House Australia Pty Ltd
20 Alfred Street, Milsons Point, NSW 2061

Sydney New York Toronto
London Auckland Johannesburg
and agencies throughout the world

First published in 1995


National Library of Australia
Cataloguing-in-Publication Data

Llewellyn, Caro, 1965– .
Jobs for the girls.
Includes index.
ISBN 0 09 183096 6.
1. Women in business–Australia–Interviews. 2. Success in business. 3. Women executives–Australia–Interviews.
I. Rogers, Skye. II. Title.

650.1082

Designed by Mark Davis, text-art, Melbourne
Typeset by Midland Typesetters, Maryborough
Printed by Griffin Paperbacks, Adelaide
Production by Vantage Graphics, Sydney

Proudly supported by Westpac

# Foreword

In reading these intimate, honest and inspiring stories of other women's businesses, I found myself challenged to examine many of my own attitudes towards my film production business and the way I run it. Often it is difficult to stand back and take stock of your goals and the manner in which you arrange your life and work. *Jobs For the Girls* encourages such an analysis.

For me, self-employment came after fourteen years working as a director and then a producer for the Australian Broadcasting Corporation. In this position I had all the security of a public servant as well as the opportunity to create and develop television which was very much from my own vision. This befitted the independent filmmaker which I had started out as and really saw myself to be. Even so, I had finally outgrown the confines of an organisation. I set off on my own with more of a sense that there were films I wanted to make which I couldn't do within that structure than a real sense of starting a business.

I worked from an office at the back of my house with a part-time assistant and two feature films in development. Within two years I had completed shooting them both and given birth to my first child. In many ways I'm very glad that my son's birth and the creation of these two films happened at the same time because it forced me to integrate my life with work in a way which typifies many women's businesses. My goal has never been to create a business entity with huge economic returns but to make films I believe in, enjoy the great gift of my husband and son and stimulating friends, and to continue to learn and develop. It would not, of course, have been possible to achieve those two years of productive work without two women directors who also believed in integration of family and friendship and life with work, a husband willing to leave his job and travel to another country to support me and, of course, excellent child care, and the extraordinarily consistent and loyal assistant I've had for the past five years.

It is my hope that 'jobs for the girls' will never be like jobs for the boys were traditionally—where an impersonal boss heads a hierarchy of return-driven employees. I'm challenged by the comments of many women in the book who carefully consider what they can give back. They recognise the need to take time out for replenishment, especially in a business which relies on one's creative judgement. I'm trying to learn to delegate or to share control and I've recently begun to experience the joy and benefit of this from a woman who talked her way into working with me so that she could learn. I don't aim at networking as a concept but I do have a number of friends (many of them women) who understand the stress and uncertainty involved when one has an idea in one's head and is in the process of accessing both the money and the right creative balance to bring it to fruition. I have the example of my long standing friend Gillian Corban, of Corban & Blair designer paper products, who is actively involved in creative business management and will sit down with me any time and help formulate a specific plan.

The challenge for me is not to take the easy way out and work long hours with that adrenalin rush which comes from achievement, but to find a balance which creates a fulfilled life as well as excellent product. It's a precarious juggle and one which many of the women in the book are attempting with integrity and imagination.

Jan Chapman

# Contents

Acknowledgments *ix*
Introduction *1*

**1. Getting Started** *8*

Jane Flett • Orda Korda *11*
Jacqui Kelly and Effy Eftimou • Bella Cosmetics *22*
Margie Budich • *Rip it Up* Magazine *28*

**2. What a Great Idea!** *38*

Emily Simpson • Full Bloom *40*
Mimi Macpherson • Maltilda Whale Watch Cruises *49*
Jill Quinlan • Jilly's Mobile Dog Watch *60*
Lisa Treen • Music Staff *69*

**3. Following a Dream** *78*

Gillian Sullivan • Opera Singer *80*
Rachael Berger • Stand-up Comedian *91*
Liz Cotter • Photographer *98*
Jodie Boffa • Fashion Designer *104*

**4. A Helping Hand** *115*

Martina Reinzner • Cabinet maker *119*
Pam George • Private Collection *130*
Katie Graham and Olivia Guntarik • Strut *140*
Trudyanne Brown • BMGART *149*

**5. Challenging Corporate Culture** *157*

Susan Chadwick • Copywriter *160*
Rebecca Cameron • Construction Contracts and Building Administration Consultant *169*
Di Jones • Real Estate Agent *179*
Flora Chiang • *Tiao* Massage Therapist *189*
Francis Trimboli • Clean With Envy *198*

**6. A Balanced Life** *205*

Cathy Scurr • Rosebud Cottage Child-Care Centre *208*
Kim O' Donnell • Namaku Bush Creations *219*
Maria Laspina and Rosalind Tasca • Rosemary's Kitchen *230*
Marieka Brugman and Sarah Stegley • Howqua Dale Gourmet Retreat *240*

**Getting Down to Business** *250*

**Further Reading** *254*

**Small Business Resource Guide** *255*

# Acknowledgments

We would like to thank all the woman whose stories you will read in this book: Rachel Berger, Jodie Boffa, Trudyanne Brown, Marieke Brugman, Margie Budich, Rebecca Cameron, Susan Chadwick, Flora Chiang, Liz Cotter, Effy Eftimiou, Jane Flett, Pam George, Katie Graham, Olivia Guntarik, Di Jones, Jacqui Kelly, Maria Laspina, Mimi Macpherson, Kim O'Donnell, Jill Quinlan, Martina Rienzner, Cathie Scurr, Emily Simpson, Sarah Stegley, Gillian Sullivan, Rosalinda Tasca, Lisa Treen, and Frances Trimboli.

There were many women to whom we spoke whose stories have not appeared here: Natalie Bowra, Helen Brinkworth, Christine Bull, Lesa Belle Furhagen, Jacqui Lane, Clare Pollard and Pauline Wright. Our sincere thanks go to you all; your stories have helped us to understand this area more fully.

We sincerely thank all the women who invited us so openly and warmly into their lives and whose words have challenged, inspired and moved us in ways we could never have imagined. It has been a privilege for us to be entrusted with these life stories and dreams. For that invitation and trust, we thank you all. For fitting us into what we know to be busy and demanding schedules, we are grateful.

We would also like to acknowledge the people with whom we discussed ideas. Self-employment is a topic close to our hearts, but it was only after talking with friends and those we interviewed, that we realised that to write about it was a big and complex task. Our thoughts and conclusions on the subject are an amalgam of many conversations, formal and informal, for which we are very grateful.

Skye would like to thank John Newton for putting her in touch with the effervescent Maria Laspina and Rosalinda Tasca. I would also like to thank the ACT Women's Advisory Centre, Anna Borzi, the Building Enterprise Centre, *Dynamic Small Business Magazine*, Employment Advisory Committee, Leichhardt Women's Health Centre, my extended family and friends who all put up with me and patiently read my essays and gave me lots of good feedback, especially Spooky, my parents, sisters Justy and Sheridan, Bronee, Frances, Aunty M, Nicky, and the ever-tail-wagging Fudgey. My thanks also go to all those women who have written inspirational books that urged me on through the printed word when I was struck with doubt.

Caro sends thanks to her son Jack who so sweetly put up with an overwrought, distracted and often grumpy mother. My parents, Kate, Becky and Richard Llewellyn, who have inspired my life and helped me in so many ways. To Frankie Lee who made my first experience of self-employment a joy and who has always been there for me. To all my family and friends who supported me through moments of doubt and exhaustion and gave without receiving very much in return. Especially to Brigid Costello and Sophia (Veuve) Beckett for calm support, confidence, babysitting and wonderful friendship. Anthony and Jennifer Wallis who ensured Jack and I had one home-cooked meal a week in the company of dear friends. Warm thanks and appreciation to Kate Westlake who transcribed my interviews so carefully and patiently and who, right through to the last week of her pregnancy, continued to put time and energy into this project.

Caro would like to give heartfelt thanks to Fiona Inglis at Curtis Brown and Skye, to Margaret Connolly, our agents, who gave us sound advice, stuck by and encouraged us right from the very beginning.

We would both like to give thanks to the wonderful support of Margaret Sullivan at Random House who believed in us and this project. And to Bernadette Foley, our editor, who helped to see this project through to fruition and whose sound advice and comments taught us a lot about the written word.

# Introduction

*'Only she who says she did not choose, is the loser in the end.'*

Adrienne Riche, *Dream of a Common Language*, 1978

Women today own approximately one third of the small businesses in Australia and are 'opening up shop' at three times the rate of our male counterparts.[1] Enterprises started by women comprise the fastest growing area within the business community,[2] so it is time we looked at this phenomenon seriously.

In the 1990s many people are questioning the hype and the ideals that go with the rhetoric of corporate organisations and there is a growing desire to find more fulfilling ways to integrate work into one's life. Corporate culture is becoming increasingly out of step with these changing values. Consequently, many people are choosing to leave the company or public service structure and start a business of their own.

As two friends discussing the problems inherent in running our own small businesses, we typify the women this book is about and for. We wanted to find out what issues are important for women in their businesses and what led them to become self-employed. While there are many small-business handbooks we decided to take a more personal approach in this collection and hear what self-employed women had to say on the subject.

Through writing this book we wanted to find out how women in their own businesses fit the pieces of their lives together successfully, and how they define the word *success*. What do they believe is a successful life? We didn't want to learn the cold facts about their economic goals but instead we wanted to gain a view of their whole lives. As we began our research we were surprised by the number of women we met who had started their own businesses, and that so many expressed a desire to be included in this book. The honesty and enthusiasm with which women spoke to us about their experiences confirmed in our minds the need for this book.

Many of the women we spoke to didn't necessarily care if their story made it into print, they just wanted to talk about it. To sit down and discuss their business with people who had similar experiences seemed a great relief.

In fact, sharing their stories led us to believe that women are keen to talk about their experiences, and perhaps through the telling it is easier to make sense of the events. For some women it was only after they had spoken about their experiences that they were able to put the pieces together for themselves in a meaningful way. And it wasn't only the interviewees who found it helpful—the interviewers were equally enlightened. Through this collection we hope to draw some conclusions and help bring together the disparate aspects of the choices and solutions available for women who want to run their own business. Self-employment is not an easy option for anyone. These stories show that it is particularly fraught for women.

We found many of the women interviewed did not dream of having their own business because of the perceived financial advantages in doing so, but for less overtly economic reasons. While walking the dog, one of us was taken by a woman who was power walking ahead, wearing a T-shirt emblazoned with the slogan 'Happiness is a positive cashflow'. It amused us both as it was reminiscent of the Eighties' obsession with the pursuit of money, and we felt that this attitude was changing. We didn't think that a 'positive cashflow' was the primary motivation for any of these women and, for the most part, women do not measure success in this way.

It is generally accepted that women are good at realising the necessity of an integrated life, one that is not rigidly compartmentalised. They may not always succeed in this but it is a goal they strive for. They have a desire to make a connection between themselves, their families and their work. These interviews help to illustrate this point as many of the women were relieved to no longer be part of a restrictive hierarchy, which seems to be a part of most corporate structures.

For some women, choosing to start their own business is a difficult decision. It almost invariably means more commitment, more time and more determination than was reserved for their former jobs. Many of these women find themselves tied to their business, working at the oddest hours, even in their dreams! The rewards brought by this diligence and commitment became apparent to those we interviewed; greater control, economic independence and a distinct sense of liberation were some of the benefits mentioned.

Women often believe that their businesses reflect who they are and that they describe their identity more fully than other jobs they might have had. Consequently, they are prepared to do their utmost for the success of their enterprise, which can involve personal and financial sacrifices.

We were particularly surprised by the amount of illness some of the women had suffered. Several found that their family commitments or unexpected challenges brought about by illness forced them to look at work alternatives.

Some women simply felt there was no alternative but to start a business of their own. Often their skills and how they wanted to use them had no place in a formal, usually male-dominated corporate structure. Maybe they were unable to obtain promotion within the workplace and so they felt it was important to change the course of their careers—the glass ceiling was becoming an oppressive reality.

Other women who had good, original ideas that could not be developed within the parameters of their existing employment, opted for the alternative of starting their own businesses. They decided they could bring their ideas to fruition better that way. Emily Simpson, for example, had a great idea which no one else was going to employ her to follow through so she did it herself.

Many felt there were new and better ways to achieve their objectives; they were willing to take a risk to see if their careers or goals could be attained in a different way. Jane Flett was so committed to achieving her aims that she sold the contents of her house in order to start up her shop! Others, like Marieke Brugman and Sarah Stegley, made deliberate lifestyle choices and established a business that would fit in around their philosophies.

The problems and distractions of caring for children during work hours was raised by many women. For some, like Rebecca Cameron, the thought of bringing their children into the workplace or having them present during meetings made them uncomfortable. Interestingly, the response from clients, and from men in particular, was often more welcoming than they had expected. These people understood that it was sometimes necessary for a working mother to bring her children along. That the women themselves had more of a problem with it than their business associates may indicate that sometimes we put the obstacles in our own way. For some women the problem is feeling split between minding the child and trying to concentrate on the task at hand.

Another issue facing self-employed women is that of isolation. However, many of the women interviewed were simply too busy to experience loneliness, while others said that a measure of isolation aided their proficiency and left them undistracted to get on with their work. Depending on the nature of their work, some women welcomed it. Kim O'Donnell found it meditative to spend hours making her jewellery and she looked forward to the time alone. Jane Flett was initially lonely when she began her shop but found, as many in retail do, that once her friends knew where she was they would come and see her there.

This touches on a situation that can actually be a problem for women working from home. Maria Laspina and Rosalinda Tasca, who run their business from their property, often lament that because they work from home people seem to think that they are not actually busy working. There may be the perception that the business is a sideline, a hobby that fills in time. Visitors dropping in can overlook the fact that these people are really in business and they have to work like everyone else does. Some who worked from home found that clearly delineating their work area from their living quarters helped others to understand that their home is also their place of work. Other women, like one of the authors, say that leasing an office makes a remarkable difference in people's perceptions of the 'seriousness' of their business.

We asked women what they thought about networking in order to establish business connections and we discovered that while many women welcomed the idea, others were somewhat averse to it. Networking, in a loose sense, helped Pam George to gain entry into her chosen field. She had great contacts with manufacturers and buyers established during her years of employment and they helped her in her own business.

Jodie Boffa refuses to do the almost obligatory networking in her field because she finds it oppressive and claims that she 'wants to have a life'. Opera singer Gillian Sullivan finds that her decision not to network but to spend her free time with her family instead, has had ramifications for her career. Women are beginning to realise the increasing possibilities brought about by networking. There are now many women's professional associations and clubs that provide women with these opportunities.

Statistics show that businesses run by women are a good prospect for banks and other financial institutions that lend money. Despite the figures however, women are still faced with discrimination when securing loans for start-up capital or further capital necessary for expansion. As some of our interviews show, many women tend to borrow from their friends and families.

Others put up their own personal equity when looking for start-up capital. The irony of this is that they usually have less personal capital available than do their male counterparts. This fact also influences the capital-intensiveness of their businesses.[3] In order to accumulate enough equity to establish their businesses, some women choose to go into partnerships with others. Amongst those who have male partners we profile only those women whose partner's involvement in the day-to-day running of the business is negligible. There are many gains to be made from having a business partner. Because women's access to financial institutions may be limited, with combined collateral they have more possibilities. Some, like the women from Strut, are in partnership because they wanted the emotional and financial support that they can give each other. In the interviews we look at the benefits and disadvantages of having a business partner.

We discovered that women tend to be more conservative than men in their business ventures. They take fewer risks, employ fewer people, are better prepared in their budgeting and planning, borrow less and subsequently grow more evenly and slowly. Many of the women in this book identified strongly with this description. Jodie Boffa said it fitted her business to a T. This anecdotal evidence is supported by Anna Borzi, who suggests in her book *The Gender Finance Gap*, that these are not necessarily beneficial attributes to have in the business community, with competition being what it is.

We have found that women in the work force generally are actively redefining previously held notions of success. They are often uncomfortable with wielding authority and establishing hierarchies. Instead they are more interested in creating an egalitarian work environment. Women are rethinking how they want to approach issues like the distribution of power, hierarchy and 'being the boss'. For example, Di Jones makes sure that there is no delineation of her employees through conventional practices like having 'big chairs' exclusively for the employer.

When it comes to starting a small business, more women are beginning to realise that they can do it, that there are many possibilities open to them. We were both enormously inspired by this optimism and our discussions with the women in this book challenged us in ways we could not have imagined. In sharing their experiences, women are helping each other to see the possibilities and opportunities that are available. The frankness and honesty with which they spoke in these interviews has moved and changed us. We feel honoured to have been trusted with their stories, many of which are extremely personal.

Having control over our economic situation is integral to our continuing success in our fight for equality. We have watched women of our mothers' generation grapple with their identities because work outside the home was not always an option. Having economic freedom through paid work has surely liberated women from their previously constricting apron strings. Starting a business has extended this feeling of liberation and control for an increasing number of women.

We invite you to make this journey of discovery with us and hope this book will stimulate some discussion.

**Notes**

1. Boddington, 'Women Mean Business', in Leonie V. Still, *Enterprising Women*, Sydney: Allen & Unwin, 1990, p.5.
2. Anna Borzi, *The Gender Finance Gap*, Sydney: Borzi Smythe, 1994.
3. Anna Borzi, *ibid.*

# Getting Started

*'Some people make things happen, some people watch things happen and some people say what happened. Be in the first category.'*

Casey Stengel

We would like to introduce you to the women who have started their own businesses against the odds, with little or nothing. These women explain some of the difficulties they faced initially and how they worked to overcome them.

For the four women interviewed in this chapter, the typical profile of a woman establishing her own small business appears to hold true. They tended to start slowly and feed all their income back into the business. They were slow to expand and preferred instead to proceed in increments, reaching business maturity cautiously. This sometimes meant that they were living on very little while they were establishing their businesses. Also, they often didn't have a particularly well-formed business plan.

A woman starting her own business will inevitably encounter gender-related problems. We spoke to many women who experienced some or all of the following difficulties: lack of management skills and training; inequalities in gaining sufficient access to finance, which led them to rely on their own finances for start-up capital; insufficient business networks and support for their career aims; and a lack of information, particularly that which is relevant to women's business issues. As we have found, information is power and without it women are disadvantaged.[1] Some of the women we interviewed however, like Jane Flett and Margie Budich, were not fazed by their lack of formal knowledge and training. They set about instinctively doing what they felt to be right. Personal confidence here seemed to be the key, perhaps combined with an indomitable spirit!

According to the publication *The Australian Small Business Guide*, the criteria for a successful business, in purely economic terms, is to have a realistic assessment of your's and the business's strengths and weaknesses; to ensure that both the intended market and the founding idea have growth potential; and that you have sufficient funds to cover shortfalls of working capital in the early days and for other lean periods. Some of the women interviewed didn't quite fit that bill, particularly the last part, as you will read. Margie Budich, for example, started with only $5!

In relation to the first point, women tend to underestimate their own strengths and this can lead to a crisis of confidence. Often when women announce their intention to go into a business of their own, people are astounded or incredulous but fortunately this usually won't stop them from proceeding.

Research has shown that there are many differences between small businesses run by women and those run by men. Although some of these differences are not particularly favourable, we would suggest that some are positive and encouraging. For example, women's small businesses survive at a better rate than men's despite the initial hesitations and limitations.[2] Their tendencies to slow growth and caution have been shown to increase the longevity of the business. Anna Borzi notes, and our interviews seem to confirm, that the work environments created by women are generally happy places, with their personal values brought into the workplace to the benefit of all.

The women we interviewed had to find their business feet while learning a variety of new skills, juggling conflicting responsibilities and coping with the enormous changes in their lives. There was often a great deal of questioning going on and sometimes an unparallelled fear. They often felt as though the ground beneath them was very shaky indeed.

Jane Flett started with nothing; no capital, no business acumen, no backers, just an idea that she wanted to commit herself to something of her own making. The women from Bella started their business on the premise of knowing what cosmetic styles and colours they liked personally and slowly built from there. What these women share is a vision and the commitment to keep that vision in sight despite the sometimes considerable setbacks. Some have said that in retrospect they would do things differently, but they would still do it. Starting from scratch is not for everyone, but sometimes the itch is too great to deny!

S.R.

**Notes**

(1) Leonie V. Still, *Enterprising Women*, Sydney: Allen & Unwin, 1990, p.34.

(2) Anna Borzi, *The Gender Finance Gap*, Sydney: Borzi Smythe Pty Ltd, 1994.

# Jane Flett

## Orda Kora

> *'The price of being able to find this "other" as a living wisdom within myself had been that I must want nothing from it, I must turn to it with complete acceptance of what is, expecting nothing, wanting to change nothing; and it was only then that I received those illuminating flashes which had been most important in shaping my life.'*
>
> Marion Milner, *An Experiment in Leisure*, 1986

Jane Flett is rather eccentric and has always been a bit of a wild card. She is a passionate woman but until fairly recently her energy was not terribly well directed. Now, at 32, she has used this passion to help her become the successful owner and manager of a retail gift shop.

Before starting her own business, Jane worked part-time as a sales assistant in a second-hand furniture store. One of her regular customers, sensing that Jane had flair, suggested that she could start up her own business buying, selling and restoring second-hand goods. This encouragement was the confidence boost Jane needed to help her launch her career; that was three years ago.

'I knew I had the nous to run my own shop, but I was worried about the financial side, all the overheads, etc. To begin with, to keep costs down I rented a section of an established antique business in Newport. It might sound odd but I simply didn't have the capital to outlay for stock, so I emptied my house and sold all my possessions! The makings of a shop were certainly all there.'

This process turned out to be a cathartic spring clean for Jane. 'I think it appealed to me to strip back my life and in retrospect I suppose my idea was to clean out and unclutter my life.'

She kept her part-time job because she was scared to

commit herself to the business full-time, with no guarantee of income or security. Keeping her job during this transitional stage helped Jane feel more comfortable about taking on a new venture. 'Surprisingly though, things went well and after three months of successful trading, I realised there was some potential in the idea.'

At this point relations were turning sour between Jane and the people with whom she shared the shop. Perhaps they were more threatened by her burgeoning success than they let on, so with her new found confidence, she decided to look for her own place to set up shop.

'I was always talking about new projects and ideas for my life but I was notoriously scattered. Every time I spoke to my father he'd ask me, "So what is it going to be this week?" The cycle was starting to get to me also. I knew that I didn't want to be "employed" as such, but I knew I had to earn money to live. My motivations were never overtly financial, it was more a personal desire to commit to something and achieve a goal.

'I have always felt as though I'd never completed anything before. For ten years I continually enrolled at teachers college. I deferred for years, finally giving it a go for a few semesters. I must always have sensed that it wasn't me. When I did prac teaching I realised it definitely wasn't. I found the staffroom stifling and knew the classroom was not where I was going to do "great things". I didn't feel it challenged me in the right way. For years I had expected that one way or another I would end up in teaching—now I realised I couldn't go through with it and I consequently felt very desperate and lost. What else was I going to do? It was question time again in my life.'

Jane's sister Annie was supportive of the idea of opening a shop as she thought Jane needed to find some direction. Jane had been in itinerant work for years and they both knew that she was missing her true potential. They thought this idea sounded more promising than any of the others and felt that it might just be what Jane was looking for.

Jane and Annie had some very grand ideas for the shop and set about scouring Sydney for a suitable position. They understood though, that reality dictated they take very careful steps. Like so many women in this book, they were initially cautious not to overcapitalise or get themselves into financial deep water. They asked around and, after looking at many possibilities, finally decided on the site they now have in Balgowlah. It was attractive because they didn't have to sign a long lease and the rent was cheap compared to some more commercial, high-traffic areas. A quiet residential area with a broad cross-section of people, who were largely middle class with a fairly high disposable income, seemed like a good place to start.

'The landlady kindly reduced the rent slightly because we were just starting out. We also negotiated a month's free rent in order for us to do up the shop. At this stage we were still very uncertain the venture would work. We were taking a gamble.

'After ceasing business in Newport, I had only $3000 savings and the banks were not interested in supporting my scheme—somewhat understandably as I had no track record to speak of. I'd had some advice about business from friends I'd made at the markets who were also starting up their own business, but nothing more than that. I really had no idea what I was getting myself in for!

'We needed to find a name and so tried to register all sorts of trading names, but couldn't get any of the ones we wanted. We remembered a saying an American friend of ours often used as a nonsense, "Orda Kora" and thought why the hell not? So we opened up shop with that rather odd name as our masthead.

'Orda Kora began as a shop trading in second-hand goods. I gave up my part-time job only two weeks after opening. I realised I needed to treat it as a proper business venture and that if I was going to do it well I really had to commit myself to it 100 per cent. It meant going against the advice I'd been getting from a lot of people who said it wasn't going to work, that it was a crazy thing to be doing. I needed to make an internal decision for myself about it. I thought if other people can do it, why can't I? It was one of the scariest things I've ever done!

'From the first day of trading the prospects were encouraging though. There was a gift store two doors down from me and I was quite happy to be trading in second-hand furniture so as not to compete with them. I realised however, that when Mother's Day came around three months after we opened we'd need to get some small gift lines in. I bought some of the things I'd sourced at the markets and sold them.

'To my surprise, we sold out. We went back through the books and realised that we'd made more money selling these small gifts than we had selling the furniture. The true nature of the shop's market was beginning to form. Obviously, there was a demand for another gift shop in the area. Because of the recession, people didn't seem to have the money to buy bigger items.

'I needed to make a decision about the shop's direction. I was renting month to month, playing it a bit safe. Most of the shop's goods were still on consignment but I realised that sooner or later I'd have to outlay some capital for some stock. I knew then that it was inevitable that the shop would become a gift shop. People were demanding something different. Every bit of money that came into the till went straight back out to buy more stock.

'Apart from exercising financial caution you can see that there was no method to my madness. I very much learned about business on my feet. Perhaps I was naive but I felt it was a matter of do or die. I had a great desire to succeed at something and had finally found an area that I wanted to succeed in.

'It was now winter and I'd painted the shop a charismatic bag-wash blue and stuck flower decals all over the windows. It was rather a statement for suburban Balgowlah!'

Wondering what to do next, how to get more diversity in the shop without spending too much, Jane set about finding suppliers. 'It was a very slow time and there were days that I was just so bored. If I hadn't had that time on my hands I might never have discovered a whole network of possibilities in regards to the buying for the shop. Up until that point I'd been scouring the markets, looking at stickers on the bottom of things I liked to find out who produced them. I sensed there had to be a better way but thought this was the way everyone sourced their goods! On one of those dull, winter days I flicked through the yellow pages and came across an entry for The Australian Giftguide.

'This was a real turning point! I asked them what they did and they told me they put out an up-to-date catalogue of all the importers and wholesalers in Australia. I couldn't believe it! The snag was that it would cost me $50, which I just didn't have. I thought long and hard about that decision. I eventually decided to bite the bullet and do it. In retrospect I realised it was the wisest business decision I'd ever made! When the catalogue arrived I was like a child in a lolly store. So this was how other shops bought their stock! I devoured it!'

Jane began by buying small quantities and was careful not to stock similar lines to the shop nearby. Nevertheless, they were not impressed. They had been there for thirty-odd years, selling mostly 'olde worlde' type gifts. 'I was careful not to tread on their toes initially, but learned that business was business and I had to do all I could to help mine survive.

'I was forced to think very carefully about every purchase, a practice which has since stood me in good stead. I had to make wise choices, and in doing this it helped me define the look of the shop. My latent decision-making skills were brought out because I wasn't able to go on impulsive decisions. I just didn't have the money to throw around. I was learning about commitment and frugality.'

Although the shop was still quite bare its character had begun to take shape and was beginning to reflect Jane's personal style. She was interested in creating a unique look and would never have paid for interior designers, even if she could have afforded them.

'There were days I wouldn't clear $100. The fact that I was just making ends meet kept me going. There were some very desperate days. People would come into the shop, amazed that we were still in business. At that stage I made a point of never falling behind in the rent, and I never took any money out of the business. There was a time I couldn't afford the luxury of $30 for dinner. Annie and I struggled on together, I couldn't have done it without her constant physical and emotional support.

'Thankfully, come Christmas of that year there was finally

some financial relief to be had. After the successful turnover of the Christmas period I went back to the bank who were now willing to give me access to an overdraft facility. That was a real turning point.'

The shop has a lovely sunny atmosphere which is quite infectious. It is a riot of colour, with vibrant kites out the front beckoning the curious inside to investigate Jane's creation. As I was interviewing her many customers piped in with little quips about the unique style of things found in the shop and the attentive service they receive. Jane seems to know most of her customers by name, and has become very much a part of the community. When I rang to check some details, Jane told me she'd been awarded a Small Business and Pride in Work(wo)manship Award from the local Rotary Club, and was obviously touched. She was part of the community and they appreciated her.

The sisters make sure that people feel at ease in the shop. Being there every day helps them to maintain the familiar atmosphere, something which Jane thinks is valuable in a small business such as hers. There is always a lovely scent wafting through the air and some quiet music playing in the background. The formula seems to work.

'Gradually people came back more and more. They began to have confidence in us and knew we were obviously going to stick around. I would listen carefully to what my customers said. I got their feedback on the stock we had, and they'd offer suggestions. Although it may sound obvious, it is very important to listen to your customers, particularly in a small retail business like this. People in this area have very particular taste and I have to be careful that my stock reflects that.

'Understanding the price-breaks has been important in terms of my buying. There are quite firm price-breaks for what people would expect or be willing to pay for certain gifts, on certain occasions. For example, someone might consider it okay to spend $X on an engagement present but only $Y on a birthday gift. You have to cater to all demands and be aware of what people are prepared to pay for things.'

Hand-made goods, like ceramic platters, are a good example of the merchandise Jane likes to have in the shop.

She stocks a few pieces that are one-offs and distinctive. Although they don't sell every day, they do move as customers buy them for special occasions. 'I can now afford to have a few choice, more expensive pieces that help the shop maintain its individual look. I choose pieces that are very colourful and alive.'

Jane is interested in going overseas and sourcing goods for import. She feels that women have an intuitive sense about buying for other women and so she would be able to choose appropriate merchandise. 'We think more laterally and can, for example, see more than one use for a vase. Men don't always think outside the box.' Importing her own goods would give Jane greater control over the style of products in the shop rather than always relying on what other people import.

Business has been getting better and better, and after two years Jane feels confident to make other decisions. She thought, for example, that she might open a second shop later this year but has decided against it in favour of having more time for herself. Jane is now looking to open the first floor of the shop as an art studio-cum-gallery. 'Annie, who is very creative and would like to pursue her painting, would use it as a space to work from. It would work for me too because if I needed her to pop downstairs to mind the shop for a while, she'd be on hand to do that. We're thinking of calling it "Orda Kora Arting Around".'

When I first met Jane she said, 'I will always keep my first shop, no matter what else happens. I like the concept of this shop being extended to include others like it, but it is essential that any others maintain the same atmosphere. I can never see this shop fitting into a shopping complex, for example. It would have to remain informal and friendly. I'd like to have another shop, perhaps in another area. Because I am not interested in money as an end in itself, I don't want to go for the big turnover stuff. I'd like to keep it manageable. It's my baby. I was always running and searching before, now I can stay still. I'm still whimsical but more committed with it because I love what I'm doing.'

Jane's philosophy has now changed somewhat. This reflects what we have found to be true of many of the women we talked to who tended to have shifting views on their work, their business and their lives.

'Opening another shop would just mean taking on too much, in a personal sense. After this experience I know how draining it is and how consumed by it you become. Since I first spoke to you I have stepped back from it a bit and realise that the shop isn't all that I am. I want to be able to do other things too.'

Once a certain level of personal satisfaction and financial achievement have been attained, women like Jane have begun to look at other areas in their lives that perhaps had been neglected while they single-mindedly pursued their business interests.

'At first this shop was my baby, it had to be. It wouldn't have survived if I didn't give 150 per cent. It takes so much out of you to get the business to a certain point of financial success, that for a while it's all you think about. You live and breathe it. There comes a point though, where you just have to let go. Continuing to give every inch of yourself after that can become an obsession and it doesn't necessarily help the business either. I became very insular and being a free spirit, I didn't like the narrowness I saw growing in myself. I have learned that life is far bigger than the four walls of a shop. Getting rid of my pride that I'm not the only one on this earth who can run a shop has been very liberating!

'A lot of people seem to dream of owning their own shop and often tell me so. They can see me here with local customers and lots of lovely things around me, I'm sure they think it's a lot easier than it actually is. I think they see the end result, this happy, attractive shop, and romanticise it. Especially in the beginning it is a lot of hard work, long hours and total commitment, with uncertain financial rewards. It's funny but I never had that dream so many people seem to have of owning a little shop somewhere. It hardly occurred to me until it happened.

'If the shop had come along five years ago and I had been required to make this commitment, I surely would have gone broke. I just wasn't ready for it. I have a sense of contentment now and have ironically, by spending so much time in the shop, become more detached from material possessions.'

Surrounded by beautiful things all day Jane is quite happy to go home to a more spartan environment. 'Sometimes I find being confined to the shop nine hours a day, six days a week very exhausting. It used to be seven days. I find it is a continual giving of myself and my energies. The workload doesn't allow much time out for me. Having time away from work has always been vital for my sense of self. At the end of the day I'm quite happy to go home and be away from everything and everyone!

'Part of any business is risk taking. The risks I take now though, are much more informed than when I first started the business. I'm not particularly interested in playing it safe. With two years knowledge and experience behind me, I think I make sound business decisions now. I never want to feel that I have to make a particular decision because there is no other option. I'd like to always have the foresight and confidence to say "this'll be a winner"; to come from a position of strength rather than weakness.'

Jane came to her shop with little business experience but this is not what she would recommend for anyone else. In retrospect she feels she could have been much better prepared. However, her innate sense of style and her artistic talents combined with plain hard work have certainly contributed to the shop's success. In the future she'd like to take some marketing and small business courses to consolidate what she has learned through hands-on experience in these last few years.

On a personal level, Jane feels that the confidence she has gained since opening the shop is immutable. It has now freed her to explore other things. She attends university at night to keep up her interests in politics and history and she has learned to ride a motorbike, a long harboured desire. Jane likened the fears she experienced in taking up bike riding to those of starting her business. It was an interesting analogy and I asked her to explain it.

'I realise they are both things that I had a terrible fear about before I did them. Riding a bike is like running a business, because you start with no knowledge and you slowly conquer your fears. The adrenaline it creates and the need for perseverance on a bike are all similar to the qualities associated with business. Taking up bike riding was combatting another fear within me. It was another very personal challenge for me.'

Jane still has some fears, but now that she has conquered many of them she has the courage to see what else can be accepted or challenged within herself. 'When I opened the shop I was so frightened about not having the comforts of life that financial security could give me. I now have come to realise that it is better to actually lose than live in abject fear of losing. I had to go through losing material things that I'd clung onto, so that I could grow through that and accept that my belongings were not me and that I could survive without them. I think there is a tendency among people to say to themselves that if they're successful then that's the beginning and end of the story. For me, achieving a level of financial success was just part of the process of finding out what a satisfying life is, or can be.

'So many women seem so overly concerned with security in a relationship in terms of marriage and material possessions. I think you can easily lose the ability to take risks and be spontaneous if you are too caught up with acquiring these material things.'

Jane shares the view held by many self-employed women that success is not only measured by the financial rewards it can bring. Mind you, it was only when she achieved some financial security that she was able to relax a little.

After working long hours, seven days a week, buying stock on the day when she was not in the shop and doing all her own bookkeeping, Jane had little energy for the rest of her life. She sensed that perhaps she was becoming obsessive about her business and that her personal life was suffering. However, she couldn't really afford to drop back from the business even though she knew there was a life beyond the demands of the shop.

To overcome this she now employs Annie to help in the shop more often and makes sure that she has a day off for herself. For her own happiness she needed to get a better perspective on her whole life, not just part of it. After two years working solidly, she thought she deserved some time for herself, and finds she can finally afford to have that time. Jane believes that 'happiness is wholeness'.

S.R.

# Jacqui Kelly and Effy Eftimiou

## Bella Cosmetics

Until two years ago, the idea of an alternative cosmetic company was just about unthinkable. The big companies seemed to have the market completely sewn up. Their huge budgets and global marketing network left little room for any new names to emerge. Then Poppy King came into the picture with a range of products and a marketing campaign that immediately set her apart from the mainstream. Poppy King became a tall poppy herself. She opened what was a tightly closed door and now we have the chance to cheer on a team of young women who are also giving the big cosmetic companies a run for their money.

Bella is a new cosmetic company with two young women, Jacqui Kelly and Effy Eftimiou, at its helm. With an emphasis on promoting their products, not themselves, the women behind this new and innovative company have remained in the background, while their products and logo are stepping to the fore.

To date, Bella has not taken out any paid advertising, but if you sit with a group of women and start talking brands and shades, the name Bella will come up as a new favourite. Bella has relied on editorial in magazines and word of mouth to promote its products. The Bella logo is a 1950s style typographical design that is simple and very suave. Remo, one of Sydney's smartest stores, have used the logo on a range of their T-shirts. So without any capital outlay, the Bella word is spreading.

Jacqui is a red lipstick girl. Before she and Effy started Bella she had over one hundred shades of red lippie crammed in her bathroom cabinet. With so many shades in your own personal collection, you'd think you would be 100 per cent happy with at least one. But Jacqui found that if the colour was right, then the texture would be wrong or vice versa.

She wanted to develop the perfect red in both colour and texture and so with her friend Effy, she did.

Both Jacqui and Effy had previous experiences in small business. Jacqui had run a 1950s second-hand furniture and memorabilia shop, and Effy had run a nightclub. Their individual experiences in business had many of their friends wondering just why they were looking at going into partnership together and venturing back into the world of self-employment.

'The break up of the shop was like the break up of a marriage,' says Jacqui. 'Women seem to be more personal about their businesses. Men say, "Okay it's over" and walk away, but when a partnership between two women breaks up, it's far more emotional. For twelve months I was working in the shop as well as holding down a part-time job to subsidise the business. I was working six days a week, bringing up a four year old and getting absolutely nothing back.

'I'd never work those kind of hours again. When you're in that position, everybody suffers. You're stressed, which you pass on to your children and down the line it goes from there. After working six days a week for a year, everything was strained. My relationship with my child and my husband suffered. I will never do that again. I was jeopardising my family which is my life, and my relationship which is my support.

'Obviously you have to do what you can and as much as you can but as long as you're making money and you're happy then it's okay. Happiness is the most important thing to me.

'Our friends were and continue to be very supportive,' says Jacqui. 'They asked us if we were sure we knew what we were doing. A lot of people were surprised I was willing to take the risk of going into another partnership again so soon after I had come out of one that had burned me so badly. You have to trust your gut feeling though and I think women are really good at that. They know when something is right.'

The women donate a percentage of sales from one of their products to an organisation that gives direct financial support to HIV positive women. Bella recently sponsored The Second Positive Women's Conference and Jacqui and

Effy believe very strongly that they want to contribute to a section of the women's community in need of financial assistance. This is their way of acknowledging the support they have had from women in the establishment of their business. Their philosophy is about giving, not just taking. 'Women have supported us and this is a way for us to give back to them. There is a lot of community support for HIV kids and men, but positive women are often forgotten about.'

Many companies today use sponsorship as a vehicle for product promotion. Sponsorship in many arenas is just a marketing ploy, usually only going out to those who will use and promote the product or service in a highly visible way. Jacqui and Effy's choice of sponsorship shows that their decision is based on ethics and beliefs rather than personal gain.

The two women have known each other for five years, so they both knew about, and supported each other through, their previous business experiences. They have a real understanding of each other's priorities and they both learned from their previous business experiences that when work came first, life always came second.

'My daughter goes to school now and my five-month-old baby goes to creche. I work from home one day a week and we both only work four days a week,' says Jacqui.

Six months after this first interview, I spoke to the women again and found that they were now both working full-time at Bella. The business had expanded and grown into new areas.

'We are certainly learning a lot of new skills. We have different talents,' explained Effy, and they agree this has been a plus for the business. 'We are about to go overseas on a buying trip and this time we are going together. Jacqui sometimes gets carried away and wants to buy hundreds of new mascaras that tint, curl, lengthen and perm your eyelashes and I find myself pulling her back, keeping in mind just what and how much we can really afford. But then sometimes I'm too cautious when really we could go all out. Somewhere in between here we strike a really good balance.'

When I went to interview Jacqui and Effy, I was surprised by their office. I entered through an alleyway in the Sydney suburb of Paddington, climbed a set of narrow blue stairs and walked into an office the size of a match box. They were on the phone so they waved me in and sat me down in amongst boxes of lipsticks, which I had to hold myself back from rummaging through. It may have been small but it exuded the warmth and positive attitude of these two women.

Working in such a tight space would very quickly bring any tensions to the surface. 'It would be easy to get at each other's throats in here,' they agree. 'We are both really good at being very honest with each other about any problems we're having. It's really important that we talk about what's annoying us but we do it in a way that's not an attack.'

Effy explains that she has just put the baby seat into the bathroom to make more room and that I'm very privileged to have been let in here. 'Mostly,' she says, 'we don't meet people here. We have a lot of meetings in cafes or other people's offices. If people do have to come here we tell them these are our temporary offices—"our real office is being painted right now". That's our standard line.

'We both know that it is really important to keep our overheads right down. For a long time we worked from home. We took it in turns. For a while we worked from my house which put pressure on my flatmates,' says Effy.

'Then when we worked from my place,' explains Jacqui. 'I had my six year old getting into the lippies which were piled up in our living room. Working from home is not a great long-term plan. It means you end up working constantly because the phone never stops. But it is a great place to start and crucial in terms of keeping your overheads down. So many businesses go broke in the first six months because they overextend themselves in the beginning. They lease cars, equipment, big offices and before they know it they are in over their heads. We wanted to keep things as simple as possible and so far it has worked, but people always assume that women running their own businesses do it from home so having this office now is great. By December we plan to be out of here and into bigger premises where we're not sitting amongst our stock and our lives.'

Six months later, they have just made that move and they are now in what they call 'proper offices'. In fact a lot has shifted for Bella, not only their premises. When I first met Effy and Jacqui they had a range of nine lipsticks. Now there are 21 shades of Bella lipsticks and with names like Sex Kitten, Glamour Puss and Bomb Shell they're sure to make a splash. They now have an agent, a marketing company and beauty distributor, not to mention their first employee. Effy says that they find walking the fine line between friend and employer, establishing the boundaries and rules, a little precarious.

Jacqui and Effy started the business with an idea to make a product reminiscent of the 1950s' colours and textures. They put in an equal amount of money to begin with and while they didn't say exactly how much, they did say it wasn't very much. A friend of Effy's in the United States who runs a cosmetic company had been encouraging Effy to use her to help start something up.

'Most companies won't let you do anything under a run of 5000 per colour and my friend said we could do small runs to begin with which was the only way we could possibly do it. Jacqui was in the States at the time so she went to the factory and brought home a load of samples and then we sat down and chose the colours we wanted to make.' I'm intrigued just how they do that and they tell me they get their colours from all sorts of places. Sometimes it is as simple as seeing a fabric in a shade they like and that becomes the inspiration for a new lipstick.

'We made very small orders and that's how we began. We didn't have a big investor saying, "Here's $20,000, go off, it doesn't matter if you lose it, I'll just write it off on my tax". We had to be extremely careful every step of the way.'

'We always knew it would work. I was worried about being seen to be copying Poppy but we really believe there's room for competition. Nobody questions how many jeans labels there are. When we first started people would always say, "Oh, you mean like Poppy", but that happens less and less now. Opportunities come to everyone but they don't always come very often so when one does come your way, you have to do it. If you've got a good idea and there's a market for it and you think you will enjoy it, then you should just go for it,' says Jacqui.

They explain that the first few months were pretty tight and hectic. Their understanding that this was what they wanted to do and the certainty that there was a market for their idea inspired them even through the hardest times. 'We're the classic example of a business starting with a small capital investment,' says Jacqui. 'I already had a child and then I had another baby at Christmas time, which is slap bang in the middle of our busiest time. Four weeks after the birth I had him here in the office with us. Effy still had her other job, so she was juggling Bella with that job by coming in here before work, during her lunch break and nights too. It was hell for three weeks, but we got through it.

'My grandfather used to say that the worst thing that could possibly happen to you is that you could go to gaol. If you lose all your money, you're not going to die. No one has ever been shot because they tried something,' says Jacqui. 'Mistakes aren't failures and failure isn't failure. Everyone makes mistakes whether they've been in business 50 years or five days. Everything works out, it's just step by step. You can't force things. Anything that has happened you can't change or rectify, so there's no point losing sleep over it and you can't predict what's going to happen in the future so you can't worry about that either. All you can do is do what you do now and do it the best you possibly can. You just have to keep in your mind what you're doing now and a strong sense of belief in yourself. I think too many of us live in the future which you have no control over and lose sight of the now, which is in your grasp.'

'I feel like we are just touching the surface of what Bella could be in Australia. I feel like chapter one has closed and chapter two has begun. This is a scarier one because there's more at stake now. Chapter two has all new responsibilities, but we're still inspired,' says Effy.

And we, the public, look forward to chapters three, four . . .

C.L.

# Margie Budich

## *Rip It Up* Magazine

I've talked to Margie on the telephone many times. Confirming her deadlines for clients, convincing her to run editorial stories on bands I was publicising, or couriering artwork to her. From a distance, I watched her magazine grow in reputation and size. However until this interview, although our paths had often crossed, we had never met. I have always worked from Sydney and her magazine, *Rip It Up*, is based in Adelaide.

I was running late for our appointment, cursing that I didn't have a mobile, sure that she would say she was now too busy to see me. *Rip It Up* was on a deadline and I knew that day was a particularly chaotic one for any publisher. Designers want to add that last touch to their layout, journalists want to amend their articles and the printing press is waiting. I have watched it many times and know it takes nerves of steel to get through a deadline without major trauma or incident.

Margie greeted me warmly and calmly. There was no problem. She told her staff she was in a meeting, put the phone on 'do not disturb' and offered me a cup of tea.

Margie is in her early thirties—younger than the impression I had of her from our phone conversations and her position in the publishing industry. Considering her standing in the business, I was surprised to find out that this was not a venture she embarked upon with relevant training or a certificate under her arm.

'I studied physical education for four years. Rather a strange background for an editor, I admit. After my training I took a year off and did door-to-door sales. I needed to earn money, and didn't have any other skills. I wasn't trained to do anything. I had worked in a gym while I was studying but I was sick of teaching aerobics. I always intended that year off to be just that. I never imagined not going back to physical education.'

It was during this time that Margie met her partner both professionally and until recently, personally, Ian Fraser. 'We were selling cards that gave people two-for-one admittance into clubs and other gimmicks to get people along to the hotels. Through that I got to know a lot of the nightclub owners and management. Selling the cards and talking to the owners we thought there was a market for a music magazine. Initially though, we tested the water with a newsletter for club members.'

The newsletter confirmed their observation. Adelaide was crying out for a magazine that catered to the youth market. The glossy magazine, *Network*, which Margie and Ian began, focused on music and the live music industry.

'We published *Network* for four years. Two years into that we started *Rip It Up* which was, and still is, a weekly tabloid format newspaper which features stories on music and lifestyle issues. We only had $5 in the bank, so I went out door-to-door selling advertising for the magazine. I had to get all the advertising money upfront so we would be able to afford to pay for the printing of the first edition. Now, ten years later, we turn over a million dollars a year.

'I was young and silly. I was outgoing and wasn't scared of anything. So I just went out there, signed people up to advertise, took their money, went home, made their ads and produced the magazine. There's no way I could do it now though. I wouldn't have the gall. It was so exciting and I knew it was a really good idea. There were so many people positive about the idea that I guess I got wrapped up in it all. If I had stopped to think about what I was doing and hadn't been so young and naive, I wouldn't have done it at all.

'We were so positive about it and I was so full on about it, I don't think anyone dared tell us we were mad. I think we just bowled people over. We had a pretty in-your-face attitude—"We're going to do this magazine, just you watch us".'

Anyone watching the production of that first edition in Margie's lounge room, could have been excused for thinking they were in a scene from 'Play School'. The whole magazine was put together using a typewriter, scissors and glue. A far cry from Margie's production now, which is fully computerised. She also has a team of layout artists responsible for the overall look of the magazine.

'We didn't know what we were doing but we were both quite creative. Somehow it worked,' she says, pausing before adding a heartfelt, 'Thank God.'

Margie bought Ian out of the partnership two years after their personal relationship broke up.

'It was just too difficult to work together after the relationship finished. One of us had to go and Ian was a bit sick of Adelaide and was wanting to move into managing nightclubs anyway, so I bought him out. Towards the end we were clashing all the way down the line because he had very different ideas about the magazine, so it was a relief when he left.'

Many women complain they have trouble financing their businesses through traditional financial institutions and statistics show that they are more likely to get capital from family or friends. One factor in this might be the women's lack of confidence to approach banks, but that alone cannot explain why they seek other avenues. Despite the lending institutions' statements to the contrary, women are discriminated against when applying for loans for a range of reasons. While this bias may not be obvious in banks' written lending policies it is certainly evident in the unspoken rules and regulations governing many bank managers' appraisals of women's financial standing and abilities.

'No bank would finance me to buy Ian out even though the business was obviously viable and making a profit. I can't be sure that it was because I am a woman, but it certainly appeared that way to me. I am sure if it had been Ian approaching them to buy me out, they would have agreed to the loan. In the end, I had to borrow the money from my partner.'

Usually magazine editors are required to do a substantial amount of their own writing and oversee material written by the other journalists. Margie tells me that as editor, she has very little to do with the actual writing of the copy that appears in each week's edition of *Rip It Up*.

'You could count the articles I've written for the magazine on both hands. With my background it's quite unusual to be in this position. I have never studied journalism and the truth is I don't have the time to write.

'My job has always been to ensure the magazine makes money. With a free magazine like *Rip It Up*, it's important that editorial, advertising and promotion all fit together. You have to make sure that the things you are writing about are also bringing in advertising money. In a way, I am more a publisher than an editor, although I do ultimately make the decision about what appears and what doesn't.

'Because so much of my time is spent overseeing the whole production and ensuring money is always coming in, I have trained journalists to handle the editorial. I do find that intimidating sometimes. Here I am, an editor with no formal training, while my deputies have studied for at least five years and know everything there is to know about writing. It's strange to be sitting on top, knowing very little formally, yet making all the decisions.

'I used to be intimidated at music award nights and special industry events. Usually all the different editors from all the magazines have to sit together and inevitably someone would ask me about where I studied. They'd look a bit taken aback when I said, "The Institute of Sport and not as a sports writer". Now the magazine is successful enough it doesn't bother me at all because I like to show people that it is possible without the formal training, but that wasn't the case when I first started—I used to be terrified someone would pop that inevitable small-talk question.'

In ten years Margie has come a long way. She has bought out her business partner and is now the sole owner of *Rip It Up* and a sister fashion publication she has recently started, called *Attitude*. The business has outgrown several premises and is pushing the parameters of its present offices in Adelaide's Angas Street, which are not small. We discuss the issues involved in looking after the many people she employs and how she has coped with the burgeoning responsibilities of staff.

'It's scary being in charge of so many people. I'm a friendly person and I like to get on well with people. When you are in charge of so many, it's hard to be a friend and a boss at the same time. It's difficult to come down hard on them when they're being silly buggers and not doing the right thing. I get advice from people who've done it before because I have been really thrown in the deep end. I've never been a boss before nor had any training to be one, and all of a sudden it is actually what I have become and I still find it hard to come to terms with. I'm meant to know how to do it, but really I just wing it. It's a hard path to hoe but you learn on your feet.'

From here it's possible for Margie to look back on the early years of struggle with some detachment and perspective. When running your own business you experience a gamut of problems. It is interesting to find out how different people react to these problems and which particular pressures they find hardest to deal with. Margie has already told me she finds the employer–employee relationship a strain, but pinpoints financial difficulties as the most personally demanding.

'Thankfully now I don't have the financial problems I did in the early days, because they weighed very heavily on me. When you are bouncing cheques, unable to pay your staff and wondering where your next meal is coming from, it's very difficult. The fact I'm still here is testament to the fact that we always managed to pull through in the end, but it was touch and go sometimes.'

I can relate to Margie's position. I too find the financial strain the hardest to bear in running my own business. We agree that the stress is not to do with wondering how you yourself will eat, but how your financial difficulties affect others. Women seem to take on this burden more personally than men. Sometimes I consciously say to myself, 'Think more like a man. Creditors expect this, it is part of business, just let it go for a moment'.

'I used to go to my mother's farm and say, "I'm never going back, I can't handle it anymore". It's important to take a break when you're feeling like that. I used to go out with friends and cry on their shoulders, which was a big relief,' Margie said.

No matter how bad it got, Margie always came back, attacked the problems face on, chased the money she was owed and dealt with the realities.

'I was determined not to let the magazine go under. *Rip It Up* became such a big part of my life, to let it go and face bankruptcy was unthinkable.'

Financial crisis points are not exclusive to women in business. Those moments, when you stare down the barrel of financial ruin, at some point face almost everyone with their own business. Nevertheless, many people manage to pull themselves out of the mire and refuse to give in.

'It's a strange drive that brings you back to the front line. You know it's your career and that you have to make it work. You have no choice, it's something you started and something you have to follow through. I knew it was a great idea. So many people had patted me on the back and told me how much they liked the magazine so I knew if I could just hold on, it would be okay. It also came down to the question of what else would I do? I love this.'

Margie has obviously considered this question carefully and it seems very clear in her mind what the issues are and how the pros and cons of either choice weigh up. When I first spoke to Margie about this book, I told her that I hoped it would help other women recognise that problems they may be having in their own business were not necessarily exclusive to them. Many small businesses go through similar experiences and reach the same crisis points. I can tell Margie has this in mind when she talks about this time in her career and that she wants to impart these tips to other women.

'Once you get away from it and talk to other people, which is where friends are invaluable, you get back on track. It can make you see that it's not all that bad. An outsider's point of view is important. You can't just keep it all bottled up inside. Other people who aren't involved can look at your situation with a bit more perspective. Often it's only when you're in crisis that people tell you how much they admire what you have done and achieved. Just because they're telling you that, when you're drowning them in tears of despair, doesn't mean they're not sincere, and you should always keep that in mind. The options you have are to throw it away and start something else, or to work for someone else 38 hours a week and take home a wage each fortnight. Neither of those options weighed up for me. I knew it could work. It was just a matter of jumping the hurdles one at a time.'

Now Margie reaps the benefits of her decision to persevere through the hard times; she has just had her first holiday of more than a week since the magazine began. While she is better off than when she first started with just $5 in the bank, the rewards for her are so much more than financial.

'The magazine has created a whole new world for me. It's become a way of life. The nature of my business means that I have met a lot of wonderful people. I am invited to most opening nights and get tickets to concerts, which is a huge bonus to the work. When people find out I run *Rip It Up* magazine they say, "Wow, that must be so cool". I'm really thankful to have had the opportunities I have. I get flown all over the place to launches and special events. There's no doubt about it, it's a very groovy business to have.'

One would expect now Margie's business is expanding and evolving, that those around her would be happy for her. Instead, I discover that the tall poppy syndrome is not a myth, it is alive and well, challenging many women who are successful in their business ventures. I wonder if this prejudice is stronger against those who are doing well in their own business than those succeeding within an organisation. The success of the self-employed is entirely their own doing. Does that make the success all the more potent and therefore a larger target to those wielding the poppy-slashing scythe?

'Everyone reacts differently. One day you are not sure where your next meal is coming from and another you are seen to be living the high life. There were a lot of people who were very close to me in the early days, but now the magazine is very successful, many of them have drifted away. They don't like the success, they are jealous of it and they have gone by the wayside.

'Another force at work with friends is your very limited time. It is a very understandable reason why people drift away. Friends get hurt when you can't spend as much time with them as you used to. When I have time off I really enjoy spending it with my boyfriend. We have a shack up the river and like to spend most weekends there. So if you put my working week and going away on weekends together, it doesn't leave a lot of time for anyone else. It's a shame but it's a reality that can't really be avoided.

'I used to start work at eight in the morning and rarely finished before 6 or 7 pm. Even now I often don't get out of here till eight or nine. A lot of my work goes on outside the office when I have to attend launches or shows. Even though you can hardly call going to the opening night of *Jesus Christ Superstar* a chore, it is still work. If you count those hours, I often don't finish work until after midnight.'

The ABC's radio station Triple J has been playing in the background throughout the interview. Suddenly the DJ, Angela Catterns, many young women's idol, announces that she has to cut her shift short because her daughter has just fallen down the stairs. Even though Margie doesn't have children, she looks at me knowingly and says, 'It's amazing, isn't it, how much women are expected to fit into their lives.' That, of course, leads me to my next question . . .

'I would like to have kids before I'm 35. When to have children is a real dilemma for women. You toss questions like this up in your mind. When you're younger, either you go overseas and spend a few years running around being a bum, you go to university, you start your own business or you have a family. Trying to fit it all in is just about impossible.

'I'd have to keep working if I had kids now. Whether or not you can take a substantial amount of time off to have kids depends largely on who you have working for you and how good they are. My deputies are all still quite new, so if I fell pregnant now I'm not sure what I'd do, but I know I'll always have my foot in here. Eventually I'd like to go away on a yacht for a couple of years, but that's a long-term goal.

'One day I'd like to publish a national glossy magazine and just how I'd fit my aspiration to travel as well as fulfil that dream, I'm not quite sure. Right now though, I'm happy to continue building and broadening the scope of *Rip It Up*. I'm trying to make it more of a general entertainment magazine, one that reflects the many aspects of youth culture. I think we have to reflect the concerns of young people and all the issues that affect and interest them in the paper. Our emphasis for so long on music alone was simply a physical restraint. Articles about broader social issues and the concerns of young people take longer to research and in the past, we just didn't have the resources to write them.'

I wonder whether Margie's interest in broadening the scope of *Rip It Up* is linked to her age and changing interests. We discuss this idea and while she agrees that this is probably a factor, it is actually more of a conscious marketing decision. 'I think the readers are interested in so much more than just music and that it's important for us to give them a package that reflects all their interests. So we now have articles on health and fitness as well as pieces on trends like body piercing alongside the music editorial.

'I have just started a quarterly fashion publication called *Attitude*. I'm really enjoying it because I love fashion and it's a change from the music industry. I'm a bit burned out and a bit old for the music industry. I leave the music to the younger writers, who are all in their early twenties and really into the scene. I think I'm at the point where I'm too old for it and I don't appreciate it in the same way I used to. I still love things like the Big Day Out [a national series of concerts where many local and international bands perform on the same day at the same venue—usually a large stadium] but now I don't know all the new bands and am not up to date on the scene. It's important that the journalists writing the articles are really submerged in the industry otherwise we wouldn't be able to keep the interests of the kids.

'So I'm beginning to hand more responsibility to the deputies. I want them to make more decisions because they do know more about the industry. I want to continue working on the fashion magazine and slowly put more of my energies there. It's a quarterly which means I can spend a lot of time on each issue which I enjoy after the hectic schedule we have making sure *Rip It Up* comes out each week.'

Like many other women in this book, Margie believes, 'the sense of achievement is the most rewarding aspect of what I do. In terms of hours, running your own business is much worse than working for an employer. I have to stay until the job is done. I know I work longer hours than friends of mine who are employed, but the freedom is great. It's my business and I can do with it what I like.'

It is strange that this sense of freedom is so high on many women's list of the benefits of owning their business. In some ways Margie, and anyone who has made the decision to become self-employed, is more encumbered than others in the workforce. Her sense of freedom seems to fly in the face of her statement about the hours she works and the fact she has only had one major holiday in ten years. Perhaps then, it is the freedom to make choices rather than the ability to come and go at will. Margie agrees and defines her idea in terms of decision making. If work is 60 to 70 per cent of our lives, then the decisions about how we want to run our business must flow through to our sense of control and freedom in our personal lives.

'The most wonderful feeling for me is watching my staff grow. Many people who start here have no idea about the work but in time their confidence grows and they leave here, qualified and confident enough to get work on big glossies based in Sydney. It's great to be able to give people jobs. Seeing how excited they get when you tell them they're employed is a real buzz. Their parents come in and say, "Wow, you've got a full time job, let's go celebrate". I love it when that happens.

'I think I'll always want to keep *Rip It Up* for that sense alone. There are so few openings for young journalists or even kids who love music and want to write about it or get involved in some way. It's a wonderful feeling to be able to give someone the opportunity they have been looking for and at the same time to be in control of something so personally rewarding.'

C.L.

# What a Great Idea!

'Why didn't I think of that', or 'why wasn't that thought of before', are remarks often made about new ventures or ideas. It is sometimes the simplest ideas that become truly great.

Because the doors of the scientific world have for many years been firmly shut behind men, the area of great inventions has largely been a male domain. Although there have been outstanding examples of women who have managed to squeeze through the crack, and invent things we now take for granted, Marie Curie being the most notable, it is still an arena from which we are generally excluded.

So, it is not surprising that the stories that follow are about women who have had great ideas and made them a reality, rather than those who have invented absolutely new products. You can stop a woman from doing lots of things, but not thinking, dreaming and adapting. These are women who have seen a niche in a market and who have gone for it. And their businesses are diverse indeed: from whale watching to underwear for pregnant women! While there is seemingly a huge diversity in the services or products these women provide, there is also a commonality between them.

The cord that binds their experience starts from the recognition of the need for their product or service, then wraps around researching their market, investigating their competitors, on to a lot of hard work and devotion, and ends in the creation of something many of us will use, buy or take part in.

The great idea is a strange business. Lisa Treen's idea of starting an employment agency in the middle of a recession seems a little incongruous, but it worked. Sometimes the fact that it hasn't been done before throws doubt into the mind of the person who thinks of it. Surely, if it hasn't been done before, there must be a reason why, goes the thought pattern. But these are ideas that did not go away.

Mimi Macpherson decided to start her whale-watching business even though she didn't have a permit, a boat or capital. What she did have was the eye to see that there was a niche in the market if only she could get her foot in the door and prise it open. She achieved this after a year of hard work, a lot of determination and fast talking to convince someone to let her use their boat.

Emily Simpson found her niche through pregnancy. Unlike the others, she never dreamed of starting a business herself and tried to pass her idea onto a manufacturer. She was not able to coax them into producing the product, but as she was trying, she utterly convinced herself of the viability of her idea.

Jill Quinlan, on the other hand, saw a product with limited and specific use and decided to expand it. She was looking for a change in her life and thought there was a market for her idea. That hunch proved to be correct.

The great idea starts innocently enough. Before it entered your mind, you were a well-rounded human being who could speak on many subjects. Now you are a woman with a mission, your every thought honed on the hows, whys, whens and wheres of your new venture. You have no time for small talk and your friends are worried about you, you don't come over any more—you're dog washing or in a meeting, or testing a new fabric or watching whales. You are a changed person, or perhaps as these stories show, you are becoming the person you always wanted to be.

While the 'great idea' is a risky business, one you may never really be sure will work until it does, it is sometimes a gamble well worth taking.

C.L.

# Emily Simpson

## Full Bloom

When I was pregnant with my son Jack, I had two upsetting experiences. I tried to buy a pair of stockings from a department store for a very special outing and was shown to the maternity pantihose section. They were brown and not exactly what I had in mind. I was 22 years old. When I said I was in fact looking for stockings and black ones no less, the woman refused to serve me. I went into shock and then proceeded to cry. The second incident, shortly after, was trying to buy a maternity bra. I searched high and low in vain for something that didn't make me look like my grandmother, no disrespect to her intended.

These were traumatic experiences for me and made me wonder if society's views on pregnant women had moved an inch since the Dark Ages. Emily Simpson had similar experiences but thankfully she decided to do something about it. She was so outraged that she now manufactures a range of maternity underwear that is comfortable, attractive and black!

'The idea came from being pregnant. I used to climb in the cupboard to stop my husband seeing me in my maternity underwear. He'd walk in the room and I'd yell "Stop!" I was quite happy for him to see me naked but not in those things. I mean, please, may we meet the woman with that skin tone. No, because she's an alien, she does not exist.'

Emily has thought a lot about society's views on pregnancy, and her reasons for doing what she has are embedded in a political philosophy.

'There's something unpredictable and dangerous about a pregnant woman. One minute you are a sophisticated woman, the next, you are a baby doll. The more I thought about the issues, the more I realised it wasn't just a frivolous idea. We have baby showers and we're given rattles and bottles which is great because it means in that first year you don't actually have to buy very much, but there is nothing that celebrates the event and the mother.

'The baby shower was traditionally a time when the women got together in a passing on of wisdom ceremony. The elder women would talk about what to expect, what it all meant, what was expected of the mother. She was given the rules and a guide.

'The Japanese do have a small ritual for the mother in the fifth month of pregancy. The grandparents and parents prepare a traditional meal for the mother and father-to-be and present the mother with a special *omi* sash. It's not a big deal, but it is some recognition of the mother and it's a nice ritual before the journey really hits the big time.

'Pregnancy and childbirth are issues feminism hasn't addressed. None of the feminist writers ever say anything about pregnancy. They, like the rest of society, just pretend it doesn't happen. It's been put in the too-hard basket. How can you be pregnant and a feminist at the same time? How can you be pregnant and strong?

'It is as though we are ashamed of it. We try to slot it invisibly into our lives. We have these huge tummies but we all try to ignore it. It's a monumental event and the most important time in most women's lives and we go around trying to pretend it doesn't exist. There's nothing more life changing than becoming a mother. It's the most fundamental rite of passage to womanhood. I don't think there's anything that compares to the experience of growing and then expelling that child. It's wild. The wildest time of your life. Yet there are no rituals, religious or otherwise that celebrate it, which I think is incredibly sad. Surely it deserves some acknowledgment.'

We are drinking tea at Emily's home, which at the moment is also her office, and I am nodding furiously, wishing that I had met Emily when I was pregnant.

She says she got a bee in her bonnet about the whole issue and the more she talked to other women, the more convinced she became that this was an important issue and one that women would back financially. To confirm her thoughts she interviewed over 400 women. Many said they were wearing their husband's Y-fronts or size 44 Cotton Tails and nearly all of them were feeling horrible because of their awful underwear. The most surprising finding in her research was the amount of underwear women bought during their pregnancy. I wondered just how much you could sell to one women for nine months of her life (assuming she is having one child) and whether this would be enough to sustain a business.

'They all bought much more than I thought. On average, pregnant women buy four bras and six pairs of underpants. The research went against the traditional wisdom that women don't want to spend money on themselves when they are pregnant. It's true that you do want to save money to prepare for the baby but at the same time, do you want to spend six months in uncomfortable underwear? Would a man spend six months in underwear that didn't fit him properly? I call it the "burnt chop theory". Women always give themselves the burnt chop and everyone else the nicely cooked ones. You can't drink, can't smoke and it's hard to find anything glamorous to wear and you don't want to spend $500 on a dress that will only fit you for six months. But underwear is different because it is something you can reasonably afford.

'I went to see the general manager of one of the large underwear manufacturers who liked the idea. He showed my rather flimsy proposal to the head designer who had four children and she also thought it was a great idea. My sketches were pathetic, I can hardly draw, but they both agreed it was a great idea.'

The company held onto Emily's proposal for three months and eventually they told her they would not be able to do it.

'They said it would be a multimillion dollar exercise and they weren't in the financial position to do it at that time. He offered me his advice if ever I decided to do the idea on my own, and told me to get back to him in a year.'

Emily's marriage was breaking up at this point and she forgot about the whole idea until she did a personal development course.

'I'd just left my husband and I was in a mess. A friend suggested I do the course and it was just what I needed. A dumping ground for emotional baggage. I took a year out of my life to get over a five-year marriage that had been like living in a blender. I gave myself time to re-balance my life, get back on the rails and work out where I was going and what I was going to do.'

It wasn't until the last weekend of the course that Emily actually made up her mind what she wanted to do and be.

'We had to do a vision for our lives. To decide what it was you really wanted to do on this earth if there were no restraints. I imagined there was a magic fairy who would take away any barriers stopping me from doing what I wanted to do, and being what I wanted to represent. If nobody said "no", what would I want to do? I found it an incredibly hard task to complete. To think, okay, what do I represent, what do I think, what do I feel, what do I believe and what do I want to do? It's like being given a huge menu—what do you choose? It took twelve hours for me to work it out. Eventually I told the group I had been thinking about a range of underwear for pregnant women called Full Bloom.'

The course was a very important experience for Emily. It helped her to decide what she wanted to do, but it was also where she found the encouragement and practical help to actually bring it all together. When Emily spoke about her dream, Barbara, one of the other women in the course who had been a designer and couturier, said she would make her a prototype for her proposal.

'Barbara is wonderful. She's a designer, she's 50, she's a grandmother, she runs 10 kilometres a day and she's an inspiration to me. When the prototype was made, we found a model from a prenatal clinic. A photographer I also met on the course took some beautiful pictures, so this second proposal was a far cry from my first. It looked professional.

'I was feeling a lot more confident about myself by this stage and I rang the general manager of that company again. I told him I wanted to discuss the idea again, that I was thinking about doing it on my own. He said, "Don't, don't do it! It'll break your back, your heart and your bank account and it'll probably kill you". He told me I'd be gobbled up by the big guys in a minute and that the rag trade was just too difficult.'

It was just as well Emily was feeling self-confident before contacting anyone about her idea again. With a reception like this it is a wonder she ever took it any further.

While Emily made us a cup of tea, we talked generally about the ways of women in business. What we didn't discuss then, but is screamingly obvious to me now as she speaks about her own work, is the way women casually make statements about quite remarkable achievements. It goes something like this, 'Well then I just . . . '

So then Emily just . . . set up a meeting with the marketing manager of one of the largest lingerie manufacturers in the country, had her lawyer draft a confidentiality agreement to ensure her idea was protected, and sent it to the manager asking that it be signed and returned to her before they met. Unfortunately he didn't quite get around to that and after many reminder calls she finally phoned her original contact, the general manager, to ask what was happening. He was unaware that the marketing manager hadn't returned Emily's confidentiality agreement, and said he would get on to it straightaway. This was two hours before the meeting was scheduled to start. By the time Emily received her agreement by courier an hour later, she had made up her mind to manufacture the products herself. She had announced in her personal development course that it was what she wanted to do, so she took this moment as a sign.

Her decision shows that a lot can happen in a short space of time. Within an hour a new partnership had been born and a new product was seeing the light of day. Emily and her friend Barbara, now business partner as well, were on their way. Quite what to do next, once the decision had been made, had them stumped but only for a moment.

'We knew we needed someone who could set up systems for us. I know nothing about computers and Barbara, well she's creative—all right side of the brain. We were introduced to Tracy, who had been working as a treasurer for a publishing firm and was looking to do something she felt more passionate about. She set up all the systems for the business.

'It was hard to find an existing factory interested in going into production for us. We could only afford to do small runs of each range to begin with and most of the factories weren't interested in doing that. They were looking for volume. Barbara drew up all the patterns in a week and finally we found a factory who agreed to a run of 500 of each item.'

The manufacturer they found was a woman who, Emily says, 'took a great leap of faith'. As the number of businesses run by women increases, so too does the amount of support and networking available to newcomers.

'As all the garments were designed from scratch, on a pregnant women—not from traditional lingerie blocks—we needed a lot of teamwork to get it right. The manufacturing process was fascinating to watch. I expected it all to be done by computer but our factory cuts and finishes the garments by hand. The wonderful thing is that the results are more precise than any computer could achieve.

'Everyone at the factory was wonderful, full of support and tips. The head seamstress gave us a lot of advice about stitching and materials, all of which saved an awful lot of time and money. They took a risk with us but now they are growing as we expand, so it has worked well for everyone. Still though, with all this help it took six months for us to set up.'

Through a friend, Emily managed to compile a list of all maternity and lingerie stores in the country. Quite how she got her hands on such a list, she is unable to disclose but it proved an invaluable asset. From a mailout to 400 stores, they established 96 outlets for their range. Full Bloom garments first appeared in stores on 1 August 1994.

When I met with Emily she had just begun to sell to David Jones. The second time we spoke she was about to crack Myers, and I'm sure by the time this book is published she will be on her way to other milestones.

'I'd never done any selling before, but I managed to convince nearly all the stores I approached directly, to accept the range. I don't know any of the tricks or sales jargon which actually seemed to work in my favour. Someone said to me, "It's so nice to talk to someone who obviously isn't a professional sales rep". I just told people what I was doing and why, and they agreed it was a great idea and the quality of our products helped to sell them.'

When Emily was twenty she attended NIDA (National

Institute of Dramatic Art) where she learned to be an actor. She appeared in programs like 'GP', 'The Flying Doctors' and many other Australian productions.

'I was good at acting but I didn't like being an actor. I was never very comfortable saying I was an actor, because people look at you and replace the word "actor" with "bimbo". I'm no bimbo and I didn't like the games you're expected to play as an actor.'

Announcing to people she meets now that she runs her own business does sit well with her. How to describe herself after the initial 'I'm in business' is still a little perplexing for her though.

'It's really nice to say what I am now and to have people say, "Wow, that's great". I'm not boxed as a type now because I'm an unknown quantity.

'I joined a gym the other day and on the registration form they asked for your profession. I had to think long and hard about it. What am I? Am I a manufacturer, retailer, underwear mogul . . . we're not used to standing up and saying "I am". We always qualify it with "well . . . I'm just . . . I have this little . . . I'm sort of . . . "'

Emily is now trying to entice people into the stores to buy the range. Here I can see that her background in acting has been a great asset to her.

'We went on "Midday" with Derryn Hinch which was a lot of fun and a huge publicity coup. People are still ringing us after seeing the segment to find out our stockists. I've never done PR, I just ring up and blab at people. I rang the producer of Derryn's show and told them I could bring in two models both of whom were eight and a half months pregnant. They agreed, and we appeared within a week.'

For someone with no promotional experience, her 'I just' seems to have worked very well for Emily. I first read about Full Bloom in *HQ* magazine and shortly after this interview Emily rang to say that they were appearing the next day on another daytime talk program. Through my own experience as a publicist I know exactly how difficult it is to 'crack' a midday program.

Emily is in the process of contacting every obstetrician in the country, all 1200 of them. She's sending them each a brochure with a leaflet outlining where their nearest stockists are, and hopes that they will put them in their waiting rooms. Two rules of business: never leave a stone unturned and think laterally.

'I didn't have any skills related to what I am doing but I think anyone can learn anything. If you have something and you believe in it, you somehow work out how to do what's necessary for it, or find someone who can, if you can't.

'Every week there is a new wall of fire to go through. Often the others are busy or I'm the only one here and I have to tackle some seriously scary stuff. Ringing lace merchants and screaming at them when something goes wrong is not something I enjoy, but it's necessary sometimes and so I just do it.'

I asked her how she came back from walking through those walls of fire each day to her four-year-old son, Jackson.

'Jackson's at kindy three days a week and day care two days. I'm better at closing the office door at five now and giving him some quality time. We have had our ups and downs though and it would be easy to work 24 hours a day. Just before we got the range out it was enormously stressful and I was working ridiculous hours. We've almost got our systems running smoothly now, which has eased the pressure and made life less chaotic.'

When Emily says she closes the office door, she is speaking metaphorically. Jackson played a big part in her decision to keep the office at home. This allows her to work the necessary hours, while at the same time gives her the flexibility to tailor her time with him. For many women with children, that is the biggest bonus for this set up. Emily admits though, that there are drawbacks.

'People ring up to chat and I get short with them and then they get offended. A friend rang up the other day and Barbara answered the phone saying, "Full Bloom, Barbara speaking". When I got on the phone my friend said to me, "Hey, this is serious isn't it?" I work very hard and people are beginning to change their perspective of me as an actor. I'm having to re-train my friends. I'm a business woman now and I don't have a lot of time to play any more, and some of them don't like it very much. I keep finding myself on the phone late at night making apology calls. I haven't worked out the etiquette of it all yet.'

With her son and her business, Emily doesn't have a lot of time left for a personal or social life—a sacrifice she is more than willing to make for the moment. Often our sense of self is dependent on those around us and we need their attention to convince us of our place in the world, hence we need the continual company of others. Since Full Bloom, Emily has found that this has changed, she is now content to work and to have time with Jackson.

'When I was acting I was always dependent on someone else—usually the whim of a director or producer. Now I'm in control of my life, and my self-esteem and sense of self doesn't hang on someone else's opinion of me. Even if we fail, I don't think it will affect my self-esteem because at least I know I have tried. I know I have gone way out on a limb but I'd rather live on the edge of a cliff and have a view than live down on a rock in safety and never see anything.

'The learning experience alone makes it worth it. You are always discovering hidden talents and achieving things you never dreamed you'd be able to do. I can "do" meetings with bigwigs now and I think it's hysterical. It's just like acting!'

Emily has created a life that is set to challenge not only other people's understanding of her, but her own view of herself. She has embarked on a journey that will be forever changing and expanding, requiring her to re-evaluate her strengths and weaknesses and to channel those into the myriad of demands and roles her business requires of her. Full Bloom has taken her from sales rep, to manufacturer, to PR person, eventually to underwear mogul and then perhaps on to something quite different again!

C.L.

# Mimi Macpherson

## Matilda Whale Watch Cruises

Hervey Bay in Queensland is part of the National Marine Park along the Queensland coast. It covers an area of approximately 50 by 50 kilometres and is known to be the site of some of the best whale watching in the world. Humpback whales are drawn to the calm waters and converge there at the same time every year. Now, Hervey Bay is becoming a world model for the management of responsible and environmentally-friendly whale watching. The area is renowned not only for its natural beauty but also for the strict guidelines that are maintained there for the observation of whales, by both commercial and private vessels.

Mimi Macpherson is in the fortunate position of having been at the helm of one of the most successful whale-watching businesses in the area for four years now. Arriving at her flat in Sydney's southern suburbs I realise how important being near water is to her. Mimi always feels most at home when she is on or by the water and so when she is in Sydney, she lives right on the beachfront, surrounded by the sea. Posters of majestic and playful whales adorn the walls of her flat, evidence of her love for these creatures. Animals have played a big part in Mimi's life and she enjoys being in a business that allows her some close encounters with them. Choosing a career centred on the sea and its creatures seemed to be a natural extension of her personal interests.

'I had been managing my dad's commercial charter boat in Sydney for a while when I realised just how much I loved it and being close to the water. I started working on my father's boat in the capacity of helping out his partner, Bob. I worked my way up from doing menial jobs like cleaning toilets and putting the sails up etc., to then taking on more responsibility such as organising the printing of the company's T-shirts and co-ordinating the food. I really begged him to let me work on the boat. I was so bored with the work I had been doing in a jeans shop and felt I wasn't really getting anywhere. It was soon obvious to me that this was what I wanted to do. I had no desire to spend the rest of my life managing someone else's jeans store. It was great experience because it was so varied; I had to be able to turn my hand to almost anything. Unbeknownst to me it taught me a lot that was going to be very useful in my future career.'

Mimi started Matilda Whale Watch Expeditions at the age of 23.

'I'd started working as a general-hand on a boat up in Hervey Bay, Queensland, in 1989. At the time there were lots of little fishing boats operating as whale-watch cruises. There were really only a couple of boats set up in a vaguely professional manner. I worked on that boat for two years and then it was sold.

'In 1990 the Department of Environment and Heritage [DEH] issued nineteen permits for managers or owners to run environmentally sensitive whale-watching cruises in the Hervey Bay area. The Department felt the need to put some kind of limit on the numbers and types of boats running these businesses, or else it could have gotten out of hand. Those permits pretty much covered everyone who was currently operating, and no more besides. Most of them were fairly small-time, local operators, except the company I was working for.

'Unfortunately for them, but as it turned out, fortunately for me, they went into liquidation. I thought I might try and hang onto the permit and use it myself. It interested me to continue on with working in this area because I really didn't want to do anything else. I thought I could have a go at it. I had some understanding of how it all worked. If the operators I worked for could do it, then, I thought, why can't I?'

'It wasn't quite as easy as it sounds though. I had to fight to get the use of that permit, going through the courts for almost a year. I would never have had a chance to keep the permit if the boat I'd worked on had violated any of the rules of conduct issued by the DEH.

'Getting the permit was only the beginning. Everyone thought I was out of my head! Applying for a permit to operate a whale-watching cruise without even having a boat or any capital to do it with, must've seemed like a ridiculous idea to most people! I suppose, in a way, it was.

'In 1991, after avidly looking everywhere for a boat, I found one, and a skipper to go with it. Because the whale-watching season is only three months of the year, from July to September, I had limited time to get my act together before the next season started. One of the strictures of having the permit is that you must actually operate. You can't just have the permit and not use it. There's too many people who want to use them to do that . . . I panicked.

'Time was running out, so I went about rather frantically trying to set it all up—I got brochures printed, found somewhere to live and organised my transport up there. Being new to it all, what I didn't realise was that the boat hadn't been surveyed. In order to operate each season, every boat has to be inspected by the MSB [Maritime Services Board] for its worthiness as a commercial charter boat. The skipper had assured me that his boat was "fine". Well, it wasn't! His survey had lapsed some time before. I was really annoyed; there seemed to be so many things I hadn't thought of that were getting in the way.

'The inspections are necessarily quite strict. For example, you have to have proper fire-fighting equipment and if you're going to be serving food you have to have things like a Halon Firefighting System in the galley. You also have to obtain a liquor licence if you want to serve drinks. It has to be very safe and very professional, or else any old person with a boat could set up a business and probably end up harming the whales.

'I went to the National Parks and Wildlife Service and asked them if they would grant me an exemption from operating that year. I was very concerned that I'd lose the permit. Thankfully, they allowed me to keep the permit.

'I was quite despondent that I couldn't get the business up and running straightaway. I continued to work part-time in the jeans store in Sydney to make some money . . . but I knew I was going to need a lot more than I could earn at the store. I managed to put the brakes on the printing of the brochures, luckily. I'd bought life jackets and things like that. The whole thing was starting to cost me a lot of money!

'It was time to find a reliable boat. After asking around

everywhere I rang a friend, Tim Lloyd, who owned a charter boat in Sydney. I asked him if he wanted to start up a business with me. I told him I wanted to use his boat for the season of whale watching in Hervey Bay. I'd prepared some figures from the last boat I'd managed and explained how it all worked. To my delight and surprise, he said yes. I was so pleased that he put that trust in me. I knew I wasn't going to let him down, but still it wasn't a small thing for him to do. In fact it was quite a risk, really . . . having someone take over your boat for several months, taking it out of its usual, safe, harbour home and going on a long journey up north. It wasn't something you'd just let someone do every day. He had to cancel all cruises in Sydney to allow me to do it. I also employed his staff and took them away with me. I realised it was a big ask. Part of the deal was that it had to work out financially for him too, of course.'

This level of trust and confidence in women who had good ideas, but perhaps insufficient capital or equipment, emerged in a number of the interviews we conducted. It seems that these ideas are being taken seriously and people now realise that the financial support they offer business women is not a benevolent handout but very often a good investment. I commented on this to Mimi and she was encouraged to hear that other women were also able to instil confidence in their supporters. She seemed to think that there was now a willingness to extend this kind of assistance, financial or otherwise, to women with good ideas and ability.

'I think women who are willing to "have a go" are much more widely accepted now than ever before. I think if the opportunities aren't obvious, then women will find them or make them happen for themselves. I think once you show you have the ability then people will be prepared to get behind you; they think it's great to see a successful young woman out there doing her own thing.

'Once I'd secured the boat I had to get some money together, so I borrowed $30,000 to see me through. From the beginning I have trusted my gut instinct. On the business side of things I have been pretty much a one-woman show. I have made all my own mistakes, although I have learnt from others' mistakes too. I can't blame anyone but myself if things go wrong, and, conversely I can congratulate myself when things go well.

'My father was a great role model for me and my brother and sister. He started up Miranda Hi-Fi, which was a great success for many years. He has recently sold it to Brashs . . . My mother works in marketing and is also career-minded. She does the PR for Westfield.

'I worked for my father at one of the hi-fi stores some years ago and it taught me a lot about the nature of selling and the "ins and outs" of retail. I've always liked selling, I think I have a natural flair for it. I understand the necessity of good customer service, which is equally important for the industry I am in now.

'I have to sell my product, my business, to lots of small agents everywhere who in turn have to sell it to the public. You really need to be able to get along with all kinds of people and get them enthusiastic by being that way yourself. That part has always come naturally to me, although it can become draining at times.'

As far as a personal life is concerned, Mimi says, 'It is very difficult to maintain strong friendships let alone a relationship doing what I'm doing. I manage to see quite a bit of my family. Considering it is full of siblings, step-siblings, parents and step-parents, we actually manage to see a lot of each other. The family is important and we all make an effort to get together.'

Mimi is very proud of the cruise business and says, 'The boat itself is one of the biggest and of course I think, the best, operating in Hervey Bay. *Matilda* is a 25-metre power-driven catamaran. She has three decks, all of which allow wonderful views of the water. On the top deck you have uninterrupted 360 degree views. But the service is just as important—the food and the commentary. That is why we are successful.

'It's funny sometimes when people ask us, "Where is the best place to view the whales?" . . . How are we to know where they are going to come up? We're not mind-readers! We can be almost certain that they are going to turn up, but we don't exactly know which part of the boat they'll swim up to. Anyway, that would take the fun out of it.'

I wondered whether the whales would just turn up as if on demand like that but apparently they do. Mimi has had almost complete success in finding the whales on her daily jaunts into the bay, although sometimes they do have to give in to inclement weather.

'As much as I can, I try not to cancel a trip. People come from far and wide for this unique experience and often they've booked it over a year ahead. I hate to disappoint them. On average I lose about four days out of each season due to bad weather. During this period I'm usually up at 5 am. The captain and I go through the weather charts and forecasts and if it looks like it's going to be a rough day, we'll cancel. Some people really suffer from seasickness and you have to take that into account as well.'

Mimi has been amazed at the variety of things she's had to absorb through running her own business.

'I've learned a lot about weather patterns and the effects of winds in certain directions etc. It's been a great education! I never get bored because there's always such variety in the things I have to do. For example, I am my own ad agency; I don't have a manager or art director or anyone to guide me on what publicity or marketing to do. I love working out where all the pictures should go on a brochure, writing all the advertising copy and laying out the ad. It's great to work out successfully what best catches people's eye.

'If something is there to be done I just can't say no. I have learned all about the preparation and service of good food on the boat, about ecology, about humpback whales, merchandising, hiring and firing staff (something I still don't particularly like doing), delegating and communication. I've had to do a lot of publicity—radio and TV, for example. The list of what I've learned in the last few years goes on and on! I never would have thought I could learn so much.'

Mimi is a good example of the women who find that they have to turn their hand to many different tasks in order to keep up with the demands of the business. She sees this as a personal challenge and welcomes it.

On the cruises she is careful not only to observe the rules and guidelines that have been set for the observation of whales, but has taken this one step further and invites researchers on board.

'It is important to keep researching what is happening with the whales, how they are breeding etc. On board we have a commentary by some scientists/researchers from the Pacific Whale Foundation who are based in Maui. It helps educate people about the whales and gives them more empathy with them.'

This arrangement suits both parties well, as the public learn a little about what they are seeing and the Whale Foundation is able to carry out some research.

'Each day there are one or two researchers on my boat doing a talk, and a few in a separate "rubber duckie" out in the water doing some field work. Part of the price of each ticket goes to whale research, and people seem to be quite generous about donations once they've seen the whales. It's great because it allows research to be done that otherwise might be too expensive for the Foundation to do. It is a good exchange.

'The fact that we offer this scientific insight into the whales is one of the reasons why we are so successful. Also, the boat is one of the biggest. It has a carrying capacity of 265 people but we average about 150 passengers on a daily basis. *Matilda* is one of the most stable and comfortable boats operating in the area, and has a very good reputation. When you think of spending all day on a boat, you really want to be sure you'll be comfortable. People come for the whole day's experience—they want to eat good food and be looked after in pleasant surroundings, as well as see the whales. We average about four hours a day of sighting the whales. The whole experience is fun. We go at a nice, cruisy speed in case we see some whale activity on the way in or out.

'I employ twelve staff, some of whom I hire locally for the season. I like to do that if I can. I have a stable crew of four deckhands who I bring with me from Sydney each year and put up in accommodation in Hervey Bay. It is important that my staff are professional. Most of the staff I employ are thrilled to be working in the area of eco-tourism, and their enthusiasm is contagious. They understand that we have a reputation to maintain and they honour that.'

The enthusiasm for whale watching has certainly brought some other business to the immediate area, mostly in hospitality. It is a fairly small community, thriving on the sugarcane industry and tourism.

'It is, like any business, good to keep one step ahead of the competition. With nineteen competitors it is important to keep coming up with fresh ideas. First and foremost, though, I am proud of our professionalism. We won the Tourism Award for the Fraser region last year, which was a thrill. This year I'd like to go for the Queensland award.

'I have also been asked to be part of the steering committee for a worldwide whale-watching conference to be held in Hervey Bay in July 1995. I will be there to represent the whale-watching industry. It will involve the coming together of some government bodies, researchers, other whale-watch operators and myself on behalf of the commercial whale-watching industry, so that we can all learn more about how to conduct our business in the most environmentally-sensitive manner.

'It is good that the DEH has put out formal guidelines and rules for both the private and commercial charter vessels operating on Hervey Bay. Rules such as not motoring within 100 metres of the whales and being careful not to interfere with them in any way, are essential for the whales' continued happiness and health. I have witnessed a whale actually being run over by a boat. People can get really silly and irresponsible. Thankfully, the people we get on the cruise are aware of the eco-conciousness we need to maintain and so they don't do anything silly. My captain is very important in this aspect—he has to be aware of where the whales may be and what they might do. He has to think ahead a bit and has got to know their patterns of behaviour. If we violate any of the rules we could incur very large fines and/or lose our permit.

'When I began, the common knowledge was that the whales came on almost the same date every year; 15 August. Every year I've been in business so far I've put the cruises back a week, with successful whale sightings. I call these "whale searches" and I reduce the price, because you are not guaranteed to see them at this time. People seem to like the thrill though of perhaps spotting the first whale of the season. So, we start going out from 20 July until about the middle of October.'

Mimi is a shrewd and enthusiastic business woman. She feels her plans for the business are only limited by her imagination. 'I love the thought of expanding the business, building it and making it even better. Occasionally I have stepped over the line and over-committed myself financially, but it's been good to learn from my own mistakes. From time to time I might ask my father for some financial advice. I have a good accountant now whom I couldn't do without. I tend to work off the budget from the previous year in planning my next year's program.

'I think I am ambitious in my business because I have had to work so hard for it. I floundered there for a while when I left school and I was fighting having to work in a jeans store for the rest of my life. I knew I really didn't want that. I always wanted my own business. I think that if you haven't "failed" in some way, then maybe you don't have the strong will to succeed. In our family it was always assumed that we'd "Do Something" with our lives. Watching my sister Elle succeed as she has, has been a real inspiration for me. She's proud of what I've done and I'm proud of her. It did affect me seeing her do so well—it spurred me on to want to achieve things too. It didn't daunt me. My younger brother, Ben, has also done something a bit out of the ordinary. He is running his own very successful multimedia business at the age of 23. I think we're all self-starters.'

'Sometimes I think I don't give myself enough credit for what I've achieved. I often have to remind myself that for me it's like a dream come true. I can never stop thinking about work; there's this constant adrenalin going on, like it's some kind of race. I think you end up going into something that you know about. I went into something that I was familiar with from my previous working experience: selling and service. Sales is serving people—that was always my rule. I was fortunate enough to be able to couple this with my strong attraction to the sea and my love of animals.'

Mimi's role as a boss has never sat particularly well with her. She feels that being a woman in business can be beneficial and that denying your femininity is not necessary when you are in a position of authority.

'I don't think of myself as being a particularly good boss but I do think I'm seen as being a "nice person". For me it's more important to be well liked than to wield a big stick of authority over people. I think if you want to be taken seriously it's important to show that you work hard, that you're in touch with the grass roots of the business, that you have commitment. I think that if I "came on all strong" and wanted to use my authority in that way, I'd be seen as a bitch, or silly. I think women can use their feminine powers in a better way than that. It's good that I've had personal experience working in just about every area of the boat, it helps me understand what problems my staff might come up against. I think they respect me for that.'

Hard work, perseverance and a willingness to learn are the keys to success, according to Mimi. 'I find that the more work you put in, the better business gets for you and the more you get back from it. There's no magic formula, it's a lot of hard work and commitment. I don't think you necessarily have to know a lot about tourism to do what I've done. I just learn as I go. I didn't have any formal hospitality qualifications. I've always believed in hard work. I think this attitude has been a good model for the people working around me; they see that I try hard and work hard, that I don't take what I've got for granted.

'My business is booming now. Every year that we've been in business our profits have increased by a third again. Not bad in a recession! Our net profits have increased far in excess of the industry's expectations. I'm always looking at fine-tuning or improving the product. You can't afford to be idle. It's a challenge I enjoy to always stay one step ahead of the competition.

'If you want to take it seriously, organising a tourist business means attending travel shows, both public and for the tourist trade. I spend a lot of my time back in Sydney organising the merchandising and promotion of my product in these ways. The wholesalers will come around at a trade show and check out your product thoroughly. They insist on professionalism, which means having professional slides, a dependable booking service, a facility to tailor the rates for groups etc. They want to be sure that you're not some "flash-in-the-pan" operation.

'On the marketing front, this year I hope to produce a whale-watch calendar. I'm also getting into the area of direct marketing and developing a catalogue with merchandise related to tourism areas.'

Mimi has great ambitions for the future. She has been asked to be a host on the pay TV documentary channel, Quest. 'I present the wildlife programs and hope to make my own documentaries soon, perhaps one about the forthcoming whale conference that I'm involved in.'

Her energy and entrepreneurial skills have been responsible for the success of the venture so far and she is in no way slowing down. She realises that to make the business even better she will soon have to invest in her own charter boat.

'Everyone is urging me to do it, so I suppose I'll just have to bite the bullet! The business will tick over as much or as little as I like. How much I'm prepared to put in is directly related to how much I get out. I see people getting comfortable and lazy in their businesses. I don't want to do that. I want it to be working at an optimum level. It's not quite there yet, I feel there's so much more I can do with it. '

'I'm here for seven months and in Hervey Bay for the other five. Even when I'm here I'm just so busy planning ahead, it occupies my whole mind. At this time in my life, work comes first.'

S.R.

# Jill Quinlan

## Jilly's Mobile Dog Wash

> *'Not as the slow shaping of achievement to fit my preconceived purposes, but as the gradual discovery and growth of a purpose which I did not know.'*
>
> Joanna Field, *A Life of One's Own*, 1955

Jill Quinlan has run a mobile dog-wash business for just over two years now. She is 37 and hails originally from Alice Springs, where her love of dogs was born. If you live in Sydney, chances are you might have seen her. Jill's ute tows a large and strange-looking plastic contraption with 'Jilly's Mobile Dog Wash' emblazoned on the side.

'I must admit it is a bit of an attraction. It is necessary for the business for it to be hitched to the back of a car, but it is also quite a good marketing ploy. It's constant free advertising.'

When Jill was young she wasn't sure what she wanted to do with her life. Having lived in Alice until the age of eight, she feels a great affinity with the desert. Between the ages of 19 and 23 she travelled around Australia in an old HR Holden and then settled in Sydney for a few years. Following this Jill decided to go into her first business and for nine years she owned and managed Crusoe's restaurant on Magnetic Island, in the Great Barrier reef. 'I learned everything I know about business in that time. I had a partner whom I bought out after three years. I was lucky then that I had the money to do so. I wouldn't do it again.'

Going from the restaurant into the dog-washing business seemed to me to be an odd step, but Jill explains, 'I was ready to move on from that business for many reasons and had just happened to see these plastic dog-washing tubs up north. They were intended for breeders really, people with show dogs or those with a lot of dogs. It was as simple as seeing that there was a potential market and pursuing that.

I also thought it would be a good change.' Jill now operates two tubs around Sydney and is looking at buying a third to widen the area she can cover.

In this business Jill has to have a special affinity and understanding with her four-legged clients.

'Yes, you definitely have to love dogs to do this. I have a co-worker, Annie, who also loves dogs. It's imperative. It's important for your sake, the clients' sake and the dogs, that you have compassion for them. The dogs all have their individual personalities, just like people do. You also need to have good people skills; we are all familiar with how over-the-top some dog owners are, often they need handling gently too!'

The dog wash consists of a big plastic tub set atop a trailer. This tub is designed to take very large dogs and has its own water supply and drainage system. It's such a simple but good idea, with such a large potential market that it is hard to believe someone hasn't thought of doing it before. Jill says, 'Up in Queensland I think there are a few people running a dog-washing business as a small concern. As far as I know, I think I might be the only one running it as a full-on business though. Other people seem to come and go with it a bit and don't offer the range of services I do. You've got to be passionate about it to make something of it, I think other people get tired of it. It's my new career!'

When Jill first started out she attracted lots of publicity which helped the business to grow.

'It was a bit of a novelty and a good light news story, so I was approached quite early on by people in the media. It's the kind of human interest story everyone likes to hear. The *Sunday Telegraph* gave the story the whole of page three! I was also on the "Money Show". I couldn't believe that they had two minutes of footage after following me around for days! It's all been good exposure and it's free advertising. Doing the markets has been good in terms of exposure, too. You are so visible and there's always about twenty people watching you. It's a bit like being the Pied Piper.'

Jill realised that the Balmain markets in Sydney would be a good venue for her to set up a regular dog wash. It is quite a 'doggy' area and people often take their dogs to the markets on Saturdays.

The business suits Jill in many ways. 'I've never enjoyed being told what to do. In that regard it suits my personality. My dad is a geophysicist but I'm far too restless to do anything like that. I like the freedom to wander a bit, pottering around and coming up with ideas. I think you're either a practical person or a living-in-your-head person. All the kids in my family have turned out to be practical.

'I love the developing relationship I have with some of the dogs; there's nothing more rewarding than when they are happy to see me. I like to give my favourites a little tickle on the belly! I also like to see the difference in the "before" and "after", particularly after a haircut on a dog that really needed it. There can be remarkable results!

'Apart from having good people skills, I need a lot of patience. Consistency is important too. Some of the dogs, like Newfoundlands, can take up to five hours to groom and clip properly. You obviously have to be good at what you're doing. Although anyone can wash a dog, there are certain other things that we are now quite experienced in. I did a course in clipping and grooming. Getting to know the basics takes three or four weeks. There are certain ways to groom or clip dogs—a poodle will look good one way, while a maltese will look better with a different haircut. It is also important to be in good physical shape. It's very physically draining work. Some of those dogs are very big and you have to be able to lift them without hurting them or yourself. The most common ones we do are German shepherds.'

This brought me to the question of her handling of the more difficult dogs.

'I don't come across too many of these, thankfully. Often I will have to send the "parents" away though, because the dog will sometimes play up to them. Once they're out of sight the dogs are fine. People have such an incredible influence on their dogs at times. Although it is true that a dog will have a particular personality, I think it's also true that the dogs are very swayed by their owners.'

The obvious question everyone asks is, 'Do you get bitten?'

'Yes! Occasionally, the little ones can get a bit snappy. I've had the odd nick here and there. I must admit after a few times a day of being asked that I do get sick of it! Kids are particularly interested. I take the trailer with the dog-wash tub in it to the markets most weekends and I find myself surrounded by kids. Dogs and children seem to go together. It's good because they love to help and it creates interest. I give them little jobs to do.'

Having a dog myself, I know that dog parlours and some vets offer similar services, so I asked Jill why hers was better, or different.

'People come to us, or more correctly we go to them, because they trust us to do a good job. The convenience factor also contributes, that we go, wash or groom the dog and they don't have to lift a finger or go out of their way. They love the fact that you come to them. If they send their dog to a parlour, the dog can be there for a whole day. This way they never have to leave home.'

Jill finds herself doing the occasional job free of charge, which she doesn't mind too much.

'Some people just don't have the money to pay for these services, so sometimes I'll do people's animals for free. I get to all sorts of places that you wouldn't imagine! Some very funny people call me out. It's a real education!

'We get a lot of jobs around the city area doing dogs that people can't manage to wash themselves or don't have enough room to. I will always take my own water in case there isn't a hose. We don't waste a lot of water.'

Jill took me outside to see the business-on-wheels. 'I'll often get people asking me to take their kids in and wash them too and the obvious, "how much to wash my husband?"! Yes, I get all the clichés! That's just part and parcel of the job I suppose.'

I wondered what kind of products Jill used on the dogs.

'We do a heavy duty flea and tick wash on the dogs that need it, particularly in the summer. If requested we'll use a eucalyptus rinse instead, some people prefer us to use that. We do get some cases where dogs are just infested with fleas.'

I was amused to hear that the dogs also get a blow-dry, knowing full well that my canine would run a four-legged mile from this!

'In the winter especially, it is important to dry them. It's not an ordinary hair dryer, it's actually a blower that blows the water out of their coats rather than using hot air to do it. This also helps the long-haired dogs shed excess hair and they really don't seem to mind it, in fact they can come to love it. Sometimes, with all the long, dead hair coming out it's like it's snowing!'

As a dog owner who is not particularly fussy about grooming my dog, I have noticed that some people seem to be just as concerned about their dog's appearance as they are about their own.

'I don't actually groom dogs for shows, but I find that just before Christmas it's a very busy and intense period. Their hair is growing then and they need more attention in terms of their clipping and grooming. I also find that winter is quite busy too. People feel compassionate about their dogs and don't want to set the cold hose onto them. We warm the water up then, the tub has an element in it, so the dogs stay warm. The heat of the motor also helps the air in the blower stay warm. It also tends to be a bit hectic towards the end of the week, coming up to the weekend. Easter and Christmas are especially busy.'

Jill welcomes the new-found time and freedom that the dog-wash business allows her. Only occasionally does she miss the buzz of the restaurant.

'This business gives me a certain amount of freedom to do other things. In my last business I was pretty much chained to it.'

Common to many women's experiences in their small businesses, Jill started up her restaurant with very little capital and admits, 'The early days were very tight financially. Even in 1983 it was hard for women to borrow money from the banks. We were seriously undercapitalised and started with about $30,000. That covered the business and the equipment. I don't think it's a good idea to borrow too much to go into business. We were also very raw and didn't know much about running a business. Like everything in life, we learned as we went, there was no other way.

'My main reason for moving to the island then was for lifestyle reasons. I wanted to live that relaxed "island-life" existence we all dream about and I had to find a way to support doing that. I lived on a headland and walked around it to work. It was very laid back and peaceful. I got a bit stuck there in the end. It took two years to extricate myself and sell the business once I'd decided to leave. I sold in the recession and was lucky to come out of it debt free and with a bit of money to spare. Another reason I gave it up was that the rents were becoming unrealistic, it was time to move on.

'I got sick of the business after a while. It was very time-intensive and tiring. I was never particularly good out the front, so I tended to do most of the behind-the-scenes stuff. In some ways I miss the buzz of it, the intensity. We were there for a long time and I think we were the best! It built up to be a very successful business over time.

'The location was important too, we were in the right place. It was in the mall and we later extended it by having tables set out actually in the mall itself. This increased our turnover considerably and then we were open all day long. The food reflected the tastes of those on the island, they wanted simple and fresh food with a bias towards seafood. In the end I had about eight or nine staff in rotation. The business side of running the restaurant has since stood me in good stead for the things I need to know to run the mobile dog wash. I know the basics of bookkeeping and accounting. I'm capable of turning my hand to anything.'

Moving back from the city after such a sojourn I thought might have been difficult, but Jill says she was ready for it. She has also kept her options open by keeping the house she bought on the island.

'I'm not sure what I will do, ultimately. I enjoy the business but I don't think I'll do it forever. I think I might eventually sell it. It will be worth something because it really is viable.'

Jill explained that although in many ways it suited her, there were certainly downfalls in running the business. 'One of the problems is that it is affected by the weather. You can't do it on rainy days. I also depend on the light, so in summer I can feasibly work longer. I tend to get up when the sun does.'

Because of the nature of Jilly's work she often finds that isolation can be a problem. 'Sometimes it is difficult dealing with the loneliness you feel. It can be a fairly solitary business.

'The day doesn't finish when I get home. I spend a lot of time at night organising the next day's run and doing paperwork etc. I resent how much it eats into my personal time. However, I still live and breathe it!

'Another problem is the time factor. I can easily run late when it's busy. Sometimes in the peak periods I'm doing up to 25 dogs a day! Unless I organise my runs well and within the same sort of area, I can find myself driving around all day to different parts of the city. It can waste a lot of time. I realised this early on. It really needs to be organised well. People also expect you to be an expert, which of course I'm not. Annie is actually more trained than I am in grooming and dog training but we still don't know everything!'

Like many self-employed women have found, being tied to the job is an occupational hazard. Jill found that it was especially demanding in the beginning. 'When I began I also had a part-time job in a local shop. It was interesting because it was a seafood shop and having run a similar business I could see all the things they were doing wrong or could have done better. There was so much waste! I think I did learn so much in that first business.'

When she was starting up, Jill did lots of letter-box drops in the local area to publicise the dog-wash service and this took up a lot of her time.

'I don't really need to do that anymore. I have had some magnets made up, however. I thought they'd be a good idea because people don't tend to throw them out, so they are a constant reminder to people. I had about 2000 of them made up, costing approximately 80c each. I also find that the signwriting helps on the tubs.'

The most pressing thing for Jill is to keep up her physical health and strength. Even though she employs Annie three days a week, the business relies on her being physically able to manage it.

'Because it's in my nature to muck in and do everything, I can end up doing a lot of the heavy work. I fix the odd things that go wrong myself, like the heaters blowing. It is important to keep the vehicle in top condition too. Without it there isn't a business. For my health's sake I wear gloves, because those chemicals can be toxic. I might invest in a mask as well, because of the fumes. I wear sunblock and a hat, too!

'I have to watch out particularly for my back. I started getting to the edge because I was pushing it too hard and now I make sure I have treatment for my back. You don't often nurture yourself until you have to. I must keep up my stamina or else the business won't be able to carry on.'

The nature of the business dictates that Jill works weekends. 'I generally try to have Wednesdays off because the weekend is vital to our trade.'

Spending so much time with dogs I wondered if she sometimes preferred their company to the two-legged variety.

'I'm a bit of an animal person, I admit. I now live on my own, with my two dogs, because I got sick of living with people. Dogs are very intelligent company! I can tend to be a bit of a loner.'

She believes that dogs are sometimes given a raw deal.

'I think dogs have a hard time here in the city. There is legislation that if your watchdog bites a burglar who has entered your home they can sue you! Also, there isn't one beach you can take them to and not many parks where they are free to run around. Perhaps some people shouldn't have dogs if they haven't really the room or can't exercise them adequately. Dogs are no good if they're bored, they're no different to us in that respect. I like it that here in the city people seem to be so close to their dogs. I found that up north people didn't seem to have the same connection with their dogs. Perhaps people in the city have them for reasons more to do with companionship. It can be a good life for a dog!'

Despite the protests of the anti-dog lobby, Jill is pleased to have found that dogs are still in fashion. 'People either love dogs or they don't. Those that do will always want them. Of course, in this business I get a lot of people coming to me with strays or hard-luck dog stories. I'm always finding homes for them. It can be like social work at times!

One of my own dogs, a spaniel cross, I got that way. I also have an Irish wolfhound. I recommend that people take their dogs to training classes, although I'd have to say that it's often the owner who needs the training!'

For her office and storeroom Jill has rented an old depot-cum-workshop nearby.

'It's great because they are old stables. I keep all my materials and supplies there.

'I'd like eventually to employ someone to run the office side of it, do the phone calls and paperwork. The business has increased threefold since its beginning and is well-established now. We've even managed to put in a price rise. We now have a good client-base built up and it really ticks over by word-of-mouth. Occasionally a vet will refer someone to us, but business is pretty much self-perpetuating. We have our regulars.

'In the future I would like to increase the number of vehicles with tubs, but before we take that step I'd really need to find the right people. As I said before, organisation is the key. To set up washes in the same area on a given day is important.

'I could probably benefit from doing some dog training, which I might do in the future.'

Eventually, Jill thinks she will buy some land. 'I'd like to spend summer in the city and perhaps winter on the island. That would be just right.'

As I was leaving, Jill tells me that she was born in the Chinese Year of the Dog and that last year also happened to be the Year of the Dog. 'There were a lot of positive things happening for dogs last year!' I have the feeling she will work hard to ensure that this good fortune continues.

S.R

# Lisa Treen

## Music Staff

Lisa Treen is 28 years old and since starting her business has placed people in jobs with a salary total of over seven million dollars.

She is managing partner of Music Staff, an employment agency she started with her husband three years ago. It is her business to connect people with jobs, a service she offers exclusively to the music industry. Music Staff began in the middle of the recession and operates solely for an industry that was hit very badly by the economic downturn. Lisa herself thought it was a brave exercise and wondered whether it would work. However, her experience shows that even in times of economic hardship, good employees are an asset and sometimes for the untrained eye, hard to find.

'I was the only one who didn't think the business would work. On one hand I thought there was a definite need for the kind of service we were wanting to offer. On the other though, I knew there was such a lot of networking which I thought would mean no one would want to pay a commission to me for finding them staff for their jobs. It is such a maverick industry and I was unsure which way it would jump. I knew every other industry in the "real world" used employment agencies, but I also knew that the music industry wasn't the real world. I decided to research it nonetheless.'

Lisa posed as a person looking for work, and went to a variety of agencies to find out exactly what they did. She knew that finding out about their services from a potential employee's standpoint would only give her one side of the equation, so she also pretended to be an employer looking for staff. She realised that many of the agencies left a lot to be desired.

'I monitored each agency's response and service. Some sent me information straightaway and then pestered me incessantly.

Some I never heard back from at all. I wanted to sit somewhere in the middle of these two extremes. Professionalism without the hard sell and most importantly to offer a service that worked for all parties.

'I found out a lot of information by talking to people who had used agencies themselves either to find work or staff. I grilled them about their experiences, trying to find out how they were treated and what they thought were important services to offer. Most people didn't have very favourable reports and felt they were never treated well by the agencies. It was from this information that I decided what my business was going to be and certainly what it wasn't going to be.

'I knew though, that the most important part of the equation was very simple—whether or not people in the industry would use it. It doesn't take a genius to work out that you can have the best service in the world but if there isn't a demand, you won't get too far. I wanted the industry to stand up and take notice of what we were doing. So I rang everyone in the industry I knew personally, and many I had never met, asking them if they thought they might use the kind of service I had in mind and if so, how often they thought they might use it. I asked all about how they were currently getting staff and anything else I could think of.'

Lisa left school wanting to be a clothing designer. She was born in New Zealand and worked in a factory as a tailor's apprentice. There she learned that the life of a factory worker was not for her.

'I went around knocking on doors saying "take me, take me, take me". I wanted to learn the trade of tailoring and design more than anything. Eventually someone did take me, but I couldn't handle it and left after two weeks. I hated working in a factory and realised I knew quite a lot that I had taught myself along the way.

'After the factory, my mother encouraged me to take an office job. For three years I wasn't sure what to do with my life. I was bored working until one day I discovered what it was all about. The secret of it is to surround yourself with interesting people and that if what is going on in the bigger picture at your place of work is stimulating, you can get by. Perhaps even be stretched personally.'

So Lisa worked her way through many temping jobs, slowly crystallising what she wanted to do with her life through a process of experimentation. It is often those experiences which feel like 'fillers' at the time that later turn out to be invaluable.

'When I decided to start Music Staff I thought about all the time I'd spent going through agencies and made lists and notes. During my time freelancing and temping I worked in a couple of employment agencies, which in hindsight was a great bonus. I had an insight into the beast. I knew a lot of "inside" information.

'I spent four years working in the New Zealand music–entertainment industry. For three of those years I worked for the highly professional recording facility, Marmalade Recording Studios. There I was in the service side of the business, booking talent and running the front-of-house activities, which included secretarial duties and accounts. Most importantly, this was where I developed the skill to work with clients.

'I left New Zealand and started managing bands in Sydney which was my ticket into the music industry in Australia, which is renowned for being difficult to break in to. This was my first business and it too was a great learning experience for what I'm doing now. I established networks so when the bands I was looking after and I fell out it was relatively easy for me to find more work. I started work researching a book about great rock and roll scandals of our time.'

Her work on this project led to two of the most important events in her life: Lisa met the man she would marry and the seed of her new business was planted.

Lisa's research showed her that Music Staff was a viable idea. Now it was a matter of getting the ball rolling. Her temping work gave her a good understanding of business and she wasn't daunted in a practical sense by the task ahead of her. What did worry her though was the commitment she knew she was about to make.

'I was terrified that I'd have to do this for the rest of my life. I pictured myself with grey hair in front of yet another jobless record company executive, and it scared me to death. Then I decided that nothing was written in stone, and just because this was going to be my own business, I didn't have to see it as a lifelong sentence. I resolved that it wasn't going to be a ball and chain, and if at any point I decided that I wanted to sell up or dissolve the business, I would.'

Although Lisa had some general ideas about how she wanted her business to operate when she started, she says that the process of defining and implementing work policies is evolving as she gains more experience.

So often in vocational training and generally in life, we are taught that perserverance and an unswerving attitude will see us through. Whether that attitude is a useful tool for those in business is a question worth debating. Many of the women in this book talk about the need for flexibility in business and relate their ideas and philosophies in almost organic terms, like 'growing' and 'evolving'. This attitude is embedded in the social conditioning of women which has made them question themselves and their actions. Women are all too often ready to admit fault and re-evaluate their ideas and ways even when it is not necessary. This self-doubt is something many of us try to stamp out of our lives, as we try to undo and challenge our conditioning, but perhaps it can be an asset in business.

'I don't think you can start a business with every path laid out and think I'm not going to deviate from that, nothing's going to get in my way. You can't help the environmental things that come up, that should change the way the company operates. Obviously you have a set of standards and ethics, which are pretty rigid, but a business must evolve with you and your experiences. You're always learning, growing and the business has to reflect that growth.'

Like some other small-business people, Lisa started off at a run. As soon as the idea of the agency was announced, the work rolled in before she had time to get organised. Lisa had three jobs to fill but hadn't yet decided what to call the company. So, without a name, letterhead or business card she got down to the most fundamental task, work. She did have a computer, access to a printer, and, most importantly, a phone and a fax, though to Lisa this felt like the very bare bones.

The challenges that face those with their own businesses change and evolve but never seem to go away. That is a fact that many people find both rewarding and frustrating. Once one problem is solved, there is always another of a different nature on which to focus.

Since those early days things have changed dramatically. Lisa has registered the business as a company, has just had her letterhead and logo redesigned and her own printer sits proudly beside her desk.

When I first interviewd Lisa she was tackling a problem that bridged both her personal and professional life. Lisa married one of the more prominent men in the Australian music industry, Phil Tripp. He is responsible for publishing the industry's directory and works as a consultant and publicist to many of the major movers and shakers.

'On the one hand, it has been a terrific help. Phil's contacts and standing in the industry have made it easy in many respects. But I often ask myself if the business is successful just because of who I married.

'Deep down I know the answer to that—I know the company would be nothing without me. I set everything up, I do everything and I'm responsible for everything. Phil essentially is just a shareholder, but at times it plays heavily on my mind. I'm sure though that if I were a guy, the issue would never arise. Not for me, or for anyone else.

'The biggest thrill is when I have clients who have no idea who I am married to. My association with him professionally is perhaps the hardest hurdle for me to cross personally.'

At the time of this first interview, I could sense that this was a very real problem for Lisa. Six months later when we meet again, she is nonchalant about the issue.

'I have established a name for myself separate from Phil and the business and the work I do is recognised as mine. It's only the difficult people who insist on ringing Phil now and he is wonderful about making them ring me direct.'

Lisa has thought long and hard about the issues involved in this complex question. Self-employment poses different challenges for each person. For some, the challenge is to overcome practical problems, like bookkeeping (my own hurdle), while for others it is more personal. The role of her husband in the business challenged Lisa's sense of self and her confidence until she was able to bring it into perspective.

'I did have a big problem with it and it annoyed me because it made me feel so insignificant. I realised I had to get my head around it because it was causing me and everyone else around me too much grief. I feel at peace about it now. I just come straight out and correct people. If anyone rings up asking to speak to the boss, I just say, "You're speaking to her, how can I help you?" I correct Phil about it too now if he ever steps over the line.

'Before I would internalise all my feelings and get incredibly stressed out.' Pausing and reflecting, she laughs saying, 'I guess I've done a bit of a turn around since we last talked.

'What's important to me now is so much more—it's having a good relationship with my husband, being healthy, a bit more open and enjoying people.'

Now Lisa and Phil work much more as a team, and the delineation between their work is less rigid. Phil has just made an emergency trip to the United States and Lisa says, 'A year ago, I would have said to him, "I'm busy with my business, you sort out how you're going to keep your office going yourself".' Instead she offered to take over from him while he was away and is making sure everything runs smoothly. He sent her an e-mail saying, 'I kiss your cosmic feet for looking after everything so wonderfully.'

'Now I think we all have to pitch in together and it's been really rewarding for me too. I'm not as precious.

'Last year I realised that I wasn't having fun. I was working every weekend and I was busy all the time. A friend woke me up to myself. One day I pulled out of a lunch she had gone to a great deal of trouble over. She'd been to the fish markets, bought crabs and cooked a feast and two hours before we were meant to be sitting down to lunch, I ring up and cancel. She was furious and I felt bad,' she says, cringing. 'She made me think about who I wanted to be and what I wanted to do and it wasn't what I was.

'I wasn't paying attention or caring about my friends and my drive and my obsession with my business meant that I lost contact with a whole lot of really dear friends. I took a reality check and worked out my priorities. I realised I was letting people down, that I was being a lousy friend and a shitty wife. I don't know what made me think I could just put everyone on hold.

'Someone once said to me bring a friend and I had to say, "I don't have any anymore".'

Lisa says that not only did her attitude harm her friendships, it wasn't helping business either, a point many women raise when they come to the realisation that they have been unbalanced in their approach to life and work. 'Last year I was so busy that I lost sight of the importance of the niceties of work. I was robotic with people and not very nice to work with. I don't want to be a grumpy person, it doesn't suit me at all and it's not the image I want to put across in my business.'

Lisa works from home and her office is a true reflection of her life and personality. There are photos of her family alongside postcards and paraphernalia she has collected over the years. It is a cheerful and bright office that contrasts with the approach she says she was developing. She thinks it's important to make clients feel at ease when they come in for an interview. People often say to her, that her interviews are the nicest they have ever been to. That's not to say that she doesn't do her job properly. In fact she thinks her approach to the interview process helps her really find out about people and their capabilities.

'If someone's nervous and guarded, it's hard to gauge how they will fit in to a particular position or workplace situation. I spend a lot of time with employers establishing their needs. It's not just a matter of what an employee is capable of, but how they will fit into a team.'

Lisa has filled senior executive positions: she found the new *Rolling Stone* editor and placed secretarial and management jobs for many of the major record labels and industry icons.

A very important part of her work is treating people with respect. Most people never hear back about the jobs they apply for. After a certain period of time passes you just assume the position has been filled and get down to applying for the next job. Lisa makes sure she writes personal letters to every applicant telling them they didn't get the position. To some it may seem a small gesture, but to those waiting for employment it gives a sympathetic touch to what can be a disappointing moment.

Lisa has a very hands-on approach to her work and uses her equipment to help her. 'I have a good computer system, which I think is essential to any business. It's important not to be afraid of it and to make it work for you. I spent a lot of time just playing with my computer, learning all about it and the software packages.'

She even has a program that reminds her of her appointments, fifteen minutes beforehand. It beeps at her, reminding her of exactly what she has coming up. This is something I must get. Even though I'm surrounded by computers at my office, I admit that there is a lot I don't know. I make a mental note to take Lisa's advice myself. She's right, so often we only use a small amount of the computer's capabilities.

'Women can be a little fearful of computers. I think there are some really funny attitudes out there about women and keyboards. Some women seem to feel that if someone catches them at a keyboard they might mistake them for the office secretary. Men sometimes think that because you are at a computer, you're the typist. It's crazy. Technology is moving so fast—it's important to be able to keep up. Yesterday all our computers went down and I was the one who worked it out. Phil's office is full of computer heads and I was really proud that I was the only person who could get it up and running again. I really felt like I'd achieved something.'

The music industry is certainly one that has relied heavily on the 'jobs for the boys' attitude. Traditionally it has been not what you know but who you know. Perhaps the fact that so many of the major record labels and institutions have come to Music Staff indicates they are beginning to re-assess the effectiveness of that attitude.

'I hope that I encourage women when they come in, although in the end I have to go by every client's past employment record. In some ways I would be happy if someone came to me and said, "Your business only places women", or I was accused of bias in women's favour. That will never happen though, because at the end of the day my clients have full say on who they want to employ. I merely present them with a choice of candidates and from there it's up to them.

'I have been very lucky though, because I would find it very disheartening to recommend a woman and a man, knowing full well that the woman was the best candidate, and have the employer choose the man for political reasons. From a pool, often a very large one, my clients get to choose the best person for the job and gender doesn't come into it.

'I am proud to have been recognised as being responsible for putting great women in great jobs. That's a nice feeling. I like being at the forefront of equal opportunity. I have placed a lot of women in jobs that are very male dominated; influential positions that no one ever thought a woman would be given the opportunity to do.

'The reason isn't because they're women, and it's not because I stack the deck. Rather because I cut, and if the hand shows that the strongest suit is the woman, then I'm not shy to play that hand.'

Lisa's story highlights how women running their own business not only transform their own lives, but often the lives of those who come into their orbit. Slowly her work will help to right the wrongs and redress the gender imbalance that has existed in one industry. As Lisa says, it's not that she is biased, just fair.

C.L.

# Following a Dream

The first thing most people say to us on hearing about this book or what we do, is, 'I always dreamed of running my own business', and then with a somewhat romantic and nostalgic look in their eyes, they describe their idea and ask, 'So what's it really like?' 'Hell', is our usual reply, followed quickly by 'But we love it'.

Skye was in the enviable position of always knowing her dream and accepting that she would be self-employed early on. However, it was surely one of the strangest decisions I have made; to throw in a well-paid job to take on the risk, stress and financial strain of self-employment. In many people's eyes, not to mention my own, my decision to run my life in this way can seem almost certifiable. Whatever makes anyone do the same as we have is a question worth pondering, and it is one we ask and examine here.

None of the women in this chapter have been motivated primarily by financial considerations, which doesn't necessarily separate them from any of the others we talked to. But their main motivation was something quite different again—it was a drive to fulfil a passion or express an intrinsic part of their being.

For Liz Cotter, Rachel Berger and Gillian Sullivan, their dream wasn't always clearly known to them. Although both Liz and Rachel had flashes of it, as if their dream was sneaking up behind them, giving them a quick kick every now and again, saying, 'Hey, don't you forget about me'. They tried, for many years, to ignore those reminders until one day they no longer could. Once they took note, their lives changed and they describe here the struggle to overcome their own and other people's expectations of them. Rachel had been making costume jewellery and Liz had worked to support others' creativity in her role as an assistant to directors in the film industry. Now it was time for them to get in touch with their desires, accept them, and make it all happen on their own terms and on their own ground.

For both Jodie Boffa and Gillian Sullivan, you will see that there is a thread connecting their childhood to the careers they are in today. However, it was only Jodie who realised her big passion and worked steadily towards it from a very early age. She describes always having the dream and knowing that she would eventually become a fashion designer. Whether she had any idea of what her success would be is another point, but that her aim was always with her is undeniable. Gillian, on the other hand, tried many other things before singing. A printing press operator is about the last thing you would expect Australia's busiest soprano to have been, but like many of the women in this book, Gillian is full of surprises.

These stories show that what can often be seen to be strange choices, unusual catalysts and different roads, sometimes have rather fantastic rewards.

C.L.

# Gillian Sullivan

## Opera Singer

Whether to include people like Gillian Sullivan in this collection was a point of some debate. We decided that in a sense, performers are commodities and that their talents have to be sold and promoted in the same way as traditional businesses. The only difference we saw was that people like Gilly were selling themselves, not a separate service or product. They are their own manufacturer, product and retailer.

I have known Gilly since I was nine when she met my mother at adult matriculation school in Adelaide. Gilly was always quiet but when she sang she showed a completely different side of herself. It wasn't until I was fifteen that I saw this other persona. Someone asked Gilly to sing during a dinner party at our house and I thought there was an earthquake. The whole house shook, and my idea of her has never been the same since.

What hasn't changed about her is her modesty. Gilly has sung all over the world, from Russia to Hong Kong, but finding out about her achievements takes some prompting. Her presence on stage is captivating and the combination of that and her singing ability has made Gilly one of Australia's busiest sopranos.

She recently performed to 50,000 people at Sydney's Opera in the Park, and it was here that I thought about her as a small business. A huge video screen projected her so even those right up the back could see her clearly. It was a scene more reminiscent of a pop concert than an opera. The only difference was that the audience at this event were sitting on picnic rugs, sipping champagne. What became clear, even though this concert was free, was that her value was determined by demand. She is governed by the same economic laws that rule every small business.

Opera is an art form you either love or hate. To some it can seem highly camp, over the top and pretentious. To others it is full of drama, passion and beauty. Love and death are the most common themes and while moral issues play a part, the overriding emotions are of the heart. Red is the colour I think of when I think of opera. Passion, opulence and death.

What is interesting about Gilly is that while opera wasn't high on her family's list of priorities, it is something that, hearing her talk about her background, makes sense in the context of her life.

'Monetarily we were in no sense a priviliged family. My mother read and she liked music and was cultured, but we were by no means well off. I did go to a private school, but only because I won a scholarship. My older sister committed suicide when I was nineteen and there was a great deal of grief and trauma in my childhood. I am sure that a large part of my life has been in reaction to my childhood.'

While the death of her sister had a devastating effect on her, what was equally damaging and profound was the way the death wasn't dealt with in her family. 'The unhappiness in our home made me withdraw into myself and a world I created to deal with the chaos. Acting is about revealing emotion. As a child I hid it. When I was very young, I couldn't express myself at all. I hardly ever said anything but I built myself a big fantasy life and loved to read Victorian novels because everything in them was so calm, stable and contemplated. It took me away from the emotional mayhem that surrounded me.'

As I listen to her talking about that period, it strikes me that she has taken the fantasies of her childhood and the techniques she used to deal with the trauma and made a fulfilling career of them. The Victorian novels and her fantasy life transcend to opera: women in opulent costumes, singing about love and tragedy.

We discuss how interesting it is that someone who couldn't express herself as a child has made a career of singing. She couldn't speak, but now she is able to stand in front of thousands of people and scream.

'It's a controlled scream. You have to be able to scream and feel comfortable. When I was about ten I had a recurring dream. I had to overcome the devil and the only way to do it was to make more noise than him. Once, the dream took place in the middle of a football stadium, the other was in a picture theatre, but in both I was in a concert dress.

'I think that an element of what I do is to get the approval and love I feel I missed out on as a child. Of course it's not actually possible to get that solely from my work and I have had to find other ways as well, but singing has been very healing for me.'

Gilly's excellence is rooted to her past. It's as though the voice supressed within her has a force of its own. That all the time it was bottled up, it was building in strength and emotion. Those elements must surely be the key to a great artist. First, the strength to do it and then the strength to show true emotion in an honest and vulnerable way.

Singing was not something she always knew she would do, rather something she slowly adapted to and became comfortable with. Understanding Gilly's background explains why it happened this way. New ways of being and healing are not overnight transformations. Usually such changes are a slow process of developing trust and self-confidence.

'Doing it gradually gave me confidence. It was never something I consciously said, "I'm going to do that". I was in Adelaide, going to university and started performing in uni reviews. Then I sang in the big choirs which is where I was introduced to good music. That interested me the same way the literature I was being taught at university was moving me.

'After I left school, I did nursing, worked in the printing industry doing artwork and operating small letterpress machines. I enjoyed that work—it pleased my orderly sense. I learned the job quickly and then there didn't seem to be anywhere to go with it. I loved performing because I knew the challenge would be never-ending.

'The more I performed, the more I was able to express myself outside of what I did on stage. I distinctly remember when I was working in England, a woman remarked that I never said anything. Her comment really worried me at the time because I felt I couldn't do anything to change that about myself.'

Gilly now is by no means a loud person, although she is certainly not the introverted person she was back then. It is as though she has an old self and a new one. 'I am glad to have personally moved from being so introverted to who I am now. It makes me very, very happy to be able to express myself and to speak my mind.'

Unlike most professional singers, Gilly had no background in music. She didn't play a musical instrument and has not trained at a conservatorium. 'I've never had any of that. I guess I was a good performer right from the start and I built my singing technique while I was performing. A lot of singers learn the technique and then present themselves to an opera company and are completely inexperienced. I got my experience from the stage at the same time as learning the technique which gave me the stamina to lead the life I lead now.'

Gilly entered the ABC's competition, 'Quest' in 1977. She won the operetta section of the series and I later found out that the judges commented that, 'of all the contestants in this final, we feel Gillian will be the one to make a mark as a singer'. She went overseas with the prize money and studied in London. There she met her singing teacher, Audrey Langford, who was the youngest ever principal soprano at the world famous Covent Garden.

'Audrey taught me for fifteen years until she died last year, which was a big blow because she had also become a very great friend. She was my mentor and a great inspiration to me.

'Audrey was totally pragmatic, she taught me that you have to perfect your vocal technique, work extremely hard and that nobody is rocketed to stardom before their time. What was wonderful about Audrey and quite unique I think, was that she never taught with negatives. She never said, 'Don't do that that way, that's wrong'. She always said it in a postive—'this is how this is done' and 'if you sing in this way . . . '. What was also unusual about her methods was she taught a whole package. She taught me vocal technique but also how to analyse roles, to arrive prepared at rehearsal, to be reliable and to be self-reliant. Teaching self-reliance was important for me because it meant I could go away for periods of time and continue the learning. I would always come back to her and as my voice grew and changed, she would alter small things and then I would be safe to go for another period of time without her.

'After six months in London I got a job at Glynebourne [one of the most prestigious opera companies in England] in the chorus. It was wonderful not to have to find other employment outside singing.'

It was only after four years of working as a professional singer that it occurred to Gilly that it was in fact her career.

'I'd been singing principal roles and chorus for all that time and I thought I guess that's what I'm going to be doing.'

She is very matter-of-fact about her successes and it was only through talking to other people that I found out just how many she has had. She quietly sets herself goals and then goes about achieving them. Once she decided she was a singer, she told herself that if she wasn't singing full-time by the time she was 28, she wouldn't do it any more. She met that goal and quickly set herself another. By 32 she wanted to be singing principal roles with professional companies. She also achieved that target, with some years to spare.

'I know a lot of people who at 40 or 45 are still not making a living from their profession. I couldn't do that, so it was important for me to meet those targets. I've been singing professionally for fifteen years and now I earn a very good living from it.'

Just as those running their own businesses, for example, have to produce goods on time or to manufacture well-made items, Gilly similarly has to adopt an approach to her work that ensures she continues to earn a living.

'I think the moment a singer realises they are actually a commodity it lifts the pressure. It made me realise nobody was making comments on me personally. If they didn't employ me, it could just as easily be because they were looking for a very specific quality. The height, the looks, perhaps the spiritual quality you naturally show in a role and the sound and power of your voice are all qualities auditioners have to take into account. Often it's not any slight on you if you don't get the role. It's not worth chastising yourself if you're not the chosen one. You have two options, the first is to think people are being nasty to you which in the long run is not helpful, or secondly you can work with your management and say, 'Okay, let's tell them about that role I did and the success I had in that', or with your teacher to improve areas of weakness. The second option is positive and may actually get you that role or another down the track. Once I realised none of it was personal I found it a lot easier.'

Commodities are always being upgraded and refined, and those in control of them spend a great deal of time and money to push them into wider markets and expand their exposure. Just like the director of any business, Gilly is always considering where to go next and what steps to take in her career.

'The best example was when I was working in London. I felt I was stuck in a bit of a rut doing soubrette roles and knew that my voice was developing and that I needed to move into more challenging roles. No one in England would see me in that light though. It was a case of the chicken or the egg—I knew I could do it, but no one would hire me because I hadn't done it before. I needed the opportunity to sing different roles so I looked further afield.

'I got a contract in Germany to sing three new roles. It was a good move because they were right for my voice. When I came back to England I was able to command higher fees because I had the kudos of having worked overseas and I was singing more principal roles.

'Professionally it was a great move but personally I was very unhappy in Germany. I didn't have a love interest there and I wasn't meeting anyone because I was working all the time. I saw a lot of women in their forties who were by themselves. They were mostly Americans and they hadn't married and they had no personal lives whatsoever. They were getting older and they weren't getting as much work anymore. I could see they would be very unhappy and lonely.

'I knew I didn't want to end up in a foreign country all by myself so I thought I'd like to come home to Australia. I discussed it with my Australian agent and she thought I'd be able to get enough work here to keep me going, which in fact has proved itself over and over.

'I wanted to be with people who I knew cared about me

and who knew where I'd come from, which was important to me. No one in England knew what I was like as a child or what my childhood had been. So I moved back here and within a very short time I met my husband John.'

Gilly found the emotional happiness she had been craving overseas but admits the move did have a professional downside. 'I was ready to curtail my international career, to find a more balanced existence. What I have lost in my career I have gained in my personal life though, and I'm very happy about that. Other singers look at me and say, "Oh Gilly's so lucky, she's working all the time in Australia and she has a husband and children". They are right, I am lucky, but international performances are prestigious and do have their own rewards.

'Travelling is wonderful, but I am happy with my decision to stay here in Australia because I have a beautiful family I adore. When I have time to be with them, we have a very good family life. I've caught up with my old friends again and my social network here is very important to me. I think I need that. It benefits my work because I'm happy personally which enables me to give more freely when I work.'

Gilly lives in Newcastle with her husband John and their two children. Investigating how women juggle their schedules and family life was one of the initial aims of this book as it is obviously such an important factor for many self-employed women. This talk about her family gives me the perfect opportunity to delve.

'I know John feels the pressure of having to look after the children at night and on weekends when I'm not there. I wish I could do something different for him but my schedule means that there's physically nothing I can do about it. This year, for example, is going to be very busy for me. I usually spend 200 to 250 days a year away from home. I'm not always away the entire day but more and more of my work is interstate now which means I am away for blocks of time.

'When I married John his family didn't know me at all. I think they were a bit worried about inviting a theatrical person into the family. When John's mother heard me sing though, her attitude changed. She said to me, "You have to keep singing, you have such a beautiful voice". She died about fifteen months after we were married but her words help me when I worry about the children and how my absence will affect them and my marriage.

'If I'd had children earlier I don't think I'd be so torn, trying to be a good mother and a professional singer. I don't think I'd constantly feel so tired. I'd be able to enjoy it all more fully and John would be able to come with me and partake of the more glamorous side of my work.

'I have to psych myself up before a performance. I have to change from mother to opera singer and that takes time. Personally I'm very different to Gillian Sullivan the opera singer. I put on my opera singer's hat when I walk out the door. I put on make-up and wear clothes I would never wear at home. It's a definitive step I take when I walk into the public arena. I've learned from experience how to time it. I go away a couple of days before a concert because I have to get a few good nights sleep, which is hard with two small children at home. If I'm tired it shows in my voice and I have to be able to concentrate solely on the music and my performance. You have to show that you're vulnerable and often show tremendous weaknesses on stage. To do that you have to draw on your understanding of yourself and be prepared to let that show through. People need to be able to translate that as being you, not just a character, if they are to be really moved by a performance.'

What Gilly has described shows that there is a lot more to being an opera singer than just singing. She sees many singers with wonderful voices who don't have the acting skills to make their performances shine. Gilly recently performed *La Traviata* in Melbourne, where she received reviews saying that hers was the best performance of the role in twenty years. Obviously this comment is not only about her voice, but also and perhaps just as importantly, her ability to act in a way that convinces and moves the audience.

As a high-profile performer, she is invited to most opening nights but seldom accepts. She will take time away from her family for work but not for the extracurricular activities, which in some ways are part and parcel of her work. That decision, she says, has subtle effects on her standing in the industry.

'I think because I don't network or go out socially with the industry that the promotion I get is not the same as many of my peers. If you're not at all the functions and opening nights I think they decide you don't want the publicity. I would like to be able to spend more time at those events too. Not only because I want the publicity that goes with them but because I genuinely love them. Opera is my passion and hopefully I'll be able to go along to more as the children get older.'

Working as constantly as she does now, Gilly no longer has the regime of daily vocal practice that was necessary when she began her career. What she does have to maintain and constantly keep her eye on now, is her appearance. It seems that modelling and similar industries are not the only ones concerned with the notions of beauty and youth.

'About twelve months ago I lost a lot of weight. I thought I looked terrific and I was really happy being thin. All my clothes came in two dress sizes and I was like that for quite a while. I performed and received some good reviews. They called me, "the waif-like Gillian Sullivan" and I thought, oh hurray. Then I got a virus and was so ill I got bronchial pneumonia. I had to cancel a lot of work. Looking back on that experience now I realise there was nothing happy about me except the fact I was thin. I was anxious all the time and I realised it was madness. Physically I can not maintain a weight like that and do what I do.

'Physically singing is very demanding. Intellectually it takes intelligence to interpret operas and characters and to be able to offer something interesting. The intellectual side of the business I find relatively easy but it's a constant strain to keep healthy, get enough rest, keep fit and most importantly keep illness at bay. If I get sick it's always respiratory which makes singing impossible but it's hard to avoid with two small children, not to mention the fact that I have to work closely with lots of people.

'Getting pneumonia made me stop and think. I was putting everyone's expectations of me before my health. Once someone referred to my matronly figure in a review and it hurt a great deal. I had just had my second child and I was dressed as a boy. It happens to other women opera singers as well and I feel so sorry for them because I know just how much it hurts.'

We discuss how women have to be mothers, career women, look good, be 'waif like' and we decide that accomplishing all that would send you mad. We both quietly admit though, that we still do try.

'It is the worst put down. You're a successful career woman and you are also a successful mother but you must look like a dolly girl. It's the ultimate negation of what you've actually done.'

Gilly's personal philosophy helps her put her life and her work into perspective. An entertainer's earning power has a definite life span, tied to their ability to perform. In other professions it is possible to train employees to work to your standards and continue to produce work in your name when you are no longer willing or able to do so yourself. However, Gilly's singing career does have a shelf life and I wonder about how she faces that fact in a positive way.

'Your feelings about work and what goes on there come down to your own life philosophy. I've always had great determination that my life would be full and enjoyable. Some people think I'm pessimistic, but actually I think they confuse that with realism.

'In pursuit of enjoying my life as much as I possibly can, I try to make the best of all situations. So when I can no longer perform, I will find other things that interest me. We only have one life that we're aware of and I really love the earth. I love being here and I want to enjoy lots of things about it. I love painting, literature, the beach, beautiful surroundings, people, food and of course children. There're so many things left to interest me that I want to explore.

'I won't be able to work when I'm 65 and I can see my earnings trailing off in another ten years or so. If you look at my earnings over my whole career, I wouldn't have earned more than a secretarial salary. That's another reason that I have to work hard at the moment. My husband John and I will have to support ourselves when we retire. We won't get pensions, just as we don't get any kind of concessions now.'

People often look at artists doing well in their profession and assume they are wealthy. While some people have made incredible amounts of money from their talent, there is little understanding that the majority have to struggle. Economics, as Gilly's 'secretarial salary' shows, are not what motivates the artist. Obviously it is a wonderful thing if the two can be combined but the reality is that the rewards for an artist are so much more than financial.

'You come to understand yourself as part of humanity. To be able to release emotions in people is a wonderful feeling. That's what theatre is about. Making people think about life and society. Moving someone to the point of tears is my greatest reward.'

C.L.

# Rachel Berger

## Stand-up Comedian

There's a theory about change which is that it more often than not takes a crisis to initiate major upheavals in one's life. Either things get so bad, you get sick of it, or one event pushes you over so far, you have very little other choice but to change. It took the death of her father for Rachel Berger to take to the stage.

'My father died in 1984. He worked his arse off, retired, had a few months off, decided to do what had been a life-long fantasy to take a caravan holiday and then died of a massive heart attack three days into the holiday. I was with him when he died and I realised that there's really just one life. There's no dress rehearsal. His death inspired me to do what I had always wanted to do, to follow a dream and shortly after I started doing stand-up comedy.

'I didn't get a lot of encouragement from anybody because nobody thought I'd be able to do it and most people just thought it was a stupid idea. But I was really committed to the idea and thought I could do it. At first I didn't tell anyone that I was actually getting up and performing every week. I was too embarrassed for them to see me and I certainly didn't want them to see me die.

'I went to a place called Le Joke in Melbourne where there was a "try out night" every Tuesday, and I just got up and started doing it. The first time it was fabulous because I was doing what I had always wanted to do.'

Rachel says she was so full of adrenalin that first night she thought she would burst. Somehow even with all the excitement and terror, or perhaps because of it, the audience loved her. Her second and subsequent experiences of performing on stage weren't quite so successful. 'I just died and died and died again. Every so often though I'd get a good response and that kept me going.'

Rachel explains that it was her drive and determination that kept her going back despite those 'deaths' on stage. 'I knew I really wanted to do it. I don't know what it's like for anyone else but I think it's definitely got a bit of the "love me, love me" thing in it.' Pausing, she adds, 'Well, for me then, it did have that element. But you get beyond that because you realise that's fickle.'

'It's a bit like your first relationship, you want affection and then it's shattering the first time they turn on you. I think I'm a bit more grown up about it now because I know an audience can love you one day and hate you the next. But I didn't get much encouragement from friends, which was okay because I try to be very self-motivated, although in hindsight I realise I didn't allow anyone to encourage me.'

Self-disciplined is another way to describe Rachel Berger. We are talking at Rachel's hotel suite in the afternoon before she performs at Sydney's Belvoir Street Theatre. The room is set up with two tables. One, her writing table, is in the centre of the room, the other, for administration, is in the corner. Both are incredibly neat and stacked with papers.

I was expecting to meet a hyped-up woman and to be fed a string of punchy, smart one-liners that were more about style than content. But I should have known that just like her stand-up routine, this interview with Rachel would be full of content. The aromatherapy oils she had burning in the room and her calmness were a far cry from my expectations. Rachel is considered about what she says and thinks carefully about words, their meanings and connotations. 'I speak in conversation as I do in stand-up. I build and build and build.'

Rachel Berger hasn't been employed by anyone since 1978. When her marriage of six years broke up she left everything behind. 'I left my husband, my job as an interior designer, my home, my everything.'

'I started making costume jewellery and was sustaining myself by about 28. I started doing that simply because I had no other way of earning a living. I had never sewn on a button—I am hopeless with my hands—but I really liked jewellery. I had a whole lot of old pieces that I broke up and threaded together differently and then sold to a couple of stores.

'Over two years I learned an enormous amount; lessons I

could never have learned in employment and they were mainly to do with ethics and integrity in business. Lessons about keeping your word, delivering on time, sustaining the product, not ripping anyone off and honesty.'

Rachel says she learned from odd people at odd times. The example of her father was something to which she often referred. 'He was an incredibly hard worker and a terrific businessman who had a vision and I learned from him about the creative nature of business. He was scrupulously honest and was always devastated when people ripped him off. He had one arm blown off in the war, no counselling, no rehabilitation and yet he persisted and built up his delicatessen businesses. They were always immaculate.'

Not all Rachel's experiences during this time were good and she soon found out that not everyone has the same ethics in business. 'I learned about being ripped off. Often about being ripped off creatively but I never imagined that someone would not pay me properly.

'I knew from my father's business that you sometimes didn't get paid, but I never believed that someone could lie to you saying the cheque's in the mail when it's not. I never imagined that people would try and buy all the components of my jewellery, simply so I couldn't have them.

'There will always be people who rip you off but I don't believe one must live in a dog-eat-dog environment. I don't believe that globally it works. It is the responsibility of all of us to make changes in our own lives and when we do that it ripples. If we don't do that, we just really screw ourselves up. If you've been ripped off you learn your lesson in one of two ways. You either become like those people or you learn that there is an integrity and a reciprocity that can happen between people. And if you sustain that integrity and reciprocity for long enough you do in the end deal only with people who are like minded.'

Rachel describes herself as a very vertical thinker, which is not something she's terribly happy about. 'I think lateral thinkers are much better off.' Her vertical mind had a well thought out, carefully planned path: she would produce the costume jewellery, make a whole lot of money, go to America, attend an acting school and learn about comedy.

Like many plans though, it didn't pan out quite like she expected.

'Life doesn't work that way. I did the jewellery and I learned two things. First, that you don't have to go to acting school to be able to get up on stage and be a stand-up comedian. Secondly, that if you commit yourself to one business you don't have time to do anything else if you're going to do it properly.

'I made the jewellery, was very successful, made some money and was miserable because I wasn't doing stand-up. So eventually I realised that I couldn't do two things at the same time. I sold all my jewellery tools and started waitering and cleaning houses, so my mind wasn't distracted.'

She had scraped together a substantial amount of money from a business she began with only ten old pearl necklaces, and decided to take her comedy seriously. To do this Rachel employed a theatrical agent and again found that not everyone operates on the same level or to the same standards.

'I was confronted with a person who gave me photocopies with dog-eared corners, who had the phone technique of a piranha, who treated me with no respect as if I were a commodity to be sold, I found it impossible. I couldn't live with it. It was like giving a golden egg to a person who had no idea, you know, someone who would just drop it.

'I continued with this for two and a half years because I thought this is the way this industry works and what do I know about show business, about entertainment? I just figured I had a lot to learn. By this time I was 32, so it wasn't like I was a baby. In my own business I'd learned that if I didn't produce jewellery, I didn't eat.'

Rachel believes that you have to learn straightaway how to sell your product if that is your livelihood but she found that the people she was dealing with had different priorities.

'There were a number of people who disappointed me greatly, but for every ten that did, there was always that unique person who was honest and generous. This experience was so completely uplifting that it always rekindled my faith. Generally I found that the people who were most successful were the ones who treated others with respect, which was very reassuring. For over two years I persevered with this theatrical agent, and for over two years I was at odds with them.

As with almost anything, to do a job well, you have to be interested. This is particularly true in the area of promotion, whether it be for a product, or of a person. The promotor must have a real belief in the product in order for it to succeed. In Rachel's case, she needed someone who believed in her abilities as a comic.

'They didn't have a clear picture of what I wanted for myself. In 1989 I went to London and worked for three to four weeks off my own bat and then went to the Edinburgh Festival where I got really good reviews. After the festival I went back to London and worked again and then when I came back to Melbourne my agent didn't seem particularly excited about what I'd done. I wanted to go back to London and they thought I had a really inflated view of my value in the market place.

'I just went, "Excuse me, is this a Fellini movie or are you my agent? What are you telling me? I'm ambitious for myself, of course I am, and if I think I can do something then you should be supportive of that, not tell me that I'm impatient and that I don't know the ways of the industry".

'It was ludicrous, and I had the reviews to prove it. So I left them and approached two other people but I had the same feeling. I'm an extremely motivated person and creatively I have a strong sense of integrity and commitment to work and I realised that a lot of people in this industry don't.'

Part of Rachel's frustrations stemmed from the fact that many of the people she was dealing with saw her simply as a commodity. This idea interests me because in many ways it could be said that Rachel Berger, in the role of stand-up comedian, is a commodity. She 'sells herself' just as any product or service is sold, in that she demands a fee for her service and that price is determined by her ability to perform and deliver. What she says led to the breakdown of some of her professional relationships, was that those people saw her only in that light. They would only give to her in time what they thought they would be able to get back financially. Her understanding of the nature of her business is very different to that and she doesn't bind herself to the idea of giving to receive.

'A lot of people see me as a commodity but I do not see myself in that way and I don't see the audience as a consumer. These days too many people treat the general public only as consumers and not citizens. My father was a great inspiration for me here. He was very creative with his business so he never got bored and he never treated customers like just customers. He was generous on all fronts.'

To date Rachel has not found another agent or manager, so she still represents herself. This can be extremely difficult.

'There's a professional "script"—a dynamic which happens when managers and promoters talk about the artist, their availability, and their value. When the performer enters that realm it changes the dynamic. A venue owner doesn't feel comfortable saying to me, "Well, I don't think you can sell 5000 tickets", and me saying, "I think I can".'

Rachel doesn't mind challenging attitudes about the right and wrong way for a performer to run their career.

'I change the rules. I do it in my work all the time, so it's not an uncomfortable position for me to be in. My work is about challenging people on that level. I'm a "woman with attitude", which can sometimes be misunderstood.'

Currently Rachel works with a promoter/tour manager so she is able to step back from this type of confrontation and concentrate more on her work. It has also given her a clearer perspective on her role as an artist.

'I lost track of my value as an artist. If you're off on a side road somewhere it's really hard to know what's going on on a major highway.' Illustrating this point she tells me about a recent trip to England and her feelings about work in Australia.

'I went to England thinking I didn't have any value in the marketplace. In fact I did. People had remembered me and my work from my previous visits. The fact that the Australian marketplace is so small means that you constantly have to battle to perform and you lose track of your value. In that arena, it's very difficult to keep a gauge of your worth. It makes you doubt your worth and your creative abilities. My success in London made me realise that I had lost touch with the real picture and that I had to get help and delegate some of the responsibility.'

I ask Rachel about how she manages to keep delivering.

'There's a big difference in working at a desk and doing what I do. If I have a bad day I just can't go away and cry about it. The show must go on. In many ways it's a real liability. Sometimes I think I just can't get up there tonight but on other days it is the most buoyant feeling—anticipating the laughter and knowing that I am going to have fun.

'It comes down to exactly why you are doing it. If I've had a hell day I think my god, I have to do a show tonight and at a certain point I just switch off and concentrate on the show. That audience is my first priority and they come to see me to have a good time and I have to deliver. Everything else is diminished if I can't get up on stage and deliver. Some nights it works better than others because I am only human, a very vulnerable human being at that. You have to really know why you're doing it otherwise it's easy to lose energy and extremely difficult to sustain your motivation.'

Rachel is clear about why she does stand-up comedy. She wants to challenge perceptions and she thinks comedy is a great way to help people gain access to ideas and attitudes they may otherwise turn away from. 'Laughter is very emancipating. It takes a lot of courage for a person in an audience to leave themselves open and available enough to really laugh.'

What amazes me is the courage it takes for Rachel to be able to push those boundaries and keep on standing and delivering.

C.L.

# Liz Cotter

## Photographer

Liz Cotter has spent many years around cameras but she only recently decided to turn her photographic skills into a serious business. With the help of NEIS (New Enterprise Initiative Scheme), she has set up her own photographic studio, specialising in architectural photography.

Before I saw Liz's photographs, I couldn't quite make the connection between her strong visual arts background and architectural photography. The first page of her portfolio showed me that she had in fact combined the two and there was nothing incongruous about her choice. She makes building sites into art. The shots are practical in the sense that they portray what she is commissioned to show, but also aesthetically pleasing. Many of the photographs could be on display in an art gallery as their compositions are original and very beautiful.

Obviously architects can't cart around their projects to show new clients. Buildings are not a moveable feast and short of trekking out to all their sites with clients, photographers like Liz are their best option.

'I started photography in second form of high school and was completely obsessed with it. When I was about fifteen a close friend of my mother's died and left all my brothers and sisters and me $200 each. I went out and bought a camera with that money, and still have it today. I've taken some of my best photos with it and love it. It wasn't until last year when I decided to go into business that I bought another camera. I'd always just used that same one.

'I always knew that image making of some kind was something that I wanted to do. I went to school in the Seventies. I was part of the generation totally entranced by television, I watched enormous amounts of it, probably unhealthy amounts but it made me fall in love with pictures. Video was still quite new when I was at school and I thought it would be a really funky thing to do, but the school said, 'Oh no dear, you can't do that, video is not art'. So I stayed with photography although I did, in the end, experiment with film at art school.'

Art school is usually the place where creative spirits are let free and nurtured to explore the extent of their passions. What Liz experienced was a nervousness and a confidence crisis that took her away from the creation of images. 'All the people around me were really earnest and made really good whacky art films. I thought that I'd lost it. I decided that was it. I wasn't creative anymore. I started feeling really nervous about the technology. On one level I embraced it entirely and loved all the bits of wire, jacks, plugs and lenses. On the other hand I found it technologically horrifying. It was too hard and I didn't want to know about it. I didn't think that I could do it, so I stopped.'

Liz explains that she was both attracted and repelled by the medium and it was at this point that her path took a new turn. She moved from being a creator to an assistant to the creator and stepped into the world of film production. She worked for ten years in this field in varying capacities, from runner to production manager and producer.

'So many people had told me I was a good organiser and production was an area I thought I could get into. I knew I was good at interpreting other people's creativity. To do that though, I had to completely discount my own creativity.

'I loved it to begin with because I was involved in an industry that I was interested in. If I wasn't going to be behind the camera myself, this was the next best thing. I wanted to go to film school but I was really intimidated by it. I thought I couldn't do it. At that time to apply I thought you had to have a background in physics and chemistry. I thought, I'm an art head, I don't know what a periodic table looks like let alone how to interpret one.'

For ten years Liz worked in production before she realised that it wasn't what she wanted to do. She tried to shut out her own creativity, to put a lid on it and pretend it didn't exist, but that spirit or yearning usually remains and Liz's story is testament to that.

'I watched people in a number of different capacities who called themselves directors who didn't know one end of the camera from another, who had no more creative nous than I did. They just had the gumption to say, "Oh yeah, I can do that". That's when I thought damn it, I can do that too. I realised I had my own creative ideas and ideals and that they were as valid as anyone else's.'

There were two significant events that spurred along the positive voice in her. 'I ran into a girl who had been in the year below me at school. She was an architect doing very well for herself and remembered that I'd always done photography at school. She asked me to join her in an exhibition of artists and architects working together. It was wonderful and I remember thinking wow, I haven't done this for ages. I really do love it.'

The second major incident was the death of her father. When we met she mentioned almost in passing that this had been a large factor in her decision. About a week later though, she rang me to say that it was this event that really pushed her.

'More than anything else, his death made me realise that I had to do what made me most happy in the world. It was what I had always wanted to do, but somehow I shut it out for so many years.

'After he died, I couldn't focus on anything and someone asked me to be part of a group of people who wanted to travel diagonally across the desert from Sydney to Broome. I wasn't doing anything much at the time so I decided to go along. Most of the people on the trip were architects and I took a Bolex camera and some 16mm film and shot time lapse across the country and an enormous number of stills. I felt incredibly comfortable behind the camera.

'When we got to Broome I had a revelation. I'd often heard about people having these moments where something hits them like a lightning bolt, but thought they were a bit of an exaggeration. Now I know they're not. The trip was over and I was feeling really happy for the first time in ages. A friend and I woke up really early on the last morning and went out to the port before the sun came up. I was taking photographs and I thought, I have to do architectural photography.'

It doesn't surprise me in the least that Liz decided at this moment to do photography. However, that she pinpointed the area she would work in so specifically has me wondering.

'I think the architectural idea came so strongly to me because I had been travelling with so many architects. We talked about architecture a lot on the journey, so naturally it was in the forefront of my mind. I had always been interested in it though, and I had just completed a script for a documentary I wanted to make about Circular Quay because I saw it as a symbol of Sydney, redevelopment and settlement.

'So there I was, in Broome, photographing this fantastic port structure against the most beautiful sunrise. It was one of those really blissy moments and it became very clear to me that I belonged behind a camera, not a desk. I realised all the other work I'd been doing up until that point was a bad joke. I felt so comfortable and happy. I thought, how can I do anything else but this?'

Once the decision had been made, Liz set about putting it into action. 'I'm a bit of a schemer and I thought there's got to be some grant that I can get to set myself up.'

In 1986, Liz worked on ABC television's 'Beat Box', a program aimed at young people, full of information about kids' rights and schemes to assist them. 'From "Beat Box" I knew that there were lots of government schemes and grants available to unemployed people. I hadn't worked since my dad's death so I set about to find out if I qualified.

'I rang up the CES and asked about the schemes and how to qualify. People were really helpful, but said, "They're quite difficult to get into, dear". I just thought, yeah, yeah. I'm good at filling out application forms and saying what needs to be said. I didn't even consider that I wouldn't be accepted. I rang the architect who I worked with on that first exhibition, asked her if she thought it was a good idea and if there was a market for an architectural photographer and she said, "It's great, no one else is doing it and identifying themselves so clearly. Go for it". So I applied, went for an interview and was accepted into NEIS.'

So the self-confessed 'art head' was throwing herself into the world of marketing, bookkeeping and planning. The course may not have taught her anything new about her photography, but it did teach her how to make a living and a viable business from it.

'In many ways they assume you have no business knowledge which was great for me because even though I had experience in production, there was so much about business I just hadn't thought of. We had to sit down and actually think, is my idea a viable business, can I do this? The NEIS people were very Eighties in their gung-ho approach to marketing which I knew wasn't for me, but was interesting anyway. I wanted to be a bit more subtle in my approach to putting myself forward.

'My business idea was poles apart from anyone else's in the course, which didn't seem to matter in the slightest. The skills they taught were useful, no matter what your business. It helped me identify my competitors, taught me how to approach what had always been a hobby, as a business, and most importantly how to structure my billing. I realised if the rates I charged were too low, I wouldn't be seen as a credible photographer in the market.

'What was also really useful was it taught how to get information from government departments and such like, which are pretty important skills to have when you're running your own business. It was very thorough which I appreciated and made me take the whole thing a lot more seriously.'

NEIS gives those who complete the course an allowance for 52 weeks to help the business in that crucial first year. It's a wonderful idea that means even while you're establishing your business, you know you'll at least be able to eat. It also means that money you do make in that period can go towards the business and its needs.

It has been over twelve months since Liz returned from Broome and I wondered if her focus has broadened; whether she would like her photographs to encompass a wider view of the world.

'I do take other pictures now. As time moves on my perspective changes. I decided to specialise because architecture really interested me but I can see now my choice was rooted in something deeper than that. I thought I could only interpret other people's creativity. In these last twelve months I've come to understand that is not necessarily true.'

Many of the women in this book have talked about the personal struggle to establish their businesses, but also focus on the day-to-day practicalities they have found equally challenging. What Liz has descibed is the personal struggle and the slow process of gaining enough confidence to realise that she has her own ideas and images to create; that her interpretation of the world is valid—one that challenges and interests others.

'When I started I was often terrified and wondered what on earth I had done. But now, two years later, it *is* working. I no longer have my earlier insecurities and I now feel that I am lucky enough to successfully combine commerce and creativity.'

C.L.

# Jodie Boffa

## Fashion Designer

Jodie Boffa is the force behind some of the most sought-after, upmarket ready-to-wear clothes for women in Australia at the moment. The emphasis on exquisite cut and her use of unique fabrics has made her a big name in an area that is already saturated with ambitious 'bright-young-things'. At only 30 years of age she has accomplished, in her six years of business, a success that most clothes designers only dream of. Last year she won the prestigious Wool Award for Excellence. She is coveted by all the glossy magazines, and is encouraged yet declines to become a doyenne of the Sydney social set. Jodie has remained remarkably unaffected and level-headed, her straightforward manner is both refreshing and somewhat unexpected.

Jodie is one of those rare people who 'just knows' what it is that they must do with their lives. Ever since she can remember she has made things with fabric, either outfits for herself or for her dolls.

'My parents had a dress-designer friend who was a great inspiration. When I was about five I watched her make up some doll's clothes in a flash, I was really impressed! I've always loved clothes, although none of my family seem to have had the same passion—they are all in hairdressing. I'm not sure where this obsession came from! I did have a great-uncle who was a tailor and from the age of ten I spent some time with him, perhaps his influence rubbed off on me. He was of the old school, very exacting and precise. He was the type of man who'd wear beautiful tailored trousers just around the house. I used to take my things to him when I was at college for his advice. I remember once I took him this jacket that for the life of me I couldn't get right. He immediately ripped the sleeves out, right in front of me. It was quite a brutal act! What took him five minutes to put right took me five hours! I guess he made a mark on me.

'After school it was taken for granted that I'd go on and

do dress design at a technical college. It was a very absorbing, intensive course and a lot of plain hard work. You basically learn that a lot of what you're going to have to do if you want to be in this industry is immensely tedious. There were 36 hours of lessons a week and about the same again in homework. A lot of people just couldn't cope and dropped out. The pressure they put you under at college is good because that's exactly how real life is. If you can't hack the pace there, then you never will. I'm not sure, though, if they still teach it that way.

'At college I used to enjoy the pattern-making and I always wanted to learn more about it. It's absolutely fundamental. The more you learn about pattern-making the more control you've got over how it all translates to the final garment. I think there is not enough emphasis on the technical details here in Australia.'

I interviewed Jodie in January, which is the rag-trade's traditional holiday period.

'It seems so silly to me. I just don't think it works for us to have this big holiday at this time of the year. I can't get anything done, there's no one around to do it. Remember we are competing with Asia, do you really think that they just shut-down for a month like we do? I think the notion of "now it's holiday time" has to be gotten rid of, if we're to take ourselves seriously. You can't have it all. I admit that we do have a good life here in Australia. We're spoilt. To some extent that's also why I have chosen to live here.'

I asked Jodie if she had any 'heroes' or people that she admires.

'Jil Sander is my heroine. When I look at some of her pieces I swear I can hardly breathe! Her cut and her use of fabrics are second to none. She is the richest woman in Germany today. Her pieces are extremely expensive but I think they're worth it; you could easily pay $1600 for one of her shirts.

'I'd love to be able to accomplish what she does. It's very hard to do that here, though. Partly it's because our seasons are different—we're always working a season behind. Also we don't have access to the fabrics, or the technology to produce those incredible fabrics. Our market is just so small and our wages are high. It doesn't help that the duty on the fabrics we import is running at 31 per cent. Unfortunately the resources are just not here for us to create really special fabrics; all mine have to be imported. We still produce all the raw materials in Australia but send them off overseas once they're harvested, only to pay enormous tariffs when they get sent back to us in a more usable form. For example, if you want to produce a beautiful, weighty but "floppy", soft wool for a woollen suit you just can't do it here—we haven't got the technology set up. At times it really frustrates and depresses me that I can't do or get certain things here!

'I called my business by my own name, like Jil Sander has, because it seems to me that people want to know who the actual person behind the clothes, designing them, is. Here in Australia people like to associate the product with the person. Today, for example, I'm in the *Sydney Morning Herald*—I have to admit that this is good publicity for my clothes. Labels are important to people because of the whole volume, marketing and image built up behind them. People are still very label conscious and for the Nineties I don't see that changing much. The big names are going to remain very important, but I think there's going to be a different label-consciousness than there was in the Eighties. After all that "conspicuous consumption" that went on people seem to be calming down a bit. They still want to indulge in luxury items but perhaps they're indulging in fewer of them. They'll go and do the shopping at Franklins and then use the money they save to buy some premium smoked salmon, or some other kind of indulgence. I noticed that before all the interest rates were hiked-up again recently there was a noticeable willingness for people to spend on more expensive items. As soon as "interest rate rise" was mentioned people's purses shut tight. I actually think there is still a lot of money out there, floating around. You've just got to give people a good enough reason to spend it.

'The market here, because of the population, is still very small. I'd like to see it expand. Ten years ago things were very limited in the fashion area. Clothes were relatively boring—big, boxy linen suits that were very expensive. There are two schools of design that are obvious to me at the moment. There's the old school of George Gross, Weiss and that mob and some interesting new young blood in people I admire, like Andrew Chiodo, in Melbourne. I like his work because it isn't derivative, it's clean and has an almost Japanese feel. I also admire what Colette Dinnigan is doing.

'I tend to wear all my own clothes. I don't always design for myself, sometimes my own stuff doesn't particularly suit me. I buy the odd casual clothes, like a big workshop shirt and stretch pants.

'In Australia, we work a season behind the rest of the world. The isolation we have is good in a way; we can get on and do our own thing relatively unhindered. We aren't necessarily slacker in quality than any other country. The people here who really do try hard are as good as anyone else in the world. There is a bit of a tendency I think, because we do work a season behind, to just run overseas and buy some samples, come back and copy them. I think it happens a lot. I'm sure the reasoning is, how are the foreign designers ever going to find out anyway? We're protected by our distance. In the near future tariffs are going to come down a lot and we'll see a great deal more big, international names represented here. It will be impossible to plagiarise them then. It will help move the industry along by having those designer labels directly in competition with us. It will be good, it'll shake the industry up a bit.

'The only thing that worries me is that we will still have to pay very high tariffs on the same fabrics that those international designers pay no taxes on and we'll be competing directly with them.

'People are starting to become more educated around the world about the good things coming out of Australia. I think if you're good, it will be noticed. The buyers do have to look carefully though. I found overseas that you are working more on the threshold of design. You are very aware of the immediacy of the market around you. A lot of buyers are sourcing things out of Australia now. In some areas we are cheaper for the same sort of quality than Asia is for example.'

When asked to describe her work, Jodie offers, 'Because my influences are mostly from Asia rather than Europe, my lines tend to be clean and simple. Some of the designs coming out of Asia are almost on the edge of looking ridiculous—too fancy or clever. Largely though, the detail and the feel are good.

'It's hard to escape using clichés, but what seems to be said of my clothes is that they are "classic with a twist". I try to push simple things, although I don't want them to be boring. Perhaps they are on the conservative side but there's always something a bit different about the cut or the fabric I've used.'

In order to demonstrate what she meant, Jodie showed me an elegant shirt cut in one piece on the bias and an unusual jumper made of velvet corded tuille.

'We've only sold a handful of them because the fabric is hard to get and it's expensive. At $1000 for a small jumper I think it is one of the most expensive things we've ever done.'

When I met Jodie I was impressed with her image, she looked every bit the 'young inner-city fashion designer' to me. I told her I couldn't imagine having to wear high-heels in a workshop, running around all day. I joked that she'd be better off wearing Reeboks. She said, 'I do feel under pressure a lot to "look great". Often I just don't have the time to worry about it. For sheer comfort I used to wear trainers in the studio and "good shoes" for any meetings. It was so much more practical—you get filthy working in there all day. Unfortunately I'd always get caught out—the fashion girl from *Cleo* or somewhere would come in unexpectedly and find me in them! I had to give it up.'

When Jodie worked from home two years ago, she found it a real strain. 'It was so hard to always keep an immaculate house, just in case a client or fashion editor came over. For some reason, I think that people assume if you've got a messy house you're a pig or you're "losing it", but if you have a messy office, you're just busy. So I spent a lot of time cleaning! Working from home took a lot of organisation and your personal and professional lives tend to blur. In the beginning, though, I think working from home takes a lot of pressure off you, in terms of overheads. My husband and I were ready for a big change anyway. Living and working in the city meant always having to go out. Now we live right on the beach, it's wonderful because it's just like being on holidays when I'm at home.'

Part of this change in Jodie's life was brought about by a brush with serious illness in 1993.

'I'd had this lump on my neck, right near my Adam's apple, for about ten years. Really, it just seemed to be part of me. I left it six months to go and have a biopsy done that I'd been urged to have by a doctor. I hadn't been feeling great, but I thought it was just a vicious cycle of too much work and too many commitments cumulatively getting me down. After the biopsy, in the week or so that lapsed after I had it, I really didn't worry about it that much. I thought things like that just didn't happen to me and I was sure it'd be put down to stress.

'I was casually reading *The Women's Weekly* outside when the specialist called me in and told me that it was cancer. I was going to have to undergo surgery without delay. It really shocked everyone. I'd find Matthew, my husband, looking at me oddly all the time. It was awful having to tell my family. I didn't tell friends until it was over, I didn't want the drama. People seem to have a knee-jerk response to the word *cancer*, it isn't necessarily a life sentence you know. Fortunately cancer of the thyroid is curable, it was a very straightforward procedure. The whole thing made me wake up to myself a lot.'

Like many people who go through a potentially life-threatening experience such as this, Jodie believes, 'It's the best thing that ever happened to me. I realised how unhappy I was, how much I was running myself down and it was time to take stock. I was working at least six and a half days a week. Because I am such an extreme person I think it took something like cancer to stop me in my tracks, anything lesser I might've ignored. My message to you is don't be complacent about lumps!

'I see a specialist every three months and I try and look after myself, but sometimes I forget—I'm only human. I do make an effort to leave work at a reasonable hour. I'll work very hard all week but my weekends are sacred. Matthew and I just potter around at home. I love going to the beach, swimming and gardening. I love to get back to that feeling you used to have when you were a kid on holidays; everything seemed timeless, you just drifted and dreamed. Being in the garden I lose all sense of time and the world. I have no recollection of what I think about, I suppose it's a bit like meditating. It really refreshes me.

'I also think that if you are the key person in a business it's really important to pace yourself; if you go, the business goes. I think you can actually get used to an extraordinary level of stress, without which you can't function. It can become addictive. Take it from me, it's just not worth it! You have to take time out to give back to yourself. It's also good to treat yourself occasionally, if you can. When I won the Wool Award I treated myself partly to a trip to Paris and with the rest I bought some pearls, something I've always wanted.'

Having the support of her husband seems to have given Jodie a safe place to come back to and venture out from in her life.

'I would never have achieved all this without Matthew. It's a volatile industry and he is always very supportive. He encourages me to achieve the things I want to. We've been married for six years. He's an advertising copywriter. I knew after seeing him about three times that here was a man I would be with for a very long time!

'I don't hob-nob around with the "cocktail set". It really doesn't interest me. The media can be really insidious. You have to be careful because there is a lot of playing-off of people, it can ruin you. I think the most important thing is to just do your work and let the rest take care of itself. I admit I get a bit of a thrill at seeing my tear-sheets in *Vogue* etc., but you have to remember it is only Australia and there's a whole, great big world out there. It must be kept in perspective. You have to be careful not to believe your own publicity too much; it's all hype in the end.

'I don't want to know too much about the details of what everyone else is doing—either in what they might be designing or about how they run their businesses. You can lose speed if you're constantly being told that so and so's new range is outselling yours two to one. It can breed insecurity and I don't think that's good. I just get on and do my work.

I rarely think of what anyone else is doing, I'd become so insecure if I did. The reality of my working life is that I just have to knuckle down and do it, I really don't have time to worry about what Jo Bloggs is doing.

'I'm overseas about four or five times a year. It nearly kills me to get that organised! I mostly go to Tokyo, which I love, and Hong Kong. I hate the worry of leaving things behind. The longest stretch I've been away for is three weeks. It really is an organisational nightmare, although the girls are great. I hadn't had a holiday for five years, so last year I went away for two weeks and I've just had three weeks off now.

'There comes a time when everyone in my business just needs to have some time out. I think it's best if we all do it together—if I'm off and the girls are working I can't help myself worrying about things and so I end up ringing all the time, or going in. Besides, there are some things only I can do. This is the best time of the year to have that time off, when everyone in the industry is on holidays too. This time, coming back, it's been a challenge to get my head back in work mode! One thing I find essential is to have a comprehensive list written each morning—I can't do anything without it. I know that if I'm scatty then everyone in the workshop is too.

'We do three ranges a year, two summer ones: the first being kind of trans-seasonal and then a resorty one. Then there's a winter range. My preferences change depending on the fabric I've got. I love working with a good wool. Basically the fabric does the work. What I do with it in terms of styling is relatively simple, I like to keep the design clean. I have to tell you, I am never in some great, inspired, creative mood when I'm coming up with new collections. It's not a tampon commercial! I usually sketch ideas down. I don't take photos of clothes that inspire me or anything like that. Of course, I am influenced by what I see overseas and I have to stay aware of the trends, but mostly I do what I want. I think you have to learn how to manage the creative process for yourself. It's about putting information in and not forcing it out. You observe all the different things around you like movies, ads, art and let them all cook for a while, in terms of their influence on you, then it all slowly infiltrates your work.

'My staff and friends tell me that I'm overly pessimistic when my new collections are due out. I must admit I have a bit of a crisis. It can feel very insecure when everything you've been working so hard on for months is finally out there, hanging on a rack. Somehow it seems insubstantial. I always believe in my work fully while I'm doing it, though. I suppose I am overly critical.'

When it comes to the marketing and selling of her ranges, Jodie says, 'I really am not interested in selling things to buyers that they don't want or won't be able to sell. There is a certain protocol about selling to important buyers. I think they expect me to push, push, push, but quite honestly I couldn't be bothered. I'm not going to sell every item in a range to every customer, it isn't realistic. I think they are getting to know my irreverent ways now! I have a brother-in-law who tells me how he goes about the hard sell in his business. It seems overtly masculine and pushy to me. He just can't believe that I can actually be doing well without implementing the hard-sell approach. I think I'm good at selling my range—in an appropriate way.

'I have four full-time staff and numerous sub-contractors that I work with. Most of the people I employ I've gotten from putting the word out, or else they are people I worked with in my last job, at a place called Guanta. It is hard to find good, reliable people to work with. You pay through the nose for a good machinist, but for me it's well worth the investment. Nicole, who works with me in the studio, has been with me since the beginning and is indespensable. Staff problems are the one thing that would make me quit. It's the main area in my business that can really get me down.

'Ultimately, as an employee, I think you are in the job for yourself, because you want to be. My attitude is, well it's your responsibility to be a good and civil person in the workplace and the rest will take care of itself. It's not a school. As a boss you can't afford to play "mum" too much. It'd be great if we were always one big happy family, but it doesn't always work out that way.

'I think it's important to always be sharp in this industry, it helps to have eyes in the back of your head. The more *au fait* you are with how a good design room works, the more comfortable you are in it. Of course, by training good people up you run the risk of them going into business in competition against you. That's life, you can't worry about it too much.

'Sometimes I think the workshop can look like there's no one running the place, there's no obvious hierarchy, no boss throwing their weight around.'

Jodie, like so many of the women we interviewed, didn't like being a boss and nor did she think she was particularly good at it. She'd been reading a book called *The 'E' Myth* by Michael E. Gerber about which Jodie said, 'I swear someone had stood back and watched me in business these past few years. It said that most people who started their own business did so primarily because they wanted to sack their own boss! I'd have to agree. It also said that most people ended up doing an enormous amount of administration and all the things tied up in running a business, rather than doing the thing they actually enjoyed doing and went into business to do. All the business side of it takes you away from what you want to do. I actually find it really difficult to just sit down and design like I used to. My mind is so split worrying about all sorts of things. I come up with an idea that I'll give to Nicole to develop, which is a good way to work because I have to be very clear about it in my head before we start. It's better to be just that one step removed from it. It helps me be more objective about the process.'

At college Jodie worked part-time for a well-known fashion designer and when she had completed the course she worked for a company called Guanta.

'I had got some great experience at Guanta but decided I wanted to learn more, so I followed Matt to London where I worked for Jasper Conran for a year. We were just settling in when Matt was offered a job in Singapore.'

When asked about the future, Jodie says, 'I'd like to get into exporting. We are in the process of supplying a department store in Hong Kong. I want to be careful though, because people can get terribly enthusiastic for you. You can get swept away with it a bit. It can be scary. Part of it is finding the right person to handle you overseas. I think it's wise to avoid big waves in the business, to keep things operating at a manageable level. You can get stuck by over-estimating the market, or misjudging it because we work so far ahead.

'In the next two or three years we'd like to have kids. My husband is concerned about how it might affect me and in turn it might affect him. Too much stress around us would be quite destructive. I figure that no time's really a good time to do it. You can think too much about it, maybe you just deal with it when it happens. My Nana is always telling me how much easier it was in her day—you didn't have the luxury of pondering over it too much. I still feel like I'm in my early twenties, I don't want to rush things.'

'I think you have to have a vision to do this, a talent. The rest is just hard work! When you have a reason, you can do anything.'

S.R.

# A Helping Hand

In this chapter we look at women who went into business with a helping hand along the way. For some, this help was in the form of taking on a partner, while for others it was enrolling in a government-run course designed to launch people with good ideas into their own businesses.

According to current research, women will tend to go into a sole proprietorship when starting a business, rather than a partnership.[1] This is partly because there do not appear to be the necessary networks in place for women to readily find suitable business partners. It is also because women believe it is less of a risk, financially and personally, to go it alone. They feel they can keep their business concerns smaller and more manageable this way, without entangling another party. There are obvious rewards, however, from being in a partnership. These include a shared goal or vision, the added personal and financial support, increased networking possibilities and a greater lending potential.

Some of the women we interviewed did not have sufficient equity to start their business so they chose to go into partnerships with other women or men to increase their initial capital. Amongst those who had male partners we profiled only those whose partner's involvement in the day-to-day running of the business is negligible; or women who maintain the majority sharehold in their company.

For Katie Graham and Olivia Guntarik from Strut, partnership meant going on something of an adventure together, nutting out ideas and gaining experience along the way. Although their expertise is in different areas, their talents and contacts complemented each other's and so brought wider networking possibilities. Katie and Olivia have benefited from sharing their own skills and also learned a lot about operating their business by attending a government-run course.

There is now an awareness by both the Federal and state governments of the need to help promote and encourage small business. This is perhaps best highlighted by the emphasis placed on small business in the Federal Government's 1994 White Paper on Employment and Growth. More specifically, governments are now recognising the necessity to encourage and assist women in small business.

In terms of business ownership, women account for one in three small business owners in the country. If small businesses make up 95 per cent of all business operations, and represent 50 per cent of all employment in the non-agricultural sector,[2] then women are playing a key role in a major economic and political arena. Consequently, governments are beginning to offer monetary and advisory assistance to help women in business compete and survive. Some government schemes are aimed at the long-term unemployed while other programs are aimed at encouraging women who want to set up their own businesses.

Research has found that women are not quite as informed as men about the possibilities and range of these government schemes. But it also indicates that when their awareness is raised, women will use the guidance offered more readily than men and enrol in these helpful courses at a greater rate.[3] There are many schemes available now through community services, government departments and some private institutions. It is recognised that providing this assistance will help the long-term unemployed see that there are alternatives in the range of employment open to them.

Martina Rienzner and the women from Strut completed the NEIS (New Enterprise Initiative Scheme) and YBI (Youth Business Initiative Scheme) programs designed to help the long-term unemployed start a business. For these women the gains made in terms of confidence building, gathering sound advice, developing business acumen and an increased awareness of networking possibilities were considerable. In Martina's case the NEIS course helped her find her business feet and overcome initial hesitancy.

We have found that handing on information means handing on some power. Mentors have long been a way of handing on information to apprentices. Part of the NEIS program that Olivia Guntarik and Katie Graham undertook involved having a business mentor because it has been shown that a mentor is invaluable to women and ideally involves more than just handing on skills and experience. Through its informal arrangement a rewarding and ongoing exchange can take place. Often the mentors appointed through the NEIS are not in the same area of business and this can be a drawback, as Olivia found. Some have found that the formalised nature of the mentors established through the NEIS and the fact that they are often not in the same field make it more difficult for a truly effective mentorship to take place. The exact nature of the mentor scheme may be under debate and up for improvement in some areas, however, the concept is a good one and in many cases works well.

Pam George preferred to keep her partner as a silent backer, almost in the role of a bank, with little say in the running of the business. She needed money to get started and so asked for assistance, as many women do, from people in her personal rather than professional life. She supplemented these funds with a loan from the bank to enable her to start. In documenting Pam's story we find that these often emotionally charged partnerships are not always satisfactory and may come with strings attached. However, they are sometimes necessary. Trudyanne Brown has also followed this path of forming a partnership with a husband.

Partnerships are often a realistic alternative to sole proprietorship. We hope to uncover some of the plusses and minuses of following this path.

S.R.

## Notes

(1) Leonie V. Still, *Enterprising Women*, Sydney: Allen & Unwin, 1990.
(2) *Fourth Annual Review: Small Business in Australia*, Canberra, Australian Government Publishing Service, December 1994.
(3) Anna Borzi, *The Gender Finance Gap*, Sydney: Borzi Smythe Pty Ltd, 1994.

# Martina Rienzner

## Cabinet-maker

Martina Rienzner has run her own cabinet-making business for three years now. I discovered her through a Business Enterprise Centre where a man referred to her fondly, if a little incredulously, as 'the German woman who runs a great cabinet-making business from an old bus!'

Some friends had also told me about her, so I decided to find out just what this infamous woman did to capture people's attention. I thought it interesting that she was working successfully in a male-dominated trade and had since become renowned for the high quality of her work. Martina had quite a reputation preceeding her!

I expected someone rather eccentric but found instead a gentle, softly-spoken but determined woman. I arrived at lunchtime in the workshop and it was pleasing to see that Martina, her co-workers and Freckle the Alsatian guard-dog were sitting down together to a home-made meal. I started by asking Martina how she came to be involved in this career.

'I wasn't particularly driven to become a cabinet-maker. I found myself more or less in a corner. The expectations of my parents and school teachers didn't leave much room for who I thought I was, or might be. It was a big shock for my family to discover that this was the decision I'd made—to become a cabinet-maker. They expected me to be a doctor or teacher or something like that, not go into a trade where I'd get my hands dirty. "Nice girls" don't do things like that!

'I think my parents also had a bit of a class problem with my going into a trade. According to their way of thinking you employed tradespeople, you didn't have them working in your family; particularly if they are your daughter! Thankfully my family are over it now. Since I've started my own workshop they seem to be pleased that there is someone in the family, apart from my father, who's gone out and started their own business.

'My father's life and death have influenced my attitude towards my business a lot. You have to invest in your private as well as your professional life if you want to succeed in the long run.'

Martina was trained as a cabinet-maker while still in Germany.

'Before my apprenticeship in Germany I'd gone to art school for a year and had done furniture design, but I found it boring. The things we were encouraged to make were either uncomfortable or impractical. Many of the designers don't have a practical background and cannot put the pieces together in any useful way.

'I decided to get some hands-on experience as I thought it would be more relevant. I did my practical apprenticeship with a large joinery workshop in Munich. It was a very traditional place, the men were really of the old school. Not surprisingly I suppose, I was the only woman there. They checked me out severely at first but they got used to me after a while. I started off with my own work bench tucked away in a little corner and they would all come around at different stages to see what "this woman" was up to. I was quite nervous in the beginning and felt the pressure to prove myself to them.'

Martina left Germany to come and live in Australia four years ago, deciding to return after holidaying here. She was attracted by the promise of constant blue skies and had really enjoyed meeting the people she came across, particularly in the country. The bus was an idea Martina had back in Germany to enable her to travel, work and live in the one vehicle.

'In order to do this I had to build a workshop into the bus and completely re-fit it. This bus was going to be like a travelling-working-home-type thing. It's seven metres long and absolutely bigger than life! I had to ship it out here, which took eight weeks and a lot of organisation to make sure it wasn't going to get damaged during the trip. Once the bus arrived customs wouldn't let it through for four months because they couldn't work out what it really was—there was no single, apt description for it. They weren't sure if it was a camper-van or a workstation etc., so they couldn't put the appropriate duty on it. I got very frustrated! Once I got the bus out of customs I lived in it for a year, parked in the workshop I rented.'

Martina has been in business for three years now. She came to Australia on the Skilled Migration Program set up by the Federal Government to recruit skilled workers from overseas to work in under-resourced occupations.

'When I arrived in Sydney I spent a lot of time at the CES trying to find work as a cabinet-maker. The man who looked after me there said I wouldn't have a chance because there was not much work in that area, and also because I was female. After going to a variety of CESs, searching through the newspapers and contacting builders, the CES pointed me in the direction of a government scheme called the New Enterprise Initiative Scheme. I couldn't find any work so I thought, why not?

'I enrolled in the NEIS, which was really very helpful. It explored all sorts of things I didn't know about, like cash-flow and marketing. The teachers had quite good advice about financial matters, something I'd not had much training in in Germany. The course also gave me the confidence to communicate in a better way and people began to show more interest and excitement in what I was doing.

'After doing the course it didn't take much to get the first client in. All I had to do was to be out and about, showing people what I was doing and getting them enthusiastic about my work. I have found telling people yourself, rather than having someone else present your work, is more effective than any other form of advertising. To date that is one of the best marketing tools I have. The course was useful because I got to know a new group of people and gained some indispensable skills. I'd recommend it.

'Before I did the course I'd had one job through a builder I'd managed to contact. While doing that job I found I didn't know much about how to do things here, like getting materials etc. There were other details that are different here than in Germany, like the technical differences and the terminology. I couldn't even go to the hardware store and order what I wanted! It was a difficult time. I wasn't up to doing that first job on my own, although that's what I did. It took six or seven weeks to complete. It was a good experience in the end because I was happy with the result and so was the client.

'I had always thought that at some stage I would have my own workshop. The plan was that I would arrive here and work with someone else for a few years so I would slowly get used to it and learn about the Australian tastes etc. I thought that if that didn't work out I was quite willing to just start up my own business. With the help of the course that's exactly what I set about doing.

'I had saved some money before I left Germany. After being unemployed here for six months and doing the course I had $5000 left. With that money, little as it was, I thought I would just go for it and start my own business. It seemed to be the right thing to do.'

Although Martina had comprehensive training in Germany, she found that it was necessary to become familiar with the technical differences of working in Australia, get a builder's licence, and learn about issues such as builder's liability.

'For me it was the perfect opportunity to say, "Okay, now I've got five weeks to prepare myself and really learn all the rules and regulations and everything I've got to comply with". In that time I applied for my builder's licence, which was not very hard. I showed them my trade certificate, all kinds of work I had done and sat for an exam as well. This was a few years ago, I'm not sure if it's changed now. That was how you went about obtaining a gold licence then. It's run by the Building Services Corporation who give you a gold card entitling you to work legally as a builder.'

After getting the licence out of the way the next big hurdle for Martina was the financial aspect and setting up the business.

'I found the building jargon hard to grasp and so I enrolled in a TAFE course in English. They threw me out of the course after a few weeks because my English was too good. At least I was doing something right! I really did it because I wanted to know things like how to write business letters and how to start a conversation in a hardware store to ask for the things I needed. I had quite a good vocabulary, but I didn't have very good English communication skills. In the end I managed to just pick it up as I went along.

'I got my first "real" job doing a fit-out for a whole house, which took me an entire year. I got it by taking my portfolio around to all sorts of people—designers and architects etc. The response to the work has always been good. No one has ever said, "Oh, no we're really not interested in things like that". I think the quality always speaks to people. We've been asked back by that very first client to do some additional work. That makes it clear to me that we are doing a great job.'

There are not many women cabinet-makers around and so I was interested to hear how people reacted to her working in such a male-dominated trade.

'When I went into some of the cabinet-makers' workshops when I arrived they just couldn't believe their eyes. "What, a woman wanting to be a cabinet-maker?" They do tend to stare at you a lot! I have also noticed this same kind of incredulous reaction in Germany, but at least they are a bit more reserved and, well, polite about it.'

Martina finds that her all-female workshop is still viewed as 'highly unusual'. She says the reasons why it is all-female are varied; it is partly because of her personal preference to work with women and also because she wants to give women a chance in this traditionally male area. Martina finds that many of her clients also prefer to have women working on the site.

'Some people like to work with just female cabinet-makers. Once they get used to the idea of having tradeswomen in the house they think it is great. Still, it can be hard to get past people's prejudices that women have a biological disadvantage in this area.'

On building sites the feeling is similar to that created in the workshop. There is a lot of trust given to her and her co-workers. 'For example, people always leave us with a key. They do things like invite us to stay for cups of tea. I think it's quite different for the clients than having the male workers around. We seem to be treated better. It also works the other way around, I think we treat the clients better as well. We always take a lot of care to clean up after ourselves for example and spend a lot of time talking to the client about what they really want. It works out that a lot of the clients become good friends. They keep coming back to us for subsequent jobs.

'When we design the projects ourselves, which is roughly 50 per cent of the time, we start with someone who has only a vague idea of what they want. We then begin an intimate process of working out how to achieve this. It is necessary to gather all sorts of details about their personal habits; what they like to eat, how they like to cook, where they like things to be, if they entertain a lot etc., so that we can make informed decisions about the space we are designing. It can mean getting inside the person's head and for that you need to have an understanding or empathy with your client.

'These days I have four staff, three full-time and one part-time, which has only been the case quite recently. The full-timers work a four-day week because that way it also allows them to study.

'My staff come to me basically by just knocking at my door; I haven't had to advertise or anything. They usually turn up for work experience or an apprenticeship because they have heard about me. If a woman is interested in this trade, sooner or later she'll hear about me because as far as I know I'm the only woman running an all-female workshop, well, in Sydney at least.

'I am pleased to say the girls usually get hooked after a short period of time and want to stay! It has to work on a personal as well as professional level for me. Either we get on or we don't. It's essential that they have a certain amount of nous. I find it easier to take on people who have had no prior experience in the industry because that way I can train them from the start. They haven't had a chance to get into any bad habits. Because we do high quality work it is important that I show them exactly what I want. It's more important that the girls are keen, interested and learn by experience, rather than have a lot of technical know-how. I've found that a lot of people do their trade courses and just aren't able to cope with the reality of working life. I think this happens in a lot of trades, not just cabinet-making. Often it's good to come and get some hands-on experience to see if you're really suited to it.'

'Now the business is at a stage where I couldn't do it on my own. I rely on my staff because my turn-over is now bigger than it was. For the first two years the growth was very slow. It was terribly frustrating and there was always a struggle with the cash-flow. Every two months I had to ask someone to give me a thousand dollars just so I could pay the rent. It was terrible. Since then things have picked up and now we have a constant flow of jobs coming in and our turnover grows by 100 per cent each year.

'In those first two years we did not implement our marketing plan and we developed very slowly as a result. I've come to realise that it takes time to develop a reputation for quality. You have to be prepared to hang in there.

'Last year I had a crisis about not getting any new work and so rather than place an ad, I took around my portfolio. As I have previously found to be the case, it is really paying off now with commissions from all sorts of unexpected areas.

'I find it important to keep up your contacts in the industry and to maintain a network if you can. It's good to keep up with what is happening, attending woodworking shows and events. There was an exhibition not long ago at the showgrounds called "Timber and working with wood", at which I set up a stand. I thought it might bring in some business, but it didn't because most people came to gather ideas rather than to commission work. I will try again this year though at a show called "Designex" where I'll be taking a stand. It is a trade show for all those involved in interior design or products. There is a section for designer-makers which I think might generate us some work. It is an expensive exercise but I think it's worth it. I also stay in touch with what's happening through the Woodworkers Association. You have to keep up your marketing and unfortunately that means spending money.'

Martina believes women can do anything they set their minds to. She'd like to see more women take up traditional male professions or trades if that's what they want to do. 'Women are slowly becoming aware of opportunities for themselves. They are beginning to get more involved and are more confident about what they can do. I'd love to see women from a range of trades get together and have a support network set up for themselves. I think it's a viable thing. Lots of people would be interested in using our services. What we're doing is different and we should be proud of it.'

Martina doesn't get many opportunities for holidays since she started her business.

'This Christmas I am going back to see everyone in Germany, which I'm really looking forward to. It'll be the first time I've been back since I got citizenship. We will close down for two weeks but I'll be gone for six. At Christmas time everyone realises they need this or that done because they've had time to look around the house at what needs doing. Unfortunately most of the suppliers close down at Christmas too, so it can be difficult to get things done. I'm not especially worried, because if the girls have any trouble they can always fax me for advice ... isn't technology wonderful!'

Martina believes that the government could offer greater assistance to small businesses.

'Yes, I think the government could support small business more. There's a lot of pressure on us and we are an important sector of the business community, of the economy in general. There could be more tax incentives, for example. The implementing of schemes like NEIS are a really good idea, they really do some good.

'Twice I can distinctly remember when supporting the business financially was very touch-and-go. On both occasions I had to find someone to help me out. Thankfully, a very kind client forwarded me some money. There should be some safety-net for people in viable small businesses to enable us to ride these storms.'

Martina is delighted that the business is at a stage where she is able to pick the work she'll take on. 'We might refuse to quote for work that we really don't want, but mostly I enjoy the new challenges brought by different kinds of jobs. I am over the moon if the client is happy. I might personally think their taste is ugly, but in the end I don't have to live with it! If they keep coming back, they must be happy!'

Martina has been pleasantly surprised by the variety and quality of the Australian timbers she has come across and she uses them on jobs whenever she can.

'Rather than have any favourite timbers, I find there is always the perfect timber for the perfect job. We do use the native brushbox regularly. I get most of my timber from a local timber supplier who used to specialise in exotic timbers but now also specialises in Australian furniture timbers. Native timbers used to be very hard to get because in Australia everything gets logged and is used for the building industry, or else it gets chipped. There are timbers like Tasmanian myrtle for example, which is a beautiful furniture timber which is nearly extinct because it all got chipped up and sold to Japan. It would certainly be one of my favourites to work with.'

I was interested to ask if Martina had encountered any disasters in her business. Rolling her eyes she offered, 'There was one job that became a real nightmare, a staff problem really. I tried to give this particular worker the benefit of the doubt a few times, but in the end it was costing me too much time and money, so I had to get rid of her. It's unfortunate but it happens. I have a "three times" rule—if you keep on making the same mistake three times there's definitely something wrong!'

Working in an unusual field for a woman, Martina occasionally has problems with men's perceptions of women's abilities.

'We do encounter a bit of sexism along the way. I've had two girls come back in tears from the hardware store because they were not treated seriously, or were ridiculed when asking for things. Some men don't expect women to know what they're talking about when it comes to building materials. Now we have our well-trained, regular suppliers who know that they won't put one over us! They now treat us professionally and with respect. I do think it is that bit harder to prove yourself as a woman in this industry. Once they see the quality that we produce and realise the turnover we have, they know we're for real! At first I think they assume we're in it for the novelty value, but hey, we're still in business!'

I asked Martina if the bottom line in the business was economics.

'No, in fact the bottom line is to become really good at what you're doing and get the quality right. In the long run having that attitude proves to be economic in itself. I don't mind if the girls make mistakes or ask me how to do something a few times, as long as they are really learning. It's important that they begin to make their own decisions and to find out things for themselves. I make mistakes myself and I am always learning. It's important to try new things, to keep experimenting.

'As an employer I think it's essential to impart an overall vision of what we should be trying to achieve and what we are working towards. If my employees have a sense of this then they can't really go wrong.'

Like a number of the other women we interviewed, Martina found the more she got involved in the business side of things the less she became involved in the actual work being produced.

'Running the day-to-day business takes me out of the workshop a lot. Therefore, I don't actually get to keep a close track of the projects and their working development. When I'm gone for a few hours or a day, it is exciting to come back and see what has developed since my absence. It's good to let the girls come up with their own ingenious solutions, I can't always be towering over them. I've worked with people before who were adamant that their's was the only way. They became so dogmatic they couldn't allow people to make their own mistakes and in turn, learn from them. There are several good solutions to any single problem.'

I was curious to see how Martina viewed herself as a boss and whether or not she enjoyed that role.

'I've learned a lot about being a boss by trial and error. I find if I'm comfortable with it or not actually depends on the attitudes of those I employ. There were two women I employed early on who were used to a lot of guidance and they assumed I was happy playing the "big boss" role. I couldn't do anything right by them. They seemed to adopt an "us and them" mentality towards their working situation, which I never encouraged. Working out the boss–employee balance is difficult when you're new to it. I once worked in a display-making company and loved the absence of hierarchy there and they really encouraged equality. At the moment I think I've struck a nice balance with the girls working here. I've always believed that happy people work better.

'One day I know my employees will eventually want to start up their own businesses. I train them well so they can go and do that. It doesn't worry me that they might set up in competition with me. It is such an enormous market and I am proud if it helps increase the demand for good quality things. I also believe the more women out there giving cabinet-making a good name, the better!'

S.R.

# Pam George

## Private Collection

Pam has run Private Collection for eight years now. She has always harboured a desire to have her own business and today happily runs a very successful one in homewares.

'My father ran a general store in Western Australia for many years and as an adolescent I used to love working there. I've always loved dealing with people as customers.'

Pam had plenty of opportunity to explore that customer–retailer relationship because while working as a graduate trainee at Myer she spent a year running a department on the selling floor.

'It was great all-round training because you get to understand how the relationship with the end-customer works and the whys and hows of sales, right down the line. It's a very hands-on experience.

'I'd actually gone to university and graduated with an economics degree. After the first year I realised it wasn't for me. I loved economics but came to realise that its application was largely inappropriate.' Laughingly Pam adds, 'I did two years of accounting, which no one who's seen how I manage my books would believe! I am absolutely hopeless, I couldn't balance two columns of figures if I tried! No, numbers are not a strength of mine. My father does the books, I fax everything over to him. He's great because he's absolutely ruthless with me!

'I think I have an ability to see the big picture but somehow manage to lose all the detail. The essence or theme is clear to me but the rest just evades me. Ending up as an accountant would have been an appalling thing for me to try to do!'

'After university I worked for Myer and then Grace Bros. In those days individual states had separate buyers so I was the Perth manchester buyer. It involved a lot of travel overseas on buying expeditions and was a great experience. The job gave me lots of good opportunities. I loved it. I ended up becoming the national buyer when they decided to amalgamate all the states' buying powers and concentrate them in Sydney. Through this I met Danny, now my husband, who worked for TIA [Textile Industries Australia], the largest textile company in Australia, which encompasses companies like Sheridan.'

While she worked her way up through the ranks as a buyer Pam realised two things: first, that there was an obvious gap to be filled in the home fashion market and secondly, a realisation that her gender limited the level she could climb to within the company structure.

'I always knew I'd end up with my own business. I gained invaluable experience in my jobs leading to that inevitable end. The nature of the work in those companies enabled me to identify and focus on a specific market. I'd had enough experience to observe what people really wanted. It also became obvious that there were no women in the levels above me. In those days women just didn't get any higher. They are still conservative organisations and I think there are some token women on the boards or in senior positions now, but then it was very much a "boys' club" mentality.'

At this time Pam also met someone who would give her the opportunity she was looking for to do something more independent.

'Nigel French was a fashion forecaster from the UK who had come up with an idea similar to mine about merchandising a whole look, creating a homogeneous interior. He had the rights to Edith Holden's *Country Diary* and created a line of merchandise from it which included everything from lamps and mugs to wallpaper and stationery. Amongst women it had quite wide appeal and he'd made sure there was comprehensive marketing back-up. Nigel offered me the opportunity to bring it out to Australia and set it up here. I thought it would be a great idea as it was enormously successful in the UK, so I jumped at it.

In Pam's opinion, the homewares sold through the existing retail outlets were not co-ordinated, while the *Country Diary* range used similar themes in the designs of all its products. Pam realised that this integrated approach would appeal to the customers.

'I picked up on the whole decorating side. At that time Australia had only just been introduced to designers like Laura Ashley. I felt there was definitely a yearning for more of that kind of co-ordinated statement. I had become aware that the consumer wanted to buy complete "stories". I also realised that a large number of Australian women didn't have any confidence in their abilities with interior design, they wanted to be firmly pointed in the right direction in terms of style and what "lived" well together. It was also true that they were more inclined to get a decorator in rather than attempt to put things together themselves ... Often they didn't have the time or money to do it.

'In the early Eighties Australian women were looking at alternatives. They were becoming more sophisticated in their tastes aided by the growing influence of overseas designers. Thankfully there was a visible move away from chenille bedspreads and brown carpet! They were more interested in how their immediate surroundings described their lifestyle. The *Country Diary* collection answered some of their concerns because it covered such an enormous range of merchandise and it described a particular lifestyle. The idea for my own shop which I opened not long after, was based on this principle as well.'

Pam set up the *Country Diary* outlets by sub-leasing space in six Myer stores in New South Wales and Victoria.

'In the beginning I made an enormous amount of mistakes! It goes back to having taken so much for granted while working in a big department store. I was used to thinking big and so I made some terrible mistakes with over-ordering and well, over-everything. I'd warned Nigel that I was administratively very weak; perhaps neither of us were quite prepared for just how weak I actually turned out to be! I think I personally learned a lot, which has subsequently stood me in good stead, but I don't know how advantageous this experiment was for his business in the end.'

Nigel's company was then bought out by another company, Coloroll, with which Pam stayed.

'Coloroll had been mainly concerned with wallpaper and had decided to venture into textiles. I worked with them for a while. That business was a classic example of an entrepreneurial Eighties' style megalomania. They overstepped the line too often and went broke. I decided to leave primarily because I wanted to start my own business. I'd been planning for some time the nature and direction of my business and had identified a niche for it. It was obvious there was a demand for a retail outlet which provided consumers with a co-ordinated range of merchandise, all in the one shop. The emphasis since the early days has been on bed linen, but I thought it was important to add co-ordinating lamps, curtains, tablecloths—all the way down to tissue-box covers. That's what my research had shown people wanted.

'I'd already decided to call the business "Private Collection" because at Grace Bros I had created a home-brand manchester range which I really liked called "Private Label". I decided to keep the "Private" and add "Collection". I thought it sounded special.

'Now I needed to find a suitable venue for the shop. Earlier, while working for Nigel, I had researched possible locations for the *Country Diary* range. During that process I had looked at space in the Queen Victoria Building and thought it was a good location. I approached the building's management who said it was possible for me to have the leasehold on one of the shops. I was very lucky.'

Pam knew that in order to raise the capital needed to finance her project, she would have to beg, steal or borrow it! For the largest sum she chose to borrow from her own personal network of friends and relatives. The rest came from a bank loan.

'I borrowed money from my father, from Danny and also the bank. I'd given myself four months lead-time until the building opened, but unfortunately it opened three months late. It was a bit of a disaster because so many people had counted on the income from the first few months trading. It hit all of us hard. There was a sense of panic and a lot of money was lost due to the delays.

'Opening your first shop is a bit of a nightmare! There are all sorts of things you have to do which you haven't planned for. The buying was reasonably straightforward for me because it had been my main area and I knew all the people in the industry. Danny was a wholesaler and he knew a lot about it too, so he gave me lots of advice. Because I wanted to achieve a co-ordinated look in sheets, lamps, cushions etc., I asked the manufacturers of the sheets if they would give me extra lengths of fabric to use to cover these extra items. In hindsight I think if they hadn't have known Danny and me they would have told us to "bugger off!" It was a pain for them to run off extra fabric especially for me, they were used to set quantities and runs.

'In the first year the shop broke even. My father, in particular, was wonderful. He'd mortgaged his house and had officially retired but now found himself flying back and forwards from Perth to Sydney to help me out.

'The shop went well and the idea took off. After a while I realised the merchandise was limited by there being only one size of any particular print available and therefore the overall look was confined by that. Although my ideas had so far been successful I knew it was time to branch out. I started doing my own designs that included co-ordinating patterns so there was some variety in the scale of the print. I had contact with artists who could paint up my designs from my days at Myer and so off I went! Danny was full of good advice as he knew all the printers. When I began manufacturing my own fabrics Danny again provided finance.

'At this stage it was still a relatively small concern and I think Danny saw it as more of a hobby for me than something serious. He'd always been the wholesaler and I was the retailer, so although there were areas where we crossed over, he felt he had more expertise generally. Because of the volume of fabric produced we decided it'd be a good idea to wholesale the excess. So, two years after the shop opened at the QVB we set up the wholesaling business.

'The initial response to this was good. We became more and more involved in wholesaling. In this time we also opened another two shops. I think it was at that point I realised I'd over-committed myself, both time-wise and financially. The QVB shop was still doing well, but I'd stretched myself so thin that I had barely anything to do with it. Thankfully I had a wonderful manageress who looked after that store and it virtually ran itself. It was an extremely busy and exhausting period.

'The problem with opening more retail outlets was that the people to whom we were wholesaling began to disapprove because we were in direct competition with them. We had the cost advantage of having produced the goods ourselves, so we could retail them much more cheaply than they could. We realised pretty quickly that it wasn't fair to them.

'After having one of the new shops for two and a half years and another for about a year, we decided it was better to sell them. We kept the QVB because it was our first and for me had sentimental value. We sold the shops in the boom for a good price and managed not to lose anything on them. I've got to say that I've been exceptionally lucky in business, I put a lot of my success down to sheer luck! If this scenario had happened in the current economic climate, I'd be ruined!'

Pam decided to concentrate on wholesaling while still maintaining the first shop.

'With Danny's and my combined record we gained instant credibility with our customers. We pumped a lot of money into it.

'Danny saw the business blooming and realised it was actually capable of bringing in some *real* money. He wanted to have more control. He thought because he had more experience than I did he could make it into a super-successful business if I would just move over a bit. I found that I couldn't hand over the business to him, even if his were more capable hands. It was my baby and I wanted to hang onto it. I had worked so bloody hard to get it where it was, doing everything down to carrying huge boxes around the warehouse. I think it threatened him in some way that the business was becoming successful without him. It would have been easier for him ego-wise if I was failing so that he could take over and make it successful again for me. I think I would have been relegated to the background, like an invisible woman if I'd have let that happen. I didn't think I was much of a fighter until what I'd worked so hard for was threatened in this way.

'Danny had actually left his job to come and help me. We

also clashed because I'd make decisions that he never would have made—like putting an extra bow or frill on because it looked better, despite the extra cost. We soon realised that it wasn't going to work, being married is one thing . . . !'

Pam's story is not particularly unusual these days, as many women have to find a backer to help finance their business. She was romantically involved with her financial backer though, which consequently had its fair share of problems. The other major investor was Pam's father who believed so strongly in his daughter's ability that he mortgaged his house to help her set up her business.

'I could never have done this without my parents and Danny's contributions.

'I'd have to say that my greatest victory has been to get Danny to invest in me. I think he did it because he was completely smitten at the time! He also had a special interest in my ambitions because he was involved in the same industry.

'I wouldn't go into another partnership for anything. I think being personally involved with your business partner is fraught with difficulty and complicates the partnership. The problem being that there is a lot more emotional blackmail possible because this person knows how to "push your buttons". They are privy to all sorts of intimate things about you that no ordinary business associate would know.

'Because it is my business and I'm here on a day-to-day basis I feel the method of running it has to work principally for me. I find myself editing the facts heavily on my return home in the evening! My method of running the business seems to have been successful to date, so I can't be getting it all wrong. It's just a personality thing really, people operate differently. In order to cover those areas where I feel I'm not particularly strong I make sure that I employ people who are. I am surrounded by people who are exceptional at zooming in on the detail. Everyone here is always picking up after me!'

To organise her business management Pam takes a sensible look at where her strengths and weaknesses lie and hands over some responsibility in her weaker areas to her trusted employees.

'The temptation is, of course, to surround yourself with

similar types because it is infinitely less confronting and irritating!'

Pam thinks it is important to become as broad as possible in your approach to your enterprise.

'A problem associated with specialising only in your area, as I previously did, is there's always someone up or down the line doing things for you. It's subtle but I think it breeds a sort of incompetence. The buck doesn't stop with you, so you can afford to pass on responsibility. When you start your own business there're going to be some very rude shocks! In a big organisation it's too easy to sit there, doing your job and forget about the "invisible" people that make it all possible. There's the person who brings the mail which is waiting for you when you arrive in the morning, the person who pays the bills for you etc., etc. There's an entire infrastructure set up to make your life easier. At the end of the day all you have to do is write a damn report! In your own business you have to do those little things yourself that take up a lot of time, in fact they can take up all your time! The responsibility falls completely on your shoulders.'

I asked Pam about any trouble spots she might have had so far in the business.

'I have lost the thread so to speak, twice. A few years back I was over-confident and believed that whatever I did would automatically work. We were on a wave of success and I made some big mistakes, mostly in the design area. I became complacent and also failed to see the threat of overseas competition looming. It was a sobering lesson and I'm glad it happened. The second time I lost it was fairly recently when personal problems got in the way and I just couldn't focus enough on the business. Each time though, I have come back to it with renewed strength and vision. I am reminded of the things I love about the business.

'It dawned on me that in the past I had been quite ambitious for the business. I too, had once wanted it to be in the company of the Sheridans of the world, but now am much more relaxed about it. There are other things that are important in life. I used to put in a twelve-hour day, seven days a week. I'm not good in the mornings so now I come in later—9 am until about 6 pm.

'The business has changed a lot since I've been in it. The home fashion industry has developed considerably, partly because people's tastes have become more sophisticated and also because now there are a lot more players in the field. The demographic has expanded enormously from catering primarily to women in the 35 to 50 year-old range to now including young, upwardly-mobile kids who want their home environments to look good. This group spend more now on their homewares than they do on their clothing. People in general are becoming much more home-orientated.

'We used to produce two to four ranges a year, one in April and another in October, but things change so quickly now that we have to come up with about twenty new designs a year. As you can imagine, it is an enormous financial commitment. The profit margins are much smaller and the industry is less stable than it used to be. There are also more suppliers than there were and fewer retailers. The recession wiped out a lot of the marginal retailers. There has been a huge influx of cheap imports which has made things very competitive.

'It is important for us to consolidate our position in the market now and that's what I'm concentrating on. We are a comparatively small operation, but we've maintained our market share.'

'I primarily wholesale my goods to men, who then sell them to women. These chaps are in their forties and fifties and are terribly conservative. It is important for me to look good and dress well if I'm going to be taken seriously by them. One of the things I love about the business is dealing with all sorts of people. I have built up good relationships with my suppliers and customers now.'

We were sitting in a showroom surrounded by Pam's current range. When I asked how she sought out suitable designs Pam explained that her ideas come from trade shows she attends overseas or else she will see an image that would be suitable for a range by just observing things in her daily life. In terms of style, Private Collection is at the more conservative end of the market. Pam finds that whatever sells in the UK market also sells here, so she uses their lead as a guide. It is the details that make a difference to Private Collection's appeal.

What was the next step for Pam's business I wondered.

'The next step we take will have to be a big one. We will need to pump a lot of money into the business, sell it or get bought out. For me, once it's over it's over and I'm onto the next thing.'

On closing Pam adds, 'It has taken a great deal of luck, imagination and wherewithal.'

S.R.

# Katie Graham and Olivia Guntarik

## Strut

When the announcer on the radio began to talk about young employed people on a scheme to help them start their own business, I yelled at everyone in the office to keep quiet and let me listen. I scrawled down the contact number and called to find out more.

Through the assistance of the Youth Business Initiative Scheme (YBI) organiser, I wrote to all the women who had recently been on the scheme, telling them about the book and asking for interviewees. I received lots of faxes and phone calls from young Melbournians keen to talk and two young women, in particular, caught my attention.

Katie Graham and Olivia Guntarik are partners in a costume design and make-up business called Strut. Their studio is on the second floor of a large old building in the Melbourne suburb of Prahran. The building is a labyrinth of long dark corridors with more doors leading off them than entrances to a rabbit warren. I walked in to the lift, looked around and then just as the doors were closing ran out into the lobby, preferring instead to take the old wooden stairs, which, despite their creaking, looked and felt a whole lot more stable.

I knocked on their door and walked into a huge sunlit, open-plan studio with large arched windows looking out over the hubbub of Chapel Street. Olivia and Katie worked hard to transform what they say was a dingy and dirty space to this. They have stripped back all the woodwork, painted the walls, polished the floors and filled it with light.

The women are both in their early twenties. Olivia has been doing freelance make-up for six years since she left high school, but not in a very serious way. Until Strut, make-up was more a hobby than a serious business venture.

'My parents thought it was important for me to get an

education so I went to university and graduated with a Bachelor of Arts. After I finished my studies I did sales work and decided that I really wanted to be a make-up artist.

'My parents were a little anxious and scared about it at first. Now they're happy because they can see I've learned so many different skills. There are things you learn when you're self-employed that you'd never pick up working for someone else and I think they know and support that. I don't regret going to university and getting a degree because it taught me to be better organised and to meet deadlines. Skills I think are crucial to business.'

Katie left high school and decided to throw herself into the thing she loved best, costume design.

'I studied at the Western Australia Academy of Performing Arts for two years but deferred my last year and took off around Australia for twelve months. Then I did a business course and worked in offices for about two years. I absolutely hated it and one day I just left and promised myself I would never work in an office again.'

Katie turned her back on the professional world she had been playing with while she worked out what she really wanted to do to find her creative side again.

'I worked for the woman who was wardrobe supervisor for "Fast Forward", which gave back my confidence and polished my technique and skills. Once I had that all back in place, I decided to set up my own business.'

She enrolled in the YBI scheme in Melbourne and then went on to the NEIS. It was here, doing the course that the girls met and decided to become partners. When we start talking about NEIS, Olivia and Katie look at each other and say in unison, 'It was gruelling'. The course is full-time, eight hours a day, but they also agree that it is an excellent scheme, without which they would not have been able to put any of this into action.

When you finish the course, you are not just cast to the wolves. Current thinking on small business in Australia puts great emphasis on people learning from one another. So NEIS has a policy where every graduate of the program is allocated a mentor with whom they must meet regularly to discuss their business needs and ideas and get feedback and opinions on their progress.

Your mentor may not necessarily be in the same field as you. Katie's mentor is a psychologist and Olivia's is a caterer. Olivia says she is a bit disappointed not to be under the eye of someone in her own field, an opinion echoed lately by some sections of the media. She thinks mentors would be more useful if they understood more of the specifics of their industries. There are two points that explain why the scheme has taken its approach to mentors. First, it is the idea that there are commonalities amongst all businesses, large or small, creative or not. The second is that mentors are more likely to give sound advice to people they won't later be competing against in the marketplace.

'My mentor helps me out with the financial side of things, he knows nothing about my industry and is quite confused about exactly what I'm doing, but that's all right. I don't really need him to understand. He helps me with my books and keeps me in line, which is really helpful,' says Katie.

Olivia's experience has not been quite so rewarding. 'It has been a bit of a let down because I feel there's little understanding between us.'

Those who complete the course have responsibilities to the scheme. Each month you are required to submit a report on your takings and analyse it against your budget. The scheme concentrates on the economics of the ventures it helps establish, recognising this to be the point on which many small businesses stumble.

'If you're like us, you don't really think about money and profits. We were more concerned with our creativity. Bookkeeping is often the last thing you feel like doing but we know now how important it is to keep it up-to-date. It helps us analyse what we're doing, where we're going, where we're making money and the areas we need to turn our attention to,' says Olivia.

The course also pays special attention to marketing and Strut has an enormous range of advertising material for such a new business. They have a whole series of printed postcards they send to prospective clients. Each card shows the girls in different costumes and make-ups. One card has them as boys and it took me some time to realise that it was in fact Katie and Olivia, not two young men. They even have their own T-shirt with their business name printed very boldly across the chest.

Even though the girls are in partnership, they often work separately. Katie explains that, 'We do a lot of freelancing which means we're not necessarily in the studio all the time. We do work together, but just as often, quite separately. We work in film, on television commercials, for theatre companies, and with fashion photographers as well.' From their portfolio it is easy to see that their work is diverse. Not only are there glamorous girls in frocks, but drag queens who they design costumes and do make-up for as well.

'Although we have the partnership we are financially separate. We do have a joint business account which is specifically for studio and promotional expenses, like our cards. We also have an agent who promotes us and our business account covers that expense too. Any money we earn, we put into our own accounts and when expenses come in we deposit money into the business account.'

Although this is not a conventional partnership set-up, it seems to work well for these two women. Partnerships can be fraught with problems. Splitting assets if relationships deteriorate or the business is doing poorly is just one of the gamut of difficulties specifically related to partnerships, and Katie and Olivia's arrangement seems to safeguard them against those pitfalls. Of course when partnerships work well, they can be extremely effective. Two people focused on the one business with the same interests can be formidable.

'Really our partnership exists so we can promote each other. It works well because it means we both have a bigger base to work from. If I go out on a make-up job, I'll tell them about Strut and about what Katie does and Katie does the same,' says Olivia.

Small businesses in their fledgling stages require a huge effort to get them going, and I ask Katie about the hours they have to put in. 'Sometimes we work seven days a week from nine in the morning to ten o'clock at night. It seems to have become a 24-hour occupation. Even when we go out socially we work. A large part of the promotion and advertising we do for the business we do socially. Networking, meeting people and talking about what we do has brought us a lot of work. Then we go home and dream about it! It never ends.'

I wonder when the girls get time to socialise at all. It occurs to me that many of their peers would be spending more time thinking about boys than business. We talk about how the business has a domino effect, making its mark on other seemingly unrelated aspects of their lives.

'Our circle of friends has changed. We have become so consumed by the business that it's often all we talk about. We seem to have moved towards people in our industry, because they are obsessed like we are and understand what we're doing and why.

'I think a lot of men are threatened because they see us as independent women doing their own thing. They are a little bit scared by that, maybe even intimidated. Being in business does change who you get involved with. A lot of people just can't cope with it and it can be hard to find someone who understands the financial ups and downs of it all.

'I think we have probably offended some of our friends. People ring us at work and expect us to drop everything to go and have coffee with them. They think that because we don't have a boss standing over us we can do that,' says Olivia, looking annoyed just at the thought of that assumption.

Katie admits that having the studio has made a big difference to how others perceive them and their work. 'People don't ring as often. When we first moved in here people were always dropping in to have a look and it started to get really annoying. Now when people ring I keep it really short and make it very clear by the tone in my voice that I can't talk.'

The studio has also helped put an end to the eternal 'I was wondering if you could just whip me up something', or 'I'm going to a friend's wedding and I want to look great, can you do my make-up?' questions.

'Now people can see we have overheads, that we have to pay rent and electricity. We are very up-front about telling people we can't afford to do things for them unless they pay us, which they seem to be beginning to understand. People see that we are serious about what we're doing. It is hard to change those relationships but it makes it clearer and easier for everyone if you establish those boundaries right from the start.'

From here our conversation moves to other areas. I tell them about my experience working with a very good friend and how sometimes it was hard for us to leave our personal lives out of our work. At one point we realised large parts of our days were spent talking about our relationships and personal problems. We made a conscious decision to ban those discussions and relegate them strictly to 'after hours'. It didn't always work, but when it did we were much more productive.

'Last week Katie and I were talking about how much we do that. We're always talking about guys. It is hard to juggle your personal life with business. I think I shouldn't be thinking about boys or my social life at work, but I do, and I guess it's kind of inevitable.'

Katie and Olivia discuss an aspect of business that affects almost every self-employed person, but relates particularly to them because of the industries they work in.

'It's important for us to look good at work. We don't do the "suit bit" because that is not our market, but we always try to make ourselves look good. Sometimes I do feel like coming into the studio in a tracksuit but I can't because I never know who I might meet. What we wear is important on another level too because people judge how successful your business is by what you wear and if you don't dress well, people aren't as confident in you.'

The girls have tried to reflect the nature of the business in their workplace as well as their personal appearance. Their office would be a child's idea of heaven. There are huge mirrors, wigs hung on racks, flowing curtains and lots of dress-up clothes!

'We were both working from home before the studio and coming here has made an enormous difference. I never got out of the house and there were too many distractions at home, it was ridiculous. I think we've both found we are a lot more productive here,' poses Katie and Olivia nods firmly in agreement.

We talk about hard times and they admit they have had a few and still find some things about running their own business difficult.

'We had troubles with time management when we first started out. We often overworked ourselves which we found can be just as bad as not doing enough work. Working hard seems like a good idea and it is to a point, but if you push yourself too hard and don't take time out you get too stressed and just end up making mistakes. I feel guilty if I'm not working though,' says Katie, who admits she finds it hard to relax.

Olivia adds that she loves doing what she does, and can never imagine doing anything else but is susceptible to moments of doubt. 'There's so much pressure for women to have a career as well as everything else, sometimes I think that I'd just like to go and have babies.'

I admire Olivia for her honesty, and I think it is a sentiment most women would identify with at times, but very few would articulate. It makes me think just how the tables have turned. Thirty years or so ago it was taboo for a woman to say she wanted to work, now it's almost sacrilegious to admit you'd like to have children and not worry about a career. Damned if you do, damned if you don't.

'I've just finished reading *The Alchemist* by Paul Coelho, which is a book about following your dreams. I started reading it when I was feeling really down, wondering whether I'd achieved any of my goals. It's a great book that made me feel sure about what I was doing and confident to follow my dream,' says Olivia.

'We talk about our work and encourage each other. We give each other a lot of support because some of our other friends don't have any idea what it's like to run your own business. Writing things down, making goals and keeping a diary has also helped us both through times of doubt. With a diary, you can look back on what you've done and see how much you have achieved and what's possible in the future.'

When you are employed it is possible to defer to others.

If there is something you can't do or don't enjoy, there is usually someone else to whom you can turn for assistance. That is not always possible when you are running your own business. Olivia finds, like so many other women we spoke to, that invoicing is very difficult.

'Even though we have a set price list, I find it really hard to say my rate is $60 an hour. I am fairly new to the industry and I worry that my charges seem expensive. Even though I know other make-up artists charge the same as me and often a lot more, I still worry about it. It's all a matter of feeling confident about my abilities and what I deserve, which I try to remind myself whenever I'm quoting. It is very rewarding though, when you face and conquer those difficulties, because you know you are developing new skills.'

Confidence and self-assurance are not attributes that many women are brought up to have. While it can be a constant battle, most women find that running their own business actually builds their confidence, not deflates it.

'I think I am a changed person. My life is better than ever before, I'm stronger and a lot more independent now. It's such a rewarding experience and when you get good feedback from people it's a fantastic feeling.

'It throws you into places you've never been and at people you have never met. We're constantly working with different people which means we have to be able to accommodate a lot of different personalities and change ours to suit whoever we're with. You work together so intensely and I get to meet so many people I'd never spend time with unless I was doing this. For me, my job is not just about applying make-up to people's faces, it's just as much to do with working and relating to different people. People can get really moody and it's challenging to work in those conditions. So doing my job well and keeping a smile on my face at the same time are important for my work.'

To illustrate this point, Olivia brings out a series of photographs from a film shoot and lays them out on the coffee table. The pictures show her drawing tattoos on an enormous, bearded man who looks like he has just stepped off a Harley Davidson and more like a member of a bikey gang than an extra on the set.

'It is very intimate,' she says and I laugh. She is so small against this giant of a man. I would feel totally intimidated and frankly a bit scared spending the six hours with him that it took to draw his tattoos on for the shoot. But this is the aspect of her work that she likes the best.

Olivia and Katie have their eyes set on New York where they want to study. They show me the special folder they have with clippings of all the studios they want to visit and the people they'd like to work with. It's a scrapbook of their greatest dreams that they look at whenever their day-to-day work weighs on them. They are applying for scholarships to help them make the pilgrimage to their mecca, and I have little doubt that, with or without government assistance, enthusiasm alone will see them there soon.

C.L.

# Trudyanne Brown

## BMGART

Trudyanne is a very petite woman but what she has been through in business is huge. She owned South Australia's most famous gallery, Bonython's, took it to great heights and then watched it fall around her.

Hers is a story of success and then ruin, but what makes it astounding is the way she dealt with a disaster and came out of it with enough strength and courage to attempt it all over again.

'I lost everything when the galleries collapsed, including the custody of one of my children. You'd think I would be loathe to put my foot back in the water and attempt it all over again, but I have because I love it, I can't stop.

'I didn't have a university education and matriculated at the tender age of 38. When I first applied to do adult matric, I couldn't even fill in the form but I ended up topping English Literature at the college, and went on from there.

'Before that, I had only ever completed a commercial course and I started out as Kym Bonython's secretary, the then owner of the gallery, in 1965. I think once you enter the arts world, to use John Olsen's quote, "it's a terminal illness". There's no going back.

'My first husband was a surgeon, and we went to England for five years whilst he completed his Fellowship. When we returned, I worked for Kym again. My husband's attitude to working wives was not enthusiastic, he believed a woman's role was "a wife and mother". I decided to leave the marriage, amicably, and do Arts/Law at university, but once I was faced with the reality of raising two children on $100 a week maintenance, combined with a mortgage—all study went out the window. I returned to work for Kym, this time as his manager.

'I married again, to someone who knew how much I enjoyed my job. However, this marriage was to last a mere twelve months, probably less in retrospect. Initially we bought Kym out and I took over the business. The marriage dissolved, and I realised if I was to continue to maintain the calibre of the art the Bonython Gallery had exhibited, I would have to underwrite this with another aspect to the business. I therefore decided to move into the corporate art area. As a result, we obtained the art consultancies to fit out a number of major hotels, banks and other high-profile corporate offices. This side of the business grew so quickly that we were obliged to open another gallery purely to handle our corporate work. By this time, potential husband number three emerged and advised me in the business.

'Then I was approached by a client in the eastern states who liked the way I ran the Adelaide gallery and wanted me to open one in Sydney. After considerable thought, I took the plunge.

'It expanded very quickly and I lost control. I had someone looking after public relations, and my husband-to-be had been made financial director. The initial reasons for running the galleries disappeared and in the end I was more an administrator than anything else.'

What Trudyanne describes is a common occurrence for those running their own businesses. I often bemoan the fact that more and more of my time is spent chasing invoices, handling clients and making sure the bills are paid, and less and less doing the thing I love the most, designing. When the Sydney gallery opened, Trudyanne found she was spending more time on aeroplanes than just about anywhere else.

'My partners and artists wanted me to move to Sydney. I took the children to Sydney, showed them around, booked them into schools but in the end I didn't think it was a great environment for them, so I cancelled. In retrospect, I think if I had moved and lived in Sydney the business may have flourished. I really needed to be available for the artists and the clients.

'I tried very hard to keep the two going and ran between Sydney and Adelaide, sometimes two or three times a month. It was frantic and I hardly saw Lucy and Rupert.'

The difficult thing for women in business, especially single mothers, is that you are always torn. And it's a no-win situation; unless you have an income you can't support your children, but earning it means you don't get a lot of time with the people for whom you are doing it.

'You make decisions with your children in mind, that aren't necessarily monetarily sound. If it's a question of the needs of your business or your children I know which side wins. Now I think things have changed enormously and women are learning to balance their careers with their children, and now children find it quite acceptable to have a working mother.

'The guilt I felt about trying to run the business and have children was fantastic. Oddly enough, the people who made me feel bad about it were other women. Perhaps many of them would have liked to have been leading the kind of lifestyle they thought I had. Either they didn't have the courage to do it or it was probably just easier being married and staying at home. Staying home wasn't something I found easy and even though I missed out on a lot of time with Lucy and Rupert, the time I did spend with them was certainly quality, if not quantity, and I have no regrets.

'I tried very hard to put time aside for the children and to involve myself in their lives. Often I would get home at ten o'clock but I could organise my business schedule so that I could incorporate their interests and the business, and I also tried to involve them in the gallery. Lucy has now finished her Visual Art degree. Once you grow up in the art world there's very little escaping it. She is certainly not going to make a fortune in the arts, very few do, but that doesn't concern me as long as she's happy and fulfilled.

'I had a terrific neighbour who used to help out. I could ring up and say, "Look, I'm still stuck in Sydney" and she would just stay there with the kids. One day Lucy really spat the dummy and said, "I'm sick of being the fag end of your business life".

'Lucy, who's finished one degree and just starting another, says now that she would rather pay her own way and do what I did. She thinks that it's been good to grow up with a working mother and she understands the importance of an education and the prospect of being independent. There is certainly no lack of love.

'I was really tough on the children but I think it paid off.

Lucy, of all her contemporaries, passed her matriculation, and she is dyslexic. She also got first offering at the University of South Australia. She says that none of her friends achieved what she achieved, and believes that it was because I was so strict. Lucy says I was particularly tough on them because I felt guilty about working all the time, but she admits it was always premised by, "You have the rest of your life to go out and have fun; it is only a few years to gain an education and qualifications".'

Whatever the reasons behind that upbringing, Trudyanne thinks it has made them a very close family. Her description of the bankruptcy and the events leading up to it, shows just how unified they were.

'My third marriage came to an abrupt end after eighteen months, and the battle to ward off bankruptcy went on for about three years. It was devastating. I called the kids together and told them the business was in deep trouble and that we would have to sell the house and anything else we could. I thought that as long as we stayed together everything would be all right. I said, "If I can put that money back into the business and work very hard, with your support, everything will be fine". At the time it seemed like a fair enough proposition and I wanted to do the right thing. I thought that with good karma it would all come back.

'Well, it was totally ridiculous. The business just absorbed the money and that was it. It was all gone and it was a difficult time for us. Lucy moved into a flat with a friend and Rupert went to live with his father. Without the support of Lucy and Rupert I don't think I would have maintained my sanity. It went on for so long because I didn't want to give up.

'My bank manager and my lawyer told me the books looked very bad. We had a meeting and they didn't think it was humanly possible to turn it around. If I'd had any brains I would have listened to them and said, "Right, let's just cut our losses and stop now". But I didn't, I just kept on regardless. In the end, my enthusiasm and determination were so great that even my lawyer and bank manager came right in behind me.

'It was wild but I just thought no, these bastards are not

going to bring me down. I was so bloody minded. When you put so much into something it's hard to just give up. In retrospect I can see it was totally irrational.

'Men, I think, tend to be more cut and dried. They're more logical and rational and know where the cut-off point is. For women it's different, they're battling for so much more, not just a business. I was fighting for the business and my children's future.

'In the end, Horst, my husband now, dragged me into my lawyer's office and made me sign on the line. It was over.'

Even though Trudyanne did go into liquidation, the lessons she learned and the way she thought about and ran the business are still relevant. One of her major concerns were the good people who were caught in the financial chaos. She believes it is essential in galleries these days to have two separate accounts: an artists' trust account, and a gallery operating account, so that artists are never exposed to the turmoils of a recession period again.

What is most surprising about Trudyanne is the smile she has on her face when she tells me just how it felt when the business was doing well. It's as though none of the difficulties ever existed.

'It was like being appointed President, hoping that no one would find out that you knew nothing of politics. The only way you can find out whether or not you can do something is to give it a try. If you find out that you don't have the talent that's required in a certain area you should stop immediately and get someone in to help.

'My public relations consultant taught me a lot about image and presentation. My clothes were always suits and silk shirts. He was 6 foot 4 and an excellent business person. At one time I was going to a meeting with a company which had just awarded BMG the consultancy to supply all the art for an international hotel, and he announced he was coming with me. I was somewhat taken aback and asked him what on earth for? He said, "You have to be realistic about this. Men don't take women seriously in business, even though they may say they do. You're tiny, you're going to be the only woman there, you've beaten two other guys to the job, and there could be a bit of blood letting".

'He promised not to say anything unless he saw me heading in the wrong direction or saw someone cutting me off at the knees in a very clever male manner. He was fantastic and perfectly right. There were a few try-ons, but in the end he didn't have to say much at all. I learned a very good lesson there. I had to maintain my ground in that meeting, but I just sat, wearing glasses I did not need, another part of the dressing required, and battled it out. A lot of men are either flirtatious or think they can treat you as a fool, and many of them don't like it if you play neither of those games.'

So Trudyanne made an impression at that meeting, but has also made a more lasting impression in Adelaide that is not so favourable. When I told a friend that I was interviewing Trudyanne for this book, they said that they thought the galleries were a hobby for her which her husbands financed and ran. I was stunned at the time and outraged after the first few moments of talking with Trudyanne when it became clear that she was a business person in her own right. Trudyanne is the first person to admit that she has had help with her business from two of her husbands at different points. Adelaide is a small town and the arts world even smaller, and some people still think that Trudyanne was handed her business on a silver platter.

'When I married for the second time my husband secretly agreed to purchase the gallery from Kym Bonython as a "wedding present". I knew nothing about it until the press ran articles saying that he'd done it. It looked like I'd been given a hobby by some multimillionaire and I just about died of embarassment. Every time I tried to explain it was waved aside. The publicity was too good. The national glossies ran the story, press releases were everywhere, so it was just about impossible to convince anybody otherwise. I had negotiated the mortgage, and ran the gallery from day one with no input from my husband. He paid Kym a deposit which I returned on our divorce. He had done this with the best of intentions as he knew how much I loved my work.

'The irony was that after a few months of me working, he

couldn't stand it and asked me to give it up. I didn't want to but said that if the business hadn't made any money I would. We had a meeting with the accountant who told us I was in the black and so the marriage ended. Once we split up people started to realise that I really did work for my own business, and it wasn't a hobby.

'My third husband who had come into the business as the financial director loathed the feeling that he was "working for me", and that also finished that marriage.'

Now Trudyanne runs BMGART in Adelaide, with her husband Horst, who owns the business, and she feels very optimistic about the prospects of this venture. She also has her son Rupert back living with them and considers herself to be very fortunate. She had known Horst for 32 years, and he had been a good client of both the Bonython Gallery and BMG Fine Art.

'Horst and I have a better understanding of each other and he's always known that visual arts are my passion. There is absolutely no role playing in this partnership, Horst certainly does all the cooking, and can iron a shirt better than I, whereas I probably know my way around the gallery schedules and files better than he. But we definitely work as a team, at home and at work.

'Of course, this new venture would not be working so successfully had not Australia's most respected artists with whom I had worked for so long, prior to my crash, continued to give me their undivided loyalty and friendship. This is despite the fact that when the final crash came many of them were financially hurt because there was simply no money to pay them. Kevin Connor, in his inimitable manner, refers to me as "the Lazarus Lady"!

'Taking on areas of business that you have to learn about as you go gives you an enormous sense of satisfaction. It makes for a very rounded life. Sometimes I think it would have been nice to spend more time with the children, but I feel that we are much closer because we've been through such a tumultuous time together. I've always said to Lucy and Rupert, take the job, and then learn how to do it. If you can't do it, then at least you know you've tried, but it's the only way to find out if you really want to do something badly enough. It's advice I'd give to anyone thinking about taking on a challenge. You have to prove to yourself that you can do it, and the rewards are fantastic if you succeed!'

C.L.

# Challenging the Corporate Culture

As we approach the twenty-first century our notion of the working week is being challenged. The nature of work is changing at a rate not seen since the industrial revolution. We are all having to learn the meaning of, and come to terms with, the results of downsizing, telecommuting, virtual offices, out-sourcing and restructuring, an often used euphemism for retrenchment.

The nature of work has turned a corner; we are all looking at what the new parameters of work will have to offer us and what we will have to give in return.

While we are all re-interpreting and re-inventing our working lives, it is obvious that there are very specific gender issues which affect men and women differently. Women often have to contend with the so-called glass ceiling, which has made it difficult for competent and intelligent women to gain positions of authority. Also, women often have the needs of their children and families to consider and structure into their working lives. To maintain some kind of balance in their professional and personal lives is a great concern. Working in an ever-increasing frenzy of competitiveness goes against many women's conditioning and ethics. Despite the fact that it could well reap higher rewards, corporate culture is not equipped to encourage the less aggressive yet often more effective methods of their female employees.

Although some of these issues affect the entire Australian work force, they are having a particular impact on women. As the demand for wage labour retracts, self-employment expands, and today women are at the helm of many small businesses in this country. Unable or unwilling to break the glass in that ceiling[1] or to find challenging and rewarding work, women are creating structures that better suit their needs and ideals—both professional and personal.

Government institutions and many corporate organisations have set up committees to find out why women are not making it to the upper echelons of power. But while the committees are meeting and researching, women are taking action into their own hands. Frustrated with not being able to move up the ladder to more challenging and responsible positions, many women are leaving their jobs. A recent article in the *Financial Review* cites three forces acting against women who want to make it to the top: '. . . the competitive and often highly aggressive nature of the Western free-enterprise system; the apparent tendency for many women and many men to have different priorities with respect to the place of work in their lives; and the widely held, and tenaciously ingrained, view of the appropriate role of women and men in society'.

The article goes on to suggest that any one of these factors alone would require a fundamental shift in society as a whole. Banded together they make the task of opening the way for women seem virtually impossible.

Faced with the enormity of this task, many women are asking themselves whether it is worth the battle. Some have made the decision to stay put and not even try to compete with their male counterparts for jobs, others are trying to initiate change from within while increasing numbers are deciding to take their skills and use them to create something new.

All the women in this chapter have made the decision to get out of the corporate sector. For some it was the frustration of the glass ceiling while for others it was a choice of working for someone else or for themselves. Knowing they had the skills and deciding to employ those talents in a way that let them take control seemed appealing.

In the Eighties the ethos was for women to compete; we power dressed and played the game the male way in order to get ahead. The ramifications of that mind set have now become apparent to us. Women have more cases of stress-related diseases than ever before and at the end of the day, are still not considered equal in terms of their financial or professional remuneration.[2] So why, many women are asking themselves, bother?

If it is true, as some writers now suggest[3] and our interviews confirm, that many women see their success in a very different light to men, then even if we were being financially rewarded for our efforts in the corporate world, we would still, personally, be largely unfulfilled. If our gauge of success is measured in terms of our sense of freedom, our personal development, an increased sense of self and our contribution to others, then it is at odds with the nature of traditional employment and the qualities it rewards and fosters.

We hope this chapter will inspire women worn out by the corporate world, or looking for satisfactory ways to integrate the many facets of their life, who at the moment may be torn apart by the nature of their work, to look to new and perhaps more rewarding ways of earning a living.

C.L.

## Notes

(1) Three per cent of female wage and salary workers across Australia hold management or senior administrative posts compared to 10 per cent of males, see *Guidelines on Mentoring for Women*, NSW Ministry for the Status and Advancement of Women, November 1994.

(2) In 1969, the Federal Wages Tribunal ruled that equal pay for equal work should be implemented from the beginning of 1971. Despite that ruling, in 1991 the average weekly earnings of women in full-time employment were 80 per cent of men's average weekly earnings. Many women work part-time and if they are figured into this equation, then the rates fall further to just 66 per cent of male earnings.

(3) See 'Women, Success and Civil Society: Submission to, or Subversion of, the Achievement Principle' by Maria Markus, in Benhabib, S. and Cornell, D. (eds), *Feminism as Critique: Essays on the Politics of Gender in Late-Capitalist Societies*, UK: Polity Press, 1987.

# Susan Chadwick

## Copywriter

I have only met Susan Chadwick once, and that was to interview her about her business as a copywriter. Since that first meeting though, I have had three letters from her. These letters, 'newsletters' or 'group letters' as she describes them, are written on her computer, hand addressed to each of her friends with the body text remaining the same to each. As Susan explains in her first letter, 'I am not up to writing screeds at the moment', although each letter is actually about two pages long, full of information, news and boundless spirit. Sections of her letters had me laughing with her descriptions of the recent goings-on in her life, while others had me in tears. Susan is recovering from a mastectomy she had one month after our first interview and is currently having chemotherapy for breast cancer, which she says makes her feel 'like a sack of Zoo Poo'.

When we first spoke, Susan had no idea of the immense change that was about to take place in her life. We discussed the future of her business, which seemed extremely sure and positive. On 22 February 1995, she entered an X-ray ward as a woman with a very successful career in advertising and left thinking she would never work again.

Susan's career has been ever-changing, born from a series of quite unusual events. She came to copywriting through go-go dancing! While studying physiotherapy, she earned money on the side by go-go dancing at university functions. All her family had been in the medical profession so it seemed almost a fait accompli that she too would join the ranks of the white-robed. 'The only drawback was that I wasn't any good at physiotherapy,' she says, almost proudly.

While dancing at a function for an advertising agency she met a copywriter and 'thought what she did looked like a great deal of fun, so I asked her about her job . . . and even though at the time I had no idea what that [a copywriter] was, I thought I could do that. At the end of that year I said,

"I'm going to be a copywriter," and I went and knocked on doors until I was.'

Susan made up her mind and then made it happen. She rang advertising agencies and talked to people in the industry to find out exactly what the job entailed. The more she heard, the more determined Susan became and she changed from thinking I could do that, to I want to and I will do that. So she asked a friend of her father's who was in advertising if he would give her a test of some sort to gauge if she had a talent for coming up with smart concepts and clever words to advertise products. Susan needed to know whether to continue this quest for a new career.

When you meet Susan Chadwick it is clear to see that she would have learned the skills of advertising very easily. She thinks fast, funny and smart. The test her father's friend devised confirmed this. In fact, they thought she was so good she must have cheated and set her another test just to be sure, this time supervised. When she finished, they offered her a job.

Susan is now 47, and since that day has been working as a copywriter. At different times in her life she has worked as an employee while at others, as a freelancer, and others still, as she was at the time of our first interview, as a combination of the two. When we met, I walked through revolving doors of a rather large building on Melbourne's St Kilda Road and took the lift to the offices of a very smart advertising agency. Susan explained to me then that she was working in-house with this company but maintained her own clients in addition to the agency's.

'Being a freelancer you do sometimes have the option to work in an agency where the management know that you have your own clients, and you are free to come and go as you please. You can have other client meetings when you want to and I find it to be a terrific set up.

'Once you've been working for yourself it's hard to go back on staff anywhere. Being employed means you can lose your job at any time, and not necessarily because you are not very good at what you do. One large account coming or going can be the difference between you being gainfully employed or on the dole. That's why I have always had the fall-back position of having my own clients. It definitely gives you a sense of security, freedom and flexibility.'

Since that first conversation, Susan's attitude about 'the terrific set-up' has changed radically. 'I have had two years of immense stress in my job which I loved and did because of the ego gratification. I should never have stopped working from home but I didn't know that then! . . . I think the cause of my cancer was stress, diet and hormones . . .'

Susan began working from home when she had her first baby, who is now nineteen years old. 'When I first started as a copywriter, I did an Arts Degree part-time. Then when I was 27, I had a baby . . . and went home and did some freelance work. I was married so I didn't have to make much money so was able to finish my degree.

'Shortly after, my husband and I were divorced and I went back into the work force in a really heavy "divorcee, career woman" mode. I got a wonderful job in a fantastic advertising agency where I had overseas and interstate trips as part of my work. I loved it, and have worked with various agencies until eight years ago.

'I was working and having a wonderful time and remarried when I was 39. We both wanted to have children and my biological clock was ticking away so we didn't have a whole lot of time to do it. I resigned on my second day back at work after our honeymoon.

'I had it all worked out. I went to see my gynaecologist to tell him I wanted to get pregnant, only to be told I was infertile. Both my tubes were completely blocked the full length.

'I had resigned from my job, told everyone I was going to run a freelance business from home, had my house on the market because we wanted to buy a bigger one for the baby, and there I was, infertile! It was quite a shock. I decided to stay home and we bought a beach house instead. Then something rather strange happened. I fell pregnant the first weekend we spent at the beach house. So the original idea proceeded to roll out as planned, after all.

'Margaux was born in May and I became a freelancer working from home. I'd planned to take six months off but people didn't listen to that and my first job came in about four days after we arrived home from the hospital. When Margaux was twelve months I was offered two mornings a week at an agency, which meant I had my clients at home as well as working part-time. The year I had the baby my income dropped about 20 per cent. I had expected it to drop by 50 per cent. Every other year since has been a growth period.

'Although I only semiconsciously planned it this way, the fact that I gave quite a few months notice to the agency meant I immediately had lots of work when I went out on my own. It gave me four months to tell people that I was going to be freelance, which made a huge difference because from the day I went home I had more than enough work to keep me busy.

'Actually, as soon as clients heard I was going out on my own they started ringing me up with freelance work even though I was still at the agency. I decided to take that work which I did at night, on weekends or early in the morning, even though I was still employed.'

When setting up a small business it is not unusual to have a period of at least six months where there is little or no income. It is during this time that you are most likely to go broke. The initial expenses are usually more than expected and the time involved to establish a clientele or market often takes longer than one would hope. The lag between the completion of a job and payment for that work is sometimes a strain which many businesses cannot withstand.

So, by working what was effectively two jobs during this period, Susan took the financial pressure off her freelance work. She had a float to get her over those lean first few months. Most importantly though, this meant that by the time she was concentrating solely on her freelance work she really did have enough work for a business.

'What helped me enormously was that money flowed into the business right from day one. The jobs I did on the side while I was still at the agency started to pay by the time I set up on my own. In this business people always take 90 days to pay, sometimes 120 days and sometimes 280! Sometimes I send celebratory reminders saying, "this invoice has had a birthday—it's now 12 months old, please pay".'

Susan realised that to work freelance she needed help with her daughter during office hours. 'I couldn't work from home without help with Margaux. My work involves visiting clients, which I knew I couldn't do with a baby on my hip. So I employed a woman to look after her at home from nine till twelve each morning.'

The home office helps many people when they are starting up their businesses. It allows time for families, is a way to keep costs down, and a wonderful way to work to the schedule of your choice, for example, you can work at night when the children are asleep. Although some women do find there are drawbacks, especially if there are small children. It can mean that you never actually get away from work or out of the house. Some find that working from home has a stigma attached to it, that people look at the business more as a hobby than a serious venture.

'One of the ways I avoided the pitfalls of working from home was to have a proper and separate office set up at the front of the house. I salvaged family life by having a television in there, which I needed for work anyway. The television is an essential element of the advertising business, which was lucky because if I was talking to a client on the phone and the kids were watching television, I could get away with it. The sound of the television equalled work.

'I put the answer phone on if I wasn't at my desk or was busy with the kids and the message said "I'm here, I'm just not at the phone at the moment so leave a message and I'll get right back to you". That meant that I didn't actually have the baby crying down the phone very often. Sometimes that situation is unavoidable, and you and your client just have to deal with it.

'Having Theta [the woman she employed to help her with Margaux] made an enormous difference. Initially she came three days a week and I found it very difficult to work the days she wasn't there. I arranged client meetings to coincide with the days Theta was with us, but would always agree to emergency meetings when she wasn't. I just told them I'd have to bring the baby with me, which never seemed to bother clients.

'I remember going to a big fashion meeting with the baby in the capsule. They needed me there and said they didn't mind the baby, but I did. I didn't want to bring her into my work environment. I found it difficult and distracting and felt it detracted from the professional image I wanted to put across.'

On another occasion Susan was asked by her client to attend an emergency meeting in another state. Initially she declined because she was still breastfeeding and so couldn't just leave the baby with Theta. Her client was adamant that Susan needed to be there so flew Susan, her mother, who looked after the baby while Susan was at the meeting, and of course Margaux, to Sydney. All for a one-hour presentation! Susan thought it was a ridiculous idea but her client didn't.

'People are very flexible now. If they want you badly enough it is quite amazing how they will adapt and fit in around your schedule. In my industry it is expected that women will bring babies to work under their arms. Obviously you can't do it all the time. Apart from anything else, it drives you nuts and it can be a distraction for the rest of the people in the office, but I have done it, if I can't organise anything else.

'I think management generally realise that we're not bringing our children in by choice. When I was starting out in business, the ethos was that workplaces should accommodate children and that they stayed with you the whole day while you worked. There was the idea that the liberated woman had her baby in a basket beside the desk while she worked. Well, that doesn't work. In your own office at home, it doesn't work. It's almost impossible to concentrate with a child around, so I think they need to be in a separate room. If they're not, you just don't get any work done. It comes down to a question of efficiency. As a principle I don't think management are against children at work, but the reality is that not a great deal is ever accomplished when they are.'

Susan is now a long way away from the world of advertising and management, although she is using many of the skills she learned there to deal with, explain and move forward to the next phase of her life. With the same determination she displayed to become a copywriter and then in establishing her own business, she is setting herself to the task of getting well.

'I will beat it [with] a combination of medical and alternative methods . . . As well as the surgery and chemotherapy, I am also deeply involved in diet, meditation, vitamin thereapy and lifestyle changes that have been successful for other people. It's an absolutely fascinating business and I am fast becoming expert at alfalfa sprouting and Ross [her husband] makes the best carrot juice in town.'

Like researching a new product for which she is finding a pitch, Susan has been thorough in learning about this new freeloader in her life, cancer. She knows all the jargon, the abbreviations of the long medical terminology, the statistics and the ramifications of any decision she may make in relation to her treatment. I realise she now understands it all thoroughly because she is able to describe it all, in true copywriter style.

'I thought I knew quite a lot about breast cancer but I didn't. It is a deadly disease with no cure. All breast cancer is considered systemic and 50 per cent of women diagnosed are dead within five years, with an average life expectancy of 21 months. The other 50 per cent live longer. How much longer? They can't tell me. They don't collect the statistics because "breast cancer is usually found in women 55 plus and they are going to die of something in ten years or so anyway". Talk about not enough interest or money being spent on it because it is a woman's disease.'

Susan later goes on to describe the gruelling chemotherapy and I salute her bravery and thank her for the description which makes me throw away the packet of cigarettes I just bought. This has worked better than any Cancer Council advertising on the subject. Once a copywriter always a copywriter!

'Now to the main question that everyone seems to want to ask. What is chemotherapy like? Well, all I can say is, if you get a better offer—like lunch at Lynch's or dinner at D'Arcy's if you're a Sydney person—take it. If that's not an option however, it's not too bad. The staff at Monash

Medical Centre are really excellent—a bit like a MASH unit going into battle and all that happens is you sit in a chair for a couple of hours whilst heavily garbed medical staff drip nuclear waste into a vein in your hand. I was quite terrified but fortunately it's nothing like that cult classic movie, *Revenge of the Toxic Avenger*, and you don't turn green and start searching for a swamp to emerge from. The treatment makes you very tired—a bit like the way you feel when you come home from hospital with a new baby—you need to lie down a lot . . . During the second week after treatment, my neutrophils (no, not a Kellogg's breakfast cereal but a component of my white blood cells) will plummet . . . Then in week three they build up again and it's back to the war zone for another cycle.'

In between all that Susan has spent a week at the Gawler Foundation where 'there were 24 wonderful women . . . in various states of health—and we all felt we gained a great deal from the experience. The group dynamic was fascinating in that a majority of us were very high achievers who had life stories which had many similarities including exceptionally busy careers, families, husbands, kids and commitments. Almost all of us were happily married—(one nun, three divorcees) and had excellent support at home too—something I hadn't expected.'

Susan explains that only two of the women there with her were over 50, which was surprising. With current publicity about breast screening, Susan says she would like to make 'a quick political announcement' and encourage all women to question the notion that breast cancer is an 'older woman's' disease. 'There is no doubt that you have to become an informed and critical consumer of medicine and the medical profession . . . so just insist that you want a mammogram and refuse to be part of the silent majority who believe everything they are told . . . Here ends the political announcement.'

When I first talked to Susan Chadwick she was an inspiring business woman whose story and successes made her perfect mentor material for anyone starting a business of their own, or moving through their career as either an employed or self-employed person. Now, not only is she a role model for one's career but for life as well. She said of her own business that she was 'run ragged all the time', but happily admitted in the next breath that, despite it all, she loved it. Now she has a disease that has changed her life and challenges her in different ways. 'It's hard work but it's worth it to see Margaux grow up, I figure she needs me for a lot longer yet and I'm not impressed with five and ten years survival rates—I need to do a whole lot better than that! There are some inspiring women and stories out there—and I'm gonna be one of them!'

While Susan has obviously come to understand the ins and outs of the advertising and business worlds and more recently her disease, what she hasn't yet got a firm grip on is just what an inspiration she already is.

C.L.

# Rebecca Cameron

## Construction Contracts and Building Administration Consultant

When I rang the South Australian Builders Association asking if they knew of any women in the industry, they said, 'Not off hand, no.' Then after a pause the voice on the end of the phone continued, 'Nope, sorry, can't think of any. Unless you've got a name, it'll take a few weeks for us to track one down for you too.'

I must say I wasn't in the slightest bit surprised. I suspected that finding a builder would be one of my more difficult research tasks. As I put the phone down, my friend Babs, with whom I was staying, piped up excitedly, 'I know a quantity surveyor. Do you think she would be useful?'

'I don't know,' I said, not doubting her relevance to the book but unsure of what a quantity surveyor was. 'What does she do?' I asked, trying not to appear completely ignorant. Pause. 'Well, I'm not exactly sure, to be honest with you, but I know it's got something to do with building,' she stammered. 'Right,' I said, 'can I have her number?'

It turned out that Rebecca Cameron wasn't really a quantity surveyor, or more accurately, a quantity surveyor wasn't all she was. She is and has been for the last twenty years, deeply entrenched in what is perhaps the most male-dominated industry of all, the building industry.

As Rebecca explained to me, she is 'a construction contract consultant. I provide a construction consultancy to people in the commercial construction industry doing a number of things. Sometimes I write contracts for people, sometimes I do quantity surveying, estimating and other times I just write letters.

'I fell into this area and there's nobody else who does exactly what I do. It's unique. Often people are involved in a contractual situation, they may be a plasterer, working for a builder and they find there's something contractually required by them they are just not able to do. They don't have the knowledge mostly or they feel that they are not in a good bargaining position with their client. They need the help of someone who has more professional expertise than they do about a particular matter, which is where I come in.'

I found it very hard to imagine ever having the courage to walk on to a building site and tell builders what to do. I admit that, as with many women I know, I will cross the road or take a different route even if it's out of my way, to avoid a building site. Rebecca tells me that I have totally misconceived the situation on sites.

'Oddly enough it's really easy. Strikingly easy. My experience of working in firms wasn't always very good though. When I first started out from college, I worked for an old family company and I was never given any opportunity. They always thought I was going to have a baby and leave so they gave me all the really terrible work.

'Other people moved on left, right and centre and all the paperwork to deal with their jobs would be shoved in a box and handed to me. So I was doing the most difficult work they had and it was terrible, but actually it has been the most tremendous advantage because it has meant that I can do anything.

'They didn't give me a chance because they didn't think a woman's place was in the building industry. And I think the only reason they let me work for them was because they were under pressure from their wives. I was a cadet building student, studying building technology at the Institute of Technology here in South Australia. I studied part-time and worked for this company on a part-time basis as well. They regularly took on cadets who spent six months in every department but I was never moved out of administration. When I finally did get onto building sites, I found the fact that I had been kept away from them for so long meant that I was able to visualise my work much better.

'When I got on site I didn't have any difficulty relating to the men on the job. In fact I found they adored being told what to do by a woman. It was easy. In the course of twenty years I must have worked with 10,000 people and there wouldn't be more than four that I have had any difficulty with, who just couldn't cope with the idea that a woman actually knew what she was doing on a building site.'

We take so much for granted in our working lives today. Yes, sexual discrimination does happen, but when it does and when we can prove we are being held back because of it, we do have some recall. We may not win but at least we are able to take action; we have the option of taking our grievances to court to let a higher authority challenge archaic notions of where a woman's place is. When Rebecca was first working in the building industry there was no such recall available; she had to sit tight and accept the rough justice she was being dealt or face the unemployment queue.

To be held back within an organisation for so many years would be soul destroying for most people, and enough to send them from the work force forever. It would make the most capable question their abilities and their worth. To have the strength to walk away from that daily put-down, and say, 'I am good at my work', is one thing, to then be able to walk out saying, 'I can do this on my own' and to make a success of it as so many women have, is astounding. One of the most uplifting themes of this book and the women in it, is their strong sense of self, courage and determination to move out on their own despite their often less than supportive surrounds.

'If I knew what it was going to be like I would never have gone into the construction industry. I didn't realise that it would be so male dominated.' Rebecca pauses, rethinking her last statement. 'Well, I didn't think I'd be the only woman, put it that way. I didn't think there would be a lot of women in the industry by any means but I didn't think it would be as draconian as it was. I was repressed and discouraged just because I was a woman.'

Rebecca says it was fear of unemployment and her determination that made her stay, despite the barriers.

'When I started out, people stayed with businesses for a long time. It wasn't unusual to stay with a company for 40 years. In those days you didn't just leave companies like people do today. The company I was with was 60 years old, the industry was falling on hard times and there were a lot of retrenchments so I felt secure working for an established firm. The devil you knew was better than the devil you didn't.'

Eventually though, through what Rebecca describes as a 'very unusual set of circumstances', she went to work for another firm whose attitude was diametrically opposed to her previous employers.

'It was a Victorian based firm which was wanting to expand into Adelaide. I had once worked with one of their employees and he suggested me as someone who might be able to help them in Adelaide. They said, "It will only be you and the manager in the office, you'll only be working part-time to begin with and you will have to do everything".'

It wasn't something Rebecca had to consider for very long. She thankfully accepted the position and says it was a wonderful experience of learning and a time when she was stretched both personally and professionally.

'I learned things I'd never have had the opportunity to learn. I did everything, from estimating to quantity surveying and everything in between and beyond. It gave me the confidence to go out on my own because it showed me just what I could do. It was wonderful and gave me the background to try on my own.'

Rebecca was asked to move to Victoria but refused, seeing this to be an opportunity to work on her own.

'I made the decision to stay here in Adelaide, where I had plenty of contacts and I just thought I'd give it a go. Weekly, I was being offered lucrative employment opportunities, but I thought no, this is your chance, give it a go yourself.'

Rebecca was in the fortunate position of having a well-established career and a husband whose wage ensured there would always be food on the table even if she didn't earn a penny.

'I had tremendous confidence about going into business because there was just so much I could fall back on. I thought I'd go out on my own for six months and if it didn't work, it didn't really matter too much. I knew I could always take up one of the jobs I'd been offered.'

She had her fall-back position all worked out, which indicates a fair bit about Rebecca. She comes across as a person who maps out her moves and considers her position with realistic eyes. I can't imagine her making decisions without first considering the worst and best eventualities. As it happens, she was never out of work.

'I was very confident about what I was about to do because people kept ringing me up, asking me if I would work for them for generous amounts of money. Their offers gave me tremendous backing and my husband was supportive and was working, which also contributed to my sense of safety.'

All Rebecca's business came to her by word of mouth. She always worked for people she knew or their friends or colleagues, which she admits is a 'lovely way to work'.

'It wasn't as if I was going to be doing anything different to what I had always done, I just wasn't going to receive a monthly pay cheque for it. All the things I would have to do, I had done before on behalf of employers so it wasn't scary at all.'

The day I stumbled upon Rebecca was my last in Adelaide, so there was some urgency for us to get together. It was short notice but I was determined not to miss out on Rebecca's story. This was an interview I definitely didn't want to conduct by optic fibre. She was happy to talk to me, but she was reluctant for me to come out before she could organise a sitter for her youngest child who was home with her. 'Don't bother,' I said, quite relieved because I was about to ask her if she would mind if my son came with me to the interview. 'I have my six year old with me!'

For women with children, partnerships are sometimes a helpful option. They can act as a back-up for those times when children are demanding attention and there is an important deadline to meet or appointment to keep.

'I am a sole trader and I have never considered a partnership because of the nature of my work. People ask me to do work for them with the highest of confidence. They expect a very professional approach and I wouldn't like to be responsible for anyone else's work. I'm not confident with that, and at the time I didn't know anyone else doing the work I was doing anyway. I would never dream of going into a partnership even though with the children it would have made things easier.'

Rebecca maintains control over all aspects of her business.

'The only thing I don't do is submit my tax return. I do all the paperwork and collate all the expenses, incomings, provide statements and my accountant just puts it all together on a tax return form. I send out my invoices once a fortnight and I do that paper work at night or weekends, which takes about four hours every second week. When I first started I used to do double entry bookkeeping but I don't bother with that now. I just keep all my expense dockets and mark everything clearly and put it all in a folder.

'I am very methodical and that's why I'm good at what I do. It's my job to organise things for people whose organisation has got a bit out of hand. That is the thrust of what I do so methods and attention to detail are imperative. I keep a very detailed diary which I go through once a fortnight to log my time for invoicing because I charge my services out by the hour.

'Before the children it was easy to run the business on my own. I have always worked four days a week with one day free to deal with any emergencies clients may have. If there weren't any then I knew that I could do the other things I like to do in my life. Or it was a day for me to do chores so my husband and I could have weekends free just to relax together.

'Then children came along and everything changed. If I had had healthy pregnancies and children who slept a lot it would probably all have been okay, but I was ill and had to cut down my hours. Working from home was marvellous because I could go to sleep when things were quiet. If I had been working for someone else then I would have had to give up work altogether.

'I continued to work three days a week. I tried to work while the kids were asleep but unfortunately they didn't sleep very much so when they were small I tried to fit in my work whenever I could; an hour here and there. It was surprising that the more I worked like that, the more I was able to hone my abilities. I was able to focus my attention at the drop of a hat. Then as soon as my first child was old enough, I sent her to child care and I started work four days a week again.

'I dreaded putting her in child care. I kept stalling. The first time I took her there I thought I wouldn't be able to achieve anything that day, but I dropped her off, walked away and didn't give it another thought. She demanded me all day, for four days—"I want my mummy . . . " but after that she was fine. It was the best thing I could have done for her. She was fifteen months old and it was her first contact with other kids and she loved it.'

Rebecca's mother also works so she was unable to help with babysitting, but when her second child was born, Rebecca's mother paid the eldest's child-care fees. She had offered to do this regardless of whether Rebecca was working or not. Rebecca says, 'my mother-in-law is the child-care supremo in our family. She often has five children around. I would rather die!' But she is also extremely grateful for her own mother's support.

There are industries where you can imagine there would be some empathy and allowances made for a working woman with children. The building industry is not one that springs to my mind. There were times when Rebecca had to take her children to meetings, and her professional approach to her work makes me think it is not something she would do light-heartedly. Her feelings about those occasions hold no surprise for me.

'I think it is extremely unprofessional to bring children along to meetings, and wouldn't dream of doing it unless I absolutely had to.'

What does surprise me however, is the attitude of her clients.

'The men didn't seem to worry about it at all,' she said. 'Once I went to a meeting with eight men. I was chair and when it came time for my contribution, my daughter screamed her head off. The man sitting next to me, just said, "Here, give her to me".

'I have always tried to plan my schedule so that when I have the children, any work I have to do could be done in my own time, here at home. Once they were mobile I knew I couldn't take them along with me and I would just have to say, "No, I can't come".

Many women say that incorporating children into their work schedules is a stumbling block for them, both personally and professionally. Personally they find it draining, professionally they find it takes away from the persona they want to project to clients and colleagues. Rebecca found though, that when it came down to it, she was the only one who had a problem with crossing the personal and the professional in moments of emergency. Perhaps this illustrates the point that often we are our hardest critics.

The pressure on women today to be so many different things in so many worlds, inevitably means that these worlds we are desperately trying to segregate will cross over at some point. Perhaps we need to accept that it is virtually impossible to keep them separate and that probably we are the only ones who think we should. Whatever opinions are held about incorporating children and work, the truth is that it is an extremely troublesome issue for women. Rebecca said, 'It's the worst thing about having small children when you run your own business. It's very difficult to be professional and I do resent that.'

The pressure on mothers running their own business and indeed working mothers generally, in trying to deal with the ever-present needs of children as well as their commitment to work is something that others might find hard to comprehend. The views in society about a mother's role in her child's life and the 'proper' way for them to be raised are not always compatible with the realities that women face. We are told that early child care is detrimental to our children's needs and that 'latch key' kids become delinquents. These and a myriad of other guilt-inducing statements are thrown at working mothers. The choice working women have to make is to live their own lives and trust their instincts about their kids, or to give up their own dreams and live by the rules of society. Neither is easy or trouble free.

'I wasn't willing to put the children into care when they were very little but that decision meant my business took a dive. I kept in my mind that in the scheme of things it wasn't a very long time and I just hoped the business could withstand it.

'I have had to re-establish myself but not from scratch

because I have managed to do some work while the children have been here, at home, with me. Partly through chance and partly by design the bulk of my work over the last few years has been for solicitors and a lot of it has been research work for arbitration in legal cases. I am involved in a lot of dispute resolution and I am very interested in arbitration. I am now a member of the Institute of Arbitrators.'

I can see that Rebecca would be a fine arbitrator. She has a calmness that would work well in disputation resolution and her words are carefully considered—a trait she has either learned from, or taken to, her work.

'Construction disputes are incredibly complex and mostly they are beyond the understanding of even those in the industry. They are almost always beyond the understanding of solicitors. So I go through documents because I have eyes that see the important points and knowledge of the industry that allows me to brief them on the real issues in dispute. It's interpretive and subjective work in some ways that has allowed me to continue working even with the children. This is work I can do here at home in my own time, because it involves a lot of reading and analysing documents.'

The recession has made people in the construction industry think twice about the cost of taking disputes to court. It is an expensive and time-consuming process when the resolution could be worked out in other ways. People now see the need to resolve their disputes without expensive legal costs and realise that the only ones who make any money out of the traditional path to resolution are the solicitors. Why go to a solicitor when usually all that is needed is a mediator? Rebecca agrees that this new understanding will mean more work for her.

'I get involved in quite a lot of mediation now. By the time I am brought in, the two parties are calling each other names and it has become quite uncivilised. Usually they just need a third person who knows what they are talking about to help them reach a solution.'

Enter stage left, Rebecca Cameron. Exit stage right shortly after, two previously warring parties, in agreement and very thankful for the help of one building construction consultant with a special gift for working things out.

'In a way it doesn't matter what the result is, they are always happier because they have come to some agreement. I am called in when people have a problem they can't handle and when we finish they are always in a better position. In that way it is very rewarding work and I don't get involved with any of the political garbage those in management have to deal with. I have tremendous variety in my work. The situations and the disputes are always different. I never do anything twice, it's always different, which I love.'

The building industry is a high-risk business. There is a lot of money to be made and equally large sums to be lost. It is notorious for liquidations, bankruptcy and bad debts. I am surprised that in the ten years she has been working for herself, Rebecca has had very few bad debts.

'I am paid well for my work and I think because I do help people, my fee is never begrudged by my clients. Bad debts are a risk in any business, but it's not been my experience. I've hardly had a bad debt and those I have had have only been from liquidations, never from a client refusing to pay me.'

That surely must be a sign that what Rebecca achieves is worth its weight in gold.

The Dumbo video occupying our children while we have been talking is over, the credits are rolling and we both realise our time is running out. We look at each other knowing we have to cut to the chase and wrap this up. As the pitter patter of little feet approaches, Rebecca employs her old trick, hones her attention and just manages to say, 'I have had to keep my goals in sight and in the long run, I think the way things have panned out will help my business. I am more focused and despite the fact that the recession has meant many of the people I knew in the industry are no longer out there in the market place, I'm sure I'll never look back,' before the children burst in demanding more lemonade.

C.L.

# Di Jones

## Real Estate Agent

So much of what we are is defined by what we do. Our perceptions of people are predetermined by our notion of what they do long before we meet and get to know them. Perhaps the most challenging part of writing this book has been to put aside preconceived ideas, and to approach each person with an open mind.

I was slightly nervous about interviewing Di Jones. I knew she was a very successful real estate agent, and as someone who had only ever dealt with real estate agents as a property renter, I felt that it would be strange to visit an agent without filling out a rental reference form!

As I approached the offices of Di Jones, I found myself behaving like someone trying to rent the property of their dreams that also happened to be the dream of 40 other prospective renters. Once I remembered that I was visiting as a journalist, not a tenant, I composed myself, relaxed and entered Di's very smart offices ready to talk business.

The offices of Di Jones Real Estate are different from any other agency I have been in. A large terrace house in Sydney's palatial and leafy suburb of Woollahra, has been transformed into offices with a strong 'French country' style, with polished floor boards. I was shown into the boardroom, which also was a far cry from any other I had been in. With raffia matting on the floor, a huge table decoupaged with a 'lifesize' angel, surrounded by high backed white-upholstered chairs, the only tell-tale sign that this was an office, not a room in a French country home, was the balsa wood models of property developments and tile samples in the corner.

Di Jones Real Estate Agency is busy—the phones ring almost constantly. Di came in and I could see she had a million things on her mind. I explained that the whole idea of this book was to reflect the realities of self-employment. Real women running their own business were often interrupted or called out unexpectedly, and by deciding to write about business people like her, we accepted that there would be times when interviews just weren't possible. If she needed to attend to work commitments, I was more than happy to wait. This activity was all part of being at the helm of a business and in order to document it, we expected to see it.

Within moments of turning on my tape recorder, Di Jones was challenging my preconceived notions of real estate agents. There was a whole lot more to this woman than inventories and lease subsections.

Like many of the other women in this book, Di did not formally train in her chosen area of business. As a secretary in a real estate agency, she gained some background knowledge of the industry, but only in a very general sense. Despite this start, which some would call a drawback, Di has launched what has become one of the most successful real estate businesses in the state.

'I had never planned on being a career woman. I had always been a secretary and had some selling experience in insurance, but mainly my background was secretarial.'

Di had her first child and then her second soon after. Her youngest child, Matthew, was born with brain damage which Di attributes to human error during the birth.

'I was told to put him in a home and forget about him. That was when I realised I was a fighter. I think most mothers would have a similar reaction to mine hearing that kind of "advice".'

Obviously this was a huge turning point in Di's life, not only did it tip her own world upside down, it also changed her perceptions of professional people.

'I had always put my total trust in professionals and this made me re-evaluate my concept of what life is all about and I discovered that you are really on your own. You have to fight your own battles and fight for your children and you can't really depend on anyone.

'I searched and searched, looking for some way, some thing, to help him and I found out about a place in the States where people were doing great things with brain damaged children.'

Di and her husband Bill made up their minds that they would take Matthew to the United States and put him through the program, but the cost involved meant putting everything on the line. It was a sacrifice they were more than willing to make, but before they could do it, the business she and Bill were involved in collapsed. 'Basically, we lost everything we had.'

Di says, 'It sounds like a real hard luck story—but it is exactly what happened, and it was very hard to deal with at the time.' Di's tone implies that she has come to terms with her past, dealt with it, grown from it and let go of that which was not useful.

The ability to go through hardship and use the experience to expand rather than constrict your life, is a difficult task, but it is a common trait of many women (at least those in this book) who run their own business. The odds of jumping all the hurdles placed in your track when setting up your own business and not stumbling or knocking a few down along the way are pretty slim. The challenging task is to make those falls a positive and learning experience, rather than damaging and fearful, and those who achieve it usually excel.

At this point, after so much, many would give up but Di was spurred on. 'I had to make money to provide for Matthew so I got work as a fashion agent. I had three different lines of clothing which I sold while the children were at day care. I was driven.

'They always say, to be successful you either have to be needy or greedy. I guess I was very needy. By the time Matthew was two I had saved enough money, with the help of fundraising functions I organised, to take him to the States. We did a program run by The Institute for Human Potential in Philadelphia. Matthew was assessed and a program was drawn up specifically for his needs. Then we were taught how to do the exercises for him at home by ourselves.'

Di and her husband returned to Australia and set their house up with equipment to implement the program, the basis of which was constant stimulation. It was a seven-days a week routine and they arranged for people to come in to make sure there was no break in his treatment. Di says it was a wonderful experience because so many people rallied to their support, all working in shifts to help Matthew. 'People from the Apex Club came in their suits and rolled around on the floor with Matthew. Even the local Scouts Club helped out.

'He really did improve in this time, and for me it helped because I knew I was doing something for him, rather than just accepting it, which is what everyone had told me to do.'

The treatment helped them all enormously, but then Matthew got encephalitis and there was further damage to his brain. They had to re-assess everything and work out what to do next. They heard about a school in Dural with a reputation for doing wonderful things to help children and Di says, 'I thought it would be where we could give Matthew the best possible life.'

The drawback, of course, was the expense. Di and her husband sat down and added up what was coming in from his auctioneering and her part-time work, subtracted their outgoings, and found that there was no way they could possibly manage for Matthew to go to the school in their current situation.

'Bill was an auctioneer with Hookers Real Estate but we decided to put everything on the line. We opened up our own real estate agency. We knew that to be able to provide for Matthew we'd have to do something different, so we took a big risk. That was fifteen years ago. It was a Raine and Horne franchise in Glebe. Bill taught me everything about real estate and I took to it very well. I guess that was why I went into it.'

Di says, 'We were very successful. Nobody did auctions in Glebe at that time, they said it wasn't an auction area. Bill was very enthusiastic and we both saw the potential and we were right. The auctions were very, very successful.'

So, from the very beginning of her career in real estate, it seems Di Jones set out to do something a bit different, to push the boundaries and set new trends.

'Max Raine, chairman of Raine and Horne, was very impressed with how successful we had been in such a short space of time. He asked us to take on the Woollahra franchise, which we did, and that too worked very well.'

Within twelve months of moving to Woollahra, they had

turned the agency around and it was in the top ten Raine and Horne franchises. It wasn't long though before Bill was headhunted by another real estate franchise chain. Di didn't like the idea of working in competition with her husband, so they both took over the new Richardson and Wrench franchise in Woollahra, which they had for eight years. When they sold the business, Di remained there on contract for three years and Bill moved on to a managerial position in the same company in the city.

'I liked it there but I decided I wanted to do something different. I'd always been with a big corporation and I thought I'd like to have a boutique-style agency of my own. I had lots of ideas about marketing and ways to present properties.'

I remember the terror that set in shortly after the elation of deciding to start my own business, and I asked Di if she was overwhelmed with a similar feeling when she made up her mind to establish Di Jones Real Estate.

'I was more worried about Bill because going out on my own meant that I would be in competition with his company. He said, "Just because you're married to me doesn't mean you have to work for the same company". He was very supportive and said, "You should be able to do your own thing as if you're not married to me". I thought, if he doesn't mind and he's not holding me back, what's stopping me? So I started, thinking that it would be a very small business.

'Kathryn Morris, whom I had employed at Richardson and Wrench, wanted to come with me when I left. The business was accepted really well right from the beginning. I think the decision to do all-colour advertising was a large factor in the success of the business.'

The formula for advertising properties had been set in stone until Di came along and shook it up. No other agent had ever strayed from the predominantly black-and-white format, so when she placed her ads, they really stood out from the crowd.

'Everyone's copied us now but at that time, it was very outstanding to have all-colour advertising.' Who was it who said 'imitation is the sincerest form of flattery'? 'We consciously chose a very different kind of lay-out as well, using more photos and less writing and, along with the eye-catching French blue, that really set us apart from everyone else. The marketing company I employed said it wouldn't work, but I stuck to my guns and am very glad that I did,' she says.

It was Di's For Sale signs that first brought her to my attention. As a designer I remember being impressed with the style of her signs—so much better than the gaudy placards that most agencies erect on their properties.

'People were always saying to me, "I don't have to have one of those ugly sign boards do I?" I decided that was another important aspect to the business. I thought about what I would want from an agency and from there it was all easy really.'

I found it hard to believe that Di has only been running her business for two years—her sign boards are plastered all over Sydney's eastern suburbs and the entire operation gives the impression of being well-established.

She explains that many of her clients came to her on the basis of their earlier dealings with her at other agencies. Her fourteen years experience in the area stood her in good stead with her clients and they were only too happy to support her when she set out on her own. She wasn't a nobody who sprang up from nowhere. She already had a reputation and profile and she stresses that women were very supportive.

Di says that being a woman has worked to her advantage. 'I think the fact that so many women have set up their own businesses in the last few years has helped me. When I first went out in real estate it was very different though. When I worked for other companies, people didn't feel confident in my ability because I was a women even though I was the top performer year after year. That's changed now, but when I first started I really had to prove myself and it was a struggle to be recognised.

'I was quietly confident that I would get enough business to be financially all right. To be honest though, I never realised it would go to this. It has been amazing.'

Perhaps one reason for the high success rate of women running their own businesses is that they are more realistic in their assessment of their business needs and capacities than their male counterparts. Women, so our interviews illustrate, tend not to overcommit themselves. Perhaps by acknowledging a practical economic reality that financial backing is harder for women to come by, they are less likely to get into financial strife. Women, for example, rarely lease expensive properties or make capital investments before the business can realistically sustain them. Di explains that she started her business erring on the side of caution.

'I didn't start off here in these offices. Initially I only had a secretary in Queens Court. Later we moved into one of the rooms downstairs from where we are now. Now it's gone to this,' she says extending her arms in a sweeping arch. 'I still want to keep it small. My major competitor is a huge operation of 45 staff and I don't want to get to that. That is really not my style at all.'

Success brings with it a pressure to expand, which comes not only from friends and family but prospective clients, eager to reap the benefits of associations with 'winners'. Di is adamant that she 'wants it to stay a boutique agency that is very personalised and unique'. She says she doesn't agree to handle all the sales she is asked to. Her staff has grown from two to thirteen in a relatively short time and she is keen, for the moment, to keep it at that.

At this point Di has to see a client who wants to put a property on the market, so I wander around the offices. Most directors of companies like everyone to know that that is exactly what they are. There are many ways to convey this: one is to have an air of self-importance—the manner and the tone says to the world, 'Hey, pay attention to me, I matter'. The other is by making a distinction in the surroundings of the employee and the employer.

Di Jones has used neither of these techniques. While she is obviously the one in the spotlight, and she is at the helm, there is nothing that sets her apart from any of the other people on her team besides her name on the company plaque. Di and the other agents share a large room on the second floor of the terrace. Her desk and chair are exactly the same as all the others. There seems to be no hierarchy in this office.

'I believe in fitting in with everyone else. We work as a team. With the office set up this way, we can discuss ideas and plans all day. Hands on management is the only way to go. If you're locked up in an ivory tower away from your staff, you lose touch and miss out on important things. This way I know what's going on all the time and I'm convinced that setting yourself up as a guru apart from your staff doesn't work.'

The decision for a woman to establish her own business is never straightforward. Not only do we have to grapple with the realities of the 'how to', we also often have other people to consider and a grab bag of social conditioning that says a woman's number one commitment is to her family. To the outside world it often seems that the decision made by a woman with a family to start a business is selfish and irresponsible. To the woman making the choice, it is actually almost always the opposite. This is true in Di's case. It was her commitment to her family that made her take the plunge.

'There were people who criticised me for doing what I did. They wondered how I could possibly run a business and have a family, but the truth is, I didn't see I had any other option. I was determined not to put Matthew in a spastic centre. I'm not criticising people that have put their children in centres but it was something I just couldn't do.

'There was a lot of criticism aimed at me as a working mother. I often got snide remarks from other mothers at school, but I used to keep it firmly in my mind that they didn't understand my situation. How could they possibly have any comprehension of what the circumstances were that made me set my life up in this way?

'I think Kim, my eldest daughter, had troubles with it when she was a teenager. I must admit, if I had my time over again I would give her more attention. At the time though, I felt that she was all right. My attention was so focused on Matthew that I did overlook her a bit. She went through a bit of a rocky patch but she's fine now. She understands what we have done and why, but when she was about fourteen or fifteen I think she thought we were horrible because we were so busy. We weren't busy socialising, we were working, and I think it's given her the drive to be very successful herself.

'At the time I remember questioning myself. Was I doing the right thing? Maybe it would have been better to send

Kim to a public school and maybe I should have stayed home and tried to cope with Matthew myself, but I think that option would probably have broken up my marriage. So from where I was coming from I couldn't see any other option but to give everyone a better life and I'm glad I did it.

'Matthew is 21 now and I do feel very happy about him and I have come to terms with it. I know the choices I have made and the life I have set up have given him the best and happiest life that he could have had.'

When you are self-employed it would be easy to work 24 hours a day, seven days a week. Often this seems the only way to get through all the things piled on your plate and to attend to matters that aren't stamped urgent, but are important nonetheless.

'We never work Sundays. We have to work six days a week in this industry, but I do think you can combine family and business, you just have to make good quality time for both.

'I don't have to work as hard now as I did in the beginning because success has built my reputation and now I get recommended. That's a lovely way to do business. But when you're starting out it's so hard and I think in any business it's the same. If you always had to work as hard as you do in the first five years, you probably wouldn't get through it. Those first five years are when you have to go all out to establish yourself, and that takes time and a lot of energy.

Di says that running your own business certainly isn't for everyone. 'I can understand that lots of people want to have a career and a business and that's their driving force. Other people do it because like me, they need to, but it's certainly not for everyone.'

I agreed with Di and explained that I found the daily struggle between being too accommodating and too firm is hard to maintain.

'The velvet glove is better than the iron fist. Women can achieve what they want without being aggressive. You do have to be firm and focused and have a direction but you can do it without compromising your nature. You have to be thick skinned in business and I still go to water sometimes.

It's very hard when I feel tears coming up in my eyes but have to keep my composure.

'We are what we are and we have to put on fronts to try and hide our emotions. Sometimes it is incredibly difficult to keep everything business-like, to be firm. I remember one time particularly when I almost burst into tears. I hadn't been sleeping because I was so worried about a sale I was trying to organise for a lovely old couple who were really relying on me. At the last minute it all fell through and I was devastated. I'd done back flips to make the sale and I remember thinking at the time that a man probably would never have been so involved and wouldn't have felt that way.'

I ask Di what she finds hardest about running her own business and she answers immediately. 'The hours,' she says without a pause. 'Real estate is very competitive, especially here in the eastern suburbs. It is six days a week and I sometimes work eleven-hour days, so for me time is the most difficult part.'

I understand the constant pressure of time, the longing for a few more hours in each day (especially weekends) and ask about the most rewarding aspect, to which she also has no delay in replying but this time with rather a large beam on her face, 'To have people happy with you and the job you have done for them, is a remarkable feeling.'

Any advice for someone starting their own business I ask, before promising to turn off my tape recorder and let Di get on with her work. 'Make sacrifices and take chances,' she says, as someone who really knows.

C.L.

# Flora Chiang

## *Tiao* Massage Therapist

Flora Chiang has run the *Tiao* Centre for a year now. *Tiao* roughly translates as being in tune or harmony. As far as she knows she is the only person in Sydney practising this type of traditional Chinese massage professionally, despite the plethora of different types of massage available.

Flora was born and raised in Singapore and came to Australia in 1978 with her husband, whom she has since divorced. They applied for permanent residency before they arrived because her husband's sister had moved here and loved it. Flora considers herself very much an Australian now and as she says, she's no longer even 'new', having been naturalised for thirteen years.

To this day, Flora maintains that Sydney is, 'My favourite place in all the world! I have always felt so privileged living here. Whenever I go overseas I am always so happy to return.'

'We came to Australia for an adventure and really wanted a change in environment. I never felt as though I fitted into Asian society very well. Although I am Chinese and I respect Chinese tradition, I find that in the more restrictive Asian society I can't really be who I am, there is a limit to how I could express myself. I wanted more freedom.'

This sense of restriction has plagued Flora throughout her life. She left Singapore to escape it only to walk into a similar predicament in her first profession, accounting.

Flora was brought up in a family of five children. Her parents owned an electrical shop and she admits to always having been 'business minded'. 'We grew up around the shop as kids. I used to love playing "shopkeeper" even when I was quite young. I eventually did the accounts for the shop when I got older. It was somewhat inevitable!'

Flora did most of her training in accounting here, although she had worked in the finance and administration areas in Singapore before she left.

'I chose accounting because I thought that way I'd never be out of a job. You see, security was important to me.'

However, a life-crisis led to change and enormous upheaval in all aspects of Flora's life. She admits to me that it was like being 'born again'. Understandably, a breakdown, either mental or physical, is often the pivotal agent of change for many people. Until then they may have spent years running without arriving at their true path. Illness stopped them in their tracks, or their depression became so vast, that they were eventually forced to listen to what their bodies were telling them.

In Flora's case, the expectation that she would succeed and maintain values traditionally associated with achieving and staying on top in business wore her down and ultimately changed the direction of her life.

'I had been working for the same mining company for ten years. I was the finance administration manager and this involved an enormous commitment to the company. My job meant that I had to know about everything that happened within the company. It was very hands-on. They were a small company and it was a lot of responsibility for one person.

'Two years ago I got extremely ill and thought it was chronic fatigue syndrome because I was just so tired all the time. It got to the point that I couldn't even walk up the stairs anymore, my hair was falling out and I was having trouble breathing properly. In desperation I went to a conventional doctor, who told me I had the hepatitis B virus. I knew this was usually assigned to big drinkers, but I wasn't one!'

Flora then approached a Chinese herbalist who wrote some herbal prescriptions for her that didn't help much. When she went back to see the herbalist, Flora was told that her system was actually 'closing down' and that her entire digestive tract had seized up and was unable to absorb anything.

'This has always been my reaction to stress. Because my stomach's capacity to absorb things was so impaired, no matter what I ate it could not absorb anything.'

The herbalist recommended that Flora take a traditional Chinese remedy, swallow's nest. Flora explained to me that the bird makes its nest out of its own saliva rather than twigs and that once taken it can have exceptional results. It is expensive because it is harvested from the nests that are built high on cliffs near the sea and therefore difficult to procure. The hitch was that the remedy wasn't available in Australia and she had to go back to Singapore to get it.

'Within a few days of him telling me this I had left for Singapore to be looked after by my family. My mother urged me to come home. Once I got there I went to all kinds of specialists; I had an endoscopy, a colonoscopy and an ultrasound of the stomach, liver and intestines! My condition was so bad I knew I had to do something drastic. I slept day and night, despite the noise level which I normally find unsettling. I cooked the nest and ate it twice a day. Initially I couldn't swallow solids, but after a week I could eat again and the colour returned to my face. In the second week my appetite started to return and then I came back to Australia, cured! Post my recovery, I commenced work immediately because I felt well enough.'

Flora began to realise that her life was not fulfilling her needs and she was becoming sick as a result. This upheaval, happening as she was approaching forty, seemed interesting to me. From her description, her malaise sounded like a typical male mid-life crisis. She had been working in a male-dominated area and in order to play the game had found herself assuming a role that didn't really fit. She had spent years working her way up and being very ambitious, pursuing traditionally masculine goals, only to find an emptiness growing within her. Flora explained that she had forfeited having children because of the lifestyle that surrounded her work and the long hours. She had begun to wonder just who she was in all of this.

'My whole life had been centred on security and ambition. Yes, I suppose it was like a mid-life crisis! I had been wanting a change for a long time but didn't know how to do it. I yearned to get more in touch with my authentic self, in harmony with my true nature. People had seen me as an authoritarian and organising sort of person, but I knew inside myself that I was only doing what my job required. Come forty, I knew it was time to do something else.'

Flora had always been interested in the area of health and healing, but up until a year ago, had only a personal interest in it, having regular massage treatments. She read about an intensive four-week course studying traditional Chinese massage.

'I really just did it as an interest initially. Because the office wanted me back at work I could not do the four weeks, I could only attend the first two weeks of the course. In those weeks they covered all the fundamentals of traditional Chinese philosophy. I think subconsciously I was harking back to my roots because I was feeling so lost. I needed to make contact with my culture again in some way. Some of the basics I knew, but there was a lot to learn.'

About a year later, in late 1993, Flora decided to quit her job. She repeated the course and it wasn't until the very last day of the classes that she said, 'This is it!' Flora really felt that it was her destiny to go into this field.

'Even when I was halfway through the course, I didn't expect to go into it as a living or a business, I really thought it wouldn't be for me. Everything changed very quickly. It was such an enlightenment. I realised then that it was second nature to me.'

The course entailed a study of traditional Chinese medical philosophy as well as the application of the technique. Flora says that this particular massage is extremely powerful and works by rearranging the body's resources so that it can function and cope normally. 'It works on the massage reflex points of the body that lie along the meridian pathways. It doesn't use as much pressure as *Shiatsu* and a number of points are used in combination in order to harmonise the body. It is not just a matter of knowing the points, but knowing the ancient wisdom of their unique therapeutic effect—and if you don't know this and the way they interconnect with the meridian pathways, your work will have no real effect.'

'I am always interested in talking to the person about themselves during the massage, as this will inevitably lead me to the core of the problem. You can have a headache from stress, period pain, asthma, all kinds of reasons. You must take these extenuating factors into account while doing the massage, otherwise it may have little or no result.'

Flora had one week off after the course and flew to Singapore for the Chinese New Year.

'When I returned to Singapore and happily announced my decision to go into a practice of my own I was greeted with disapproval from my family. In order to understand this you must first understand something of the Chinese culture. Most Chinese think of a "massage business" as a front for a sex shop. My mother couldn't understand why I wanted to do it, as most people would get the wrong idea. I don't think she'd ever had a massage in her life and was a bit wary of it. Even now, here in Sydney, I won't get Chinese coming because they are sceptical about it, they think it's something else. I will get the odd phone call from Chinese men asking what "services" I provide!'

Despite her family's initial scepticism, she was determined to make a change. Flora was fortunate that she had some money from her previous job to see her through and, of course, her long-saved superannuation. Her establishment costs were not too high as she didn't need much equipment. In fact, she is one of the few women we interviewed who was not seriously undercapitalised when starting up.

'I opened the clinic in April. I wanted a street frontage because it is the sort of business that needs to be visible to remind people that you're there. I also didn't want to be tucked away upstairs somewhere, because then people might think what my mother thought!

'I've been very lucky, I think the first two days were the only quiet ones I've had. I have found that it works very much by word-of-mouth. I have also produced a brochure, which explains to people all about the methods I use and how they can be applied, which I think is helpful. This traditional form of Chinese massage is a very small, specialised field and now I have people from all over Sydney coming to see me here.'

She explains that in order to understand what she is talking about I will have to have one of her massages myself, so I booked in immediately!

Flora began by offering only the massage service and then decided to extend this to include Ventose therapy, which involves the use of glass cups. Looking around me when I arrived I had wondered what the trolley with all the heavy glass beakers was for.

'The "cups" were brought to China by the Romans and are an ancient healing method. The Greeks also used them. The Chinese have perfected the art and they are commonly used in China today. They basically work on the principle of suction. You heat them up and apply them to the body and they actually suck the skin up, bringing to the surface all the "bad energy". We use them on the back, mostly along the spine. The different sizes are for different areas. We work on what we call *Shu* points which are located along the body's meridian pathways.

'I closed the clinic and took the whole month of July off to study their use, at the same college at which I did the massage.'

She explains that the method is especially effective for those with muscle and joint pain or suffering from menstrual problems and for the very tense. She often uses them in conjunction with the massage to be even more effective.

'The procedure really allows "bad" energy to be released. It can make quite a remarkable difference, even in twenty minutes.'

I mentioned that my limited knowledge of Chinese therapies extended to the word *Ch'i*, which I knew to mean 'energy'. Flora explained that there is a problem with the different connotations and implications of language between the two cultures.

'The Chinese medical concept is so different from the Western one. The Western idea is not about going to the root of the problem and trying to solve that. It is more about "there's a germ in there, let's get it out". It isn't wholistic.

'The Chinese way is to say that we have to make the whole system work well, that there's no room in a healthy body for sickness. We have to make the entire person well again, not just treat the symptom. What is little understood is that the Chinese speak in metaphors; the "wind", the "heat", the "damp". When we say *Ch'i* we don't mean just the Western understanding of the word "energy". *Ch'i* in China has so many more connotations and a lot more depth, in fact it means the whole life-force energy. The same goes for *Hsüeh*. The West say it is just the blood and it moves the circulation around. In Chinese it means all of the bodily fluids, everything. It is a great deal more complex. The terms are linguistically handicapped. What I have learned is that what you express in words is limited by the language itself.'

Flora also has a diploma in clinical hypnotherapy which she obtained this year. She explains that it is not the kind of traditional hypnotherapy that most people would think of.

'The director of the school I attended, Lindsay Yeates, has a most extensive knowledge and background in both the medical and alternative healing areas. He trained as a radiographer and is also a practising clinical hypnotherapist. He has had 30-odd years experience and is keen to impart the true wisdom he has found through his studies.

'His form of hypnotherapy is very client-centred, permissive style. This way the client has the power and I am merely the agent of change, the guide. Usually people come with behavioural problems that they want to change. I help them go where they want to go . . . The power is with them, not me. I don't tell them what to do. I believe that so much illness is due to people's psychology, helping them empower themselves is wonderful.

'My teacher found that massage and hypnotherapy, used together, are very potent. With the conventional form of hypnotherapy, the therapist has all the power, which is odd, really, because the people are normally coming to take control of their lives, not hand it over! By accessing the power within them, you give the power back to the individuals themselves.'

Flora lives according to the philosophies she espouses. Because she was caught up in the race for success for so long, she understands what many of her clients are going through. She believes that there are a lot of people who are 'out of control'.

'I am so happy to see the transformation in the people walking out of here. What could be more satisfying or rewarding? On a one-to-one level, helping people gain personal control again is great. I could do it forever and a day. I've always been a "helping" kind of person. On a larger, global level it is wonderful to be able to contribute to society.

Shuffling paper and money around seems so empty to me now, it just doesn't compare.'

Flora maintains that she was always keen to explore a broad range of interests and read widely in addition to the financial papers. She says that her peers in her previous industry were comparatively narrow, if something didn't add up to money, they just weren't interested.

'The rewards now are certainly not financial. I think my ex-colleagues were a bit threatened. They didn't understand how I could just let go of so much. Well, of course in my eyes it was more than a fair trade-off! Some are envious. My friends can't believe the change in me, they see that my life is so much fuller.'

When Flora opened the clinic in 1994, she also became involved with a man who practises in a similar area, with whom she now lives.

'Yes, everything changed at once! I had separated from my husband eight years ago, although we only recently divorced. It wasn't acrimonious, we were just heading in different ways. It was essential for me to fill the gap when we broke up by keeping busy.'

Flora is still busy with the clinic open nine hours a day, five days a week. She is also studying a part-time course in applied psychology, which she felt would nicely complement the hypnotherapy.

'I admit at the moment I am very busy and I thought I would be able to do my study here in the clinic. I find, though, that I can't concentrate, there are too many distractions. So I leave it until after hours, often working until the early hours of the morning. Next semester I will drop back to fewer subjects, I've learned my lesson!'

However, Flora finds that she is so invigorated by the subjects she's learning that it isn't nearly as draining as it could be. She makes sure she has a regular walk on Balmoral Beach and has a beautiful painting of it in her clinic to remind her of its tranquillity.

'Although I'm so busy, I find I have so much energy. Before I had the practice I'd wake up groggy at eight. Now I find I'm up with the dawn and my sleep is much more restful. I can easily survive on five hours sleep a night now.'

As many of the women interviewed have found, particularly if they have to devote much of their own energy to their clients, it is imperative that they continue to nurture themselves also. Flora can treat between four and six clients a day, more than that is too draining as each session is over an hour long and can be very intensive. She uses her self-hypnosis in between seeing clients to keep herself well and refreshed. She cites one of the great advantages of being in her own business as having the freedom to sort out her own priorities, even choosing to close for a while so that she can attend classes or seminars.

'I'm lucky in that I can afford to close if I want to. My clients understand, they will wait for me because the service I provide is rare. They also know that they'll ultimately benefit from me learning as much as I can and passing that on. It also means I can really enjoy my business without worrying whether there is a lot of money coming in. For this I am lucky.'

There are times when Flora misses a weekly salary, but only for a moment. Her new financial position has curbed her lifestyle in some ways, but then her life is much richer. She now feels happy to be taking an uncertain path. Flora's discovery of the joy in giving to others has led her to a sense of wholeness that better suits her 'authentic self'.

'I look forward to my day now in a way I never did before. My values have changed and I even surprise myself in that way! I still see this as a stepping stone for me, I'm not sure where it will lead. The energy around me is constantly moving and changing, where I'll end up will change as I do.'

S.R.

# Frances Trimboli

## Clean With Envy

Frances Trimboli is 32 years old. At 29 she was general manager of an independent Australian record label. Now she runs her own contract cleaning business called Clean With Envy. These are two completely different worlds, but Frances' story shows that sometimes you need to experience extremes to make sense of your life.

When I first asked Frances what made her give up the kudos of a socially acceptable and influential position for the more humble and traditional job of cleaning, her answer was twofold. 'I was very sick and after a while, through my sickness, I realised that I didn't need the job and my company didn't need me.

'Towards the end of my time in the industry I was fixing everything up for the company I was with, which at the time was in a lot of difficulty. Then when it was all fixed, they wanted to take back all the power, without knowing anything about the issues. I had more of an insight into their business at that time than they did, and I think they were threatened by that and so didn't treat me very well. I was incredibly stressed and I got really sick. My body was saying to me, "Francis, it's time to check out".'

She went to the doctor one morning, thinking she had pulled a muscle in her groin, was told they suspected she had a blood clot, and was sent straight to casualty where she was admitted with suspected cancer. The doctors wanted to perform investigative surgery but Francis refused to let them. They never actually worked out what that scare was about but she suspects it was really about her stress levels. Long before the emergency dash to the hospital, she says, 'I looked like Hermann Munster. I had boils all over my face from stress. I think people probably thought I was on smack. I would look at myself in the mirror and not recognise the person looking back at me. I thought I was having a breakdown. It was terrible.

'I was in hospital for three weeks and my boss didn't even come and visit me once. After leaving hospital I was diagnosed as suffering from glandular fever and chronic fatigue syndrome. My doctor had been telling me to leave my job but it wasn't until I got well again that I would have regained enough of myself—physically and emotionally, to have the strength to take his advice. I had got caught, thinking they needed me as much as I needed them and it was hard to let go. I wondered why I had invested so much in that business when they didn't even care enough to visit me in hospital when I needed it most.'

She did find that strength and says she left 'not giving it another thought', deciding she 'didn't want to work in the music industry anymore'.

Like so many women in her position she was worn out and disillusioned with corporate culture that took so much and gave so little in return. It wasn't just the attitude of the company she was with but the whole industry, which she began to feel was morally bankrupt. It was all about 'personal gain with no thought about benefits to the community. It's scratch and claw your way to the top and no one helps each other'.

'So I got a bar job. I had never worked in the hospitality industry before and I loved it. I had lost contact with people because I was always working in an office. It gave me some breathing space, I saved up some money and I went to Central America with my girlfriend.'

Frances admits she is a workaholic, a state that often seems to curse or bless those who move to self-employment, and says she was restless even in Central America. 'I was always having to move on and around, I couldn't stay still in one spot.'

When she got back from the holiday, a friend was doing cleaning work and asked her to help out a few mornings. When the people in Paddington where she had been based in her executive job, found out she was cleaning they all asked her to do their offices and businesses.

'Before I knew it I was starting a new business. It was all based on people knowing I was trustworthy and liking me.

'I always believe it's important to be naturally friendly. I have never thought it pays off to work for people you don't like because it won't be a long relationship. Honesty is the main thing in business and to have a rapport with your clients is also very important. I am always direct and I like to operate that way and for others to be the same way with me. Respect is also very necessary for my clients and myself. It comes from the way I view myself and my position in life and flows onto the way I approach people and my work.'

Frances shows respect for the environment as well as her clients. She says though, that using green products is not only important for her conscience but her health. 'It's really bad breathing that stuff all day so I try to use more elbow grease than products. Working with them makes you realise just how bad a lot of these products are.' She tries to use environmentally safe products whenever possible and has found that the Down To Earth range are not only sound but effective too.

'I also make my own mixtures', she says, describing some of the different applications. 'For a domestic wet dust I use lemon grass oil or a combination of that and eucalyptus oil which works well and is nice to use. I sometimes take my own oil burners that I light while cleaning because I think it would be a really nice smell for my clients to come home to. I use oils whenever I can. Rosemary and vinegar for glass and vinegar and bicarbonate of soda is good for toilets.'

For ants she uses essential oils and I pipe up asking her if she has any herbal remedies or more accurately, death sentences for cockroaches. I lean forward hoping at last to have found the solution to my life's biggest nightmare. 'They are with us for ever and I'm afraid Caro, you just have to come to terms with the idea that they rent with you.' Well, it may not have solved the problem per se, but it made me feel better about the plague of insects roaming my kitchen.

I am interested in Frances' work not just because I want an answer to my cockroach plague, but I wonder about other people and how they value her work and have dealt with her move into this field.

'My mum never thought anything of it. She only wished that I had started it ten years ago, so she could have been part of it. In fact, I often wish I had too because my family would have been involved then. I think we would have had the best business. It could have been my aunties, cousins and sister as well, and we would have gone through the roof. We are all team people and my whole family is very helpful to one another. Now my mum would like me to stop because she thinks it's not good for me to be working so physically all the time. She says to me, "You've only got one body, Frances".'

With a family attitude like theirs it is easy to see why Frances found the competitive, dog-eat-dog nature of the corporate world difficult.

Her new business wasn't so readily understood and accepted by others and Frances still finds it hard to believe the reaction of some of her colleagues and acquaintances. Some thought it embarrassed them and that she was doing it out of spite, just to reflect badly on them.

'I never ever thought that people would wig out about it. They thought why is she trying to embarrass me? Some of my old colleagues told people I'd gone mad. People would say to my friends, "It's so sad about Frances, isn't it?" Which of course came straight back to me. I didn't have a problem cleaning toilets. It made sense to do cleaning because I didn't have to work twice the hours to make the same money I would have made in a cafe.'

Society is so quick to judge people by their employment. Therefore the courage and sense of self-assuredness that enabled Frances to make the move, not caring about what others thought was something I envied.

'There's a stigma involved with cleaning. I can't find staff. I guess it is a different headspace. I'm not saying, "Hey, get a career in cleaning", I'm saying, "If you're studying and you need to earn money and still have time for other things and your life, then cleaning is great". People get poor money for waitering and would earn double in cleaning and have more time for study but they don't do it because they'd rather not be known as a cleaner. I thought everyone thought like me.'

Frances eventually did find someone who wasn't worried about the stigma. 'I employed someone because I was getting lonely. After cleaning your second house of the day, you get really sad. I thought employing someone would make the business more productive but also that it would be more fun for me. What I found though, was that it took a ridiculous amount of time to get through the work. I wonder now what on earth they were doing all that time because what took me an hour to do, took them about three.'

Usually people in their own business look forward to the time when they can sit back and relax after the frenetic first few years when everything is being established and most energy is consumed. Di Jones said that if you had to work as hard as you do in the first few years, forever, you'd never do it. While Frances doesn't want to work that hard forever, she is sticking by a commitment she made to herself after leaving the record industry.

'After being so consumed by the record company, I decided that I would only spend two years doing any one thing for a while.'

Clean With Envy is in its second year now and Frances is thinking about selling the business.

'Getting your teeth into something new, that's the learning period, and that's where all the fun is for me. It's exciting to forget about what you've been doing before and launch into something else.'

I get tired just thinking about starting something from scratch all over again, but agree that it is an exciting time. It is undeniably a steep learning curve and if that's where the buzz is, then I can understand her plan.

'I went into this business because I didn't have any money to invest in anything else. It's labour intensive work but you don't need a lot of capital to get started. I have a reliable car, a back-pack vacuum cleaner, buckets, mops and dusters. I have a mobile phone even though I think they're wanky gadgets but it's security for me. Pubs are creepy at 4 am. It's easy to get spooked and imagine there are ghosts and you have to get used to all the different noises. Apart from the phone, you could get started in the cleaning business with $1500.'

Frances' willingness to eventually sell Clean With Envy shows that she has an unusually practical approach to her business. Many women wouldn't sell even if it made financial sense to do so.

'You can make a lot of money in cleaning but I missed that point on a day-to-day level. It has made me a living, not a great one, but what I realised is that I would make money when I sold up. Now I've got about twenty clients and I'm preparing to put the business on the market. When you sell a contract, you get the yearly wage you would earn from that job as good will. So if I do one job for $250 a week, when I sell the business I will get the yearly total of what that job is worth to me.

'I thought who on earth would do that? My accountant told me though, that cleaning contracts sell constantly. There's a group of people who pop out of the other end of the work force, have retired early, have their super package and are workers. They don't want to sit on their arse for the rest of their lives, they want to work. They may only be 50 years old and they really want to be useful. People with that attitude will be quite willing to pass that amount of money over to me, because they know they will be able to make money out of a business like mine. In that first year they won't make any money on the contracts I sell them but they are looking at it as a two or three year plan and have enough set aside to get them through the first twelve months, so it makes sense. If it's a husband and wife team they can make a good living from it and not feel useless when they're still wanting to work.'

The statement about a husband and wife team had me wondering whether Frances ever considered running Clean With Envy as a partnership

'If I had a partner, it would take the pressure off me. If they had been as into it as I was, there could have been money to be made. Staff lower your profit margin because it takes them twice as long to complete the work because working on an hourly basis, it's not in their interest to work fast.

'In the past I never considered going into partnership, but now I think it would be good simply because I want to have an easier life. There is a huge risk involved with partnerships but I think I have to learn to take that risk. It would be a good experience for me. It doesn't mean you both have to be "hands on". I don't mind working really hard but I would like the flexibility to be able to say to someone, "every three months, I'm having a week off to recharge my batteries". I don't want to be trapped by long hours any more. I think that with time out, you end up with a better business, because you have new ideas when you remove yourself from the grind and I think it would be nice to share it with someone.'

When I tell Frances that I think her approach to business is unusual she explains that, 'there was a point when I was really jack of doing this and I thought, I'll just let it go'. But she quickly realised that it 'would have been insane' and says she is trying to muster up a last spurt of cleaning energy to ensure a profitable sale.

Waking up at 4 am every morning would take its toll after two years, so in many ways it is easy to see why Frances is looking to sell. What she also says is hard about the cleaning business is that she works at odds with her partner who studies and works. 'We don't have quality time together any more and every three months it comes out in our relationship. When you're working the same hours you can have the wind down period together, drink and talk about each other's day. We don't have that and I guess we have put the pleasure side of the relationship on hold. I organise my free time around the relationship and won't take on work that infringes on that time but even so, we have very little time together.'

Frances tells me about some of the ideas she has for her next project and they are a melding together of her ambitions, passions, ideas about life and work, ethics and ideals. She says, 'women have been so under-represented in business', and while she says it has to come down to each individual's merits, 'if we all teamed together, we could build a bloody empire'.

C.L.

# A Balanced Life

*'The essential psychological conflict within modern western society is the conflict between our unceasing obsessive pursuit of material wealth and a deeper knowledge that this pursuit cannot bring us happiness.'*

Clive Hamilton, *The Mystic Economist*, 1994

This quote sums up for both of us writing this book, the malaise of Western society and our own concerns about life in the 1990s. We thought it most significant and particularly relevant to this chapter. It is one of the interesting and common themes that run through the interviews. However, we have not limited our search in this section to those women who have found this somewhat existential question to be their primary reason for pursuing a balanced life. Many of the women in other chapters have also considered this conflict to be an important one to unravel. There are various reasons why women search for a way to balance their needs and perhaps the needs of others. Here, we look at some of those reasons.

Achieving a balanced life can often seem like a utopian ideal; it is something that most of us believe other people manage, or something that we will be able to manage only in the future. It is a goal many of the women in this book strive for. Ironically, we have an added pressure today to not only get everything done, but to be seen to be exercising moderation and trying to achieve a balance in all aspects of work, home and social life.

The pressures of life in the 1990s may make having, or even desiring a well-balanced life seem self-indulgent. One may ask, is it a luxury or a basic human requirement? For those who have the opportunities to create this lifestyle it is a decision not often regretted.

A quote by Marion Milner in *A Life of One's Own*, that refers to the questions of seeing other possibilities, perhaps sheds some light on this question. 'Is it sometimes the feeling that the world is remote, nothing really to do with me? . . . could it be a drive to find a new way of looking at things, a kind of uneasiness that's like the feeling of a coat that has grown too tight, an awareness that some current way of seeing the world is getting worn out, has served its usefulness and become a constricting cliché?'

Surely affecting change in one's own life has the potential to echo throughout society. If we allow our work to define what and who we are, we can be left with a feeling of spiritual bankruptcy and a desire to broaden the scope of our lives. This mind-shift is slowly increasing amongst women as possibilities for achieving a balance become available or are perhaps discovered.

For one of the women profiled in this section, Kim O'Donnell, finding a balance meant considerable restructuring of her business to combine the necessities of earning an income and having a rewarding lifestyle. For others, like Marieke Brugman and Sarah Stegley, it meant moving to the country and deciding on a suitable business venture which would include their idea of the best possible lifestyle.

Often the decision to begin living a truly balanced life doesn't come to fruition until illness makes it necessary to stand back and look at ourselves. This was the case for countless women we interviewed for whom it took something of a scare to reassess their overworked lives. Unfortunately, the number of women who let ill-health and stress go too far before reading the signals are still in the majority. We sense that being a 'superwoman' is a media-driven myth. There is a limit to what is humanly achievable and acknowledging this can bring us a step closer to a kinder view of ourselves and also gives us the potential to allow others their fallibility.

Some of the women, like Maria Laspina and Rosalinda Tasca were driven to find a business that allowed them the time for others' needs; in their case it was those of their family. In their desire to follow traditional Italian values, they are sensitive to, and wish to take care of, the needs of their extended families. These women have followed through their decisions to create a balance between all the aspects of their lives. It seems that if these desires are not actively sought, where possible, the dream of a balanced life will continue to elude us as we fill our lives, our time, with unrelenting work.

S.R.

# Cathie Scurr

## Rosebud Cottage Child-Care Centre

Cathie Scurr changed her lifestyle and even her goals because of the stress of illness. Although challenged by some enormous setbacks, Cathie has achieved a happiness and independence that once she would only have dreamed of. When I spoke to her, Cathy had been the owner of Rosebud Cottage Child-Care Centre for only five months and she was still busy finding her way in this new area.

'I needed to find something that would suit my interests and pay some bills. I've wanted to have my own business for years. This is great because there is some freedom to come and go as I please most of the time.'

Rosebud Cottage is painted sunny, warm colours and has a lovely feel. When I arrived at the centre, I noticed that there were more dads hovering around than mums.

'Things have changed a lot in that regard. I find I deal with the same amount of fathers on a regular basis as I do mothers. In my day this definitely wasn't the case.'

Cathie was busy in the kitchen turning out muffins and making crumpets. The place was a hive of activity; there seemed to be a lot of staff running around and the bright, happy atmosphere of the centre was reflected in their attitude.

There is a lot of talk in the media at the moment about child-care facilities and their accreditation and consequently Cathie Scurr has found herself involved in the politics of a revolution in child care.

The main aim of the accreditation system is to weed out the centres that aren't up to scratch in terms of their facilities, conditions and activities. Safety issues like storing medicines and knives away from the children and maintaining a good staff–child relationship are examined. In order to comply with the standards there are approximately 50 principles to which a centre needs to adhere. Investigations found that a number of the existing centres were well below par and were even unsafe for the children. The changing face of child care reflects current research into children's physical and mental environments and the effect these may have on the child's subsequent development and happiness.

From the age of eighteen, Cathie suffered from severe endometriosis. It wasn't until she was 28 that she discovered it, because the contraceptive pill did a good job of camouflaging the condition. Seeking help from alternative medical practitioners, she gained some relief from her symptoms. Then, after an excrutiating operation in 1991, she was left with only a small portion of one of her ovaries, making it difficult, although not impossible, to have children.

'I was in such acute pain with the endometriosis that I physically couldn't work for four years. I was also on hormone tablets that as a side-effect made me overweight and depressed. It was a terribly stressful period because, although I was relieved to leave full-time employment for a number of reasons, it was financially shattering because my husband, John, was also out of work due to a sudden illness. He was forced to sell his business as a consequence. Honestly, we lived on the smell of an oily rag. In a six months period my whole world fell apart. Everything crashed at once.'

It took Cathie fifteen months to recover from surgery and then she was knocked down again with pelvic inflammatory disease.

'My life's situation wasn't particulary cheery, but it wasn't all bad either. I had to sell my flat and John sold his house in order to have something to live on. We existed on the interest earned on the sales; $250 a week for three and a half years. It annoys me when I think back on it, that I lived on less than a pensioner would because I chose to sell my assets to support me rather than rely on the government. Ethically I feel I did the right thing though.'

After an extended period of illness like this, a person's confidence would have had plenty of time to be eroded but Cathie's broad outlook on life helped her through this stressful time.

'I have an underlying spiritual belief that everything happens for a reason. In adversity you either die or you grow. I chose to grow. I am not ashamed to admit that during that time I thought about suicide, I was so sick of always being ill. I didn't know when it would end. John and I had our ups and downs but he always tried to be very supportive and caring, as did my grandmother, my mother, uncle and friends.'

Cathie could feel the illness lift in August 1994. 'I did a lot of work on myself both physically and spiritually during this time.'

Coming out of the gloom Cathie became aware that there was an ever-increasing demand for child-care centres as more women took up full-time work. The growth rate for private long-day care centres, like Rosebud, has increased by over 100 per cent since 1992. It was an area that interested her and she thought it would be a nice change to be her own boss.

One problem in establishing child-care centres is that there are not enough staff either with the qualifications or untrained, who are willing to endure the long hours necessary in child care, for more than a couple of years at a time. The human resources are simply not there. Cathie considers herself extremely lucky to have had the opportunity to take on the existing staff.

'I have four full-time and one casual on staff, with whom I split shifts. I was very lucky that the girls came with the business because they are just great. Sue, the director, has a Diploma of Teaching and the others have degrees or are still studying.

'The previous owners didn't seem to care too much about what happened to the staff, so when I employed them they were terribly relieved to keep their jobs. I observed how they worked for a while to make sure I thought they were suitable and it has turned out very well. Having the right staff is of utmost importance. We get on very well and have a good personal rapport, they are very happy here. They've worked at other centres that they didn't enjoy. Here it is more than just a job to them. I think the kids pick up on that as well.'

Deciding not to have children herself, Cathie has found that running a child-care centre is the perfect way to have children part-time.

'I love children and being around them here satisfies that. I also have a god-daughter, Bonnie, whom I adore. I love collecting children's artwork, especially hers. I think it says so much about what is going on for them.

'I like not being responsible full-time for the care of kids. Having been an only child I'm used to being on my own a bit, it doesn't worry me. Ideally I think kids should have both a male and female point-of-view when they are growing up. I've taught many kids from separated families and I always find that they are the ones more likely to be staring off into space and not able to concentrate. I really noticed it in the "just divorced" cases especially. I actually did counselling with the parents in my last year of teaching school. A third of the class were from separated families.'

Before illness took over her life, Cathie had been a teacher in both the private and public school systems. Her years as an infants–primary teacher at public schools ultimately frustrated her because of the bureaucracy.

'The best example I can use to illustrate this is when I got into trouble for sharpening the class's pencils! Although the person who was supposed to do it got RSI and couldn't do it, this wasn't in my job description according to the unions so I wasn't allowed to sharpen them. I suppose it was a demarcation issue. Little things like that ultimately got the better of me!

'Another drawback of the public school system is that there is no freedom within the curriculum to teach things outside it that you think might be important. For example, they don't teach the times tables anymore and I think that's a terrible shame. I am a great believer in the three "R's". To help you live in the world I think it's essential to have your basics.

'I think the independence a private school has in that regard is a good thing. They are somewhat freer to control the syllabus. Although I inherently believed in the system, after seven years in private schools I'd had enough. In the particular school I taught in there were all sorts of changes happening and the new powers-that-be weren't to the staff's liking. I was thinking of leaving anyway, when they announced they were retrenching fifteen of us without warning or reason. It was most unfair as some of those teachers were absolutely devoted to their jobs and had been of very good service to the school. Pregnant teachers or those known to be intending to become pregnant in the near future were given 48 hours to hand in their resignations! In the end it became quite bitter and the union proved unable to help us.

'A school is no good if the teachers are as unhappy with the management as we were. Often the people at the top have had no experience in teaching, only in administration and management, so they don't always understand how a teacher works. It was silly because they thought they knew more about teaching than we did. The first five years of teaching I really enjoyed, but in the last two the system got to me. It was during these two years that I learned how not to be a boss. For a long time I was happy to be told what to do, but I was starting to grow up and felt I had something to say for myself. In the end it was a relief to get out! I learned a lot about education and the needs of children in those years. They weren't always good times, but they were certainly educational!

'I'd been thinking of having my own business for years while teaching at those schools. I was ready to be my own boss. I looked in the *Sydney Morning Herald* and came across an ad for a real estate agent who specialised in selling kindergarten and child-care businesses. I wanted to get one that was already established because I thought that would be easier than starting my own. The one I chose was close to home and in a good location, quite near the city where there is a real need for child-care centres. There are a lot of working mothers in the area who need long-term day-care for their children and so I thought the business would be a viable one. I bought it with the money left over from the sale of my flat, 50 per cent deposit and 50 per cent mortgage. I had some collateral, so getting a loan wasn't so difficult this time around. I approached the banks when I was 22, for a loan for my first house and they were most unco-operative. They said, "But you might go and get pregnant, you're a high risk!" These days it's called discrimination and it wasn't that long ago!'

Not having children myself and not being able to quite recall my days in kindy, I wondered if things had changed much in child-care since the Sixties.

'The way children are treated has changed enormously in the last few decades. For instance, using words like "naughty" or "bad" is a big no-no these days.'

If this was the case I wondered how you were supposed to deal with any misbehaviour on behalf of the child and whether there was always a solution to deal with children being difficult.

'I must say, at times I am stumped and I have to admit defeat. There isn't always the perfect response. Sometimes we'll find out after the fact that the child is grumpy and misbehaving because he or she is unwell. The thing is that you mustn't imply that the child itself is bad, rather that their behaviour or actions are less than desirable. You aren't supposed to label them.'

It sounded like a bit of a tall order when the heat of the moment is upon you.

'The girls and I have a code which is to say, "Oh deary me!" with some gusto when we're really pushed to the limit. We all laugh because we know what we'd much rather say!

'Other things that have changed since my days at kindy are that when I was misbehaving I was sent to a "naughty chair" or told to sit behind the piano. There was no doubt in my mind that I had done wrong! Now those practices are considered archaic and damning. We say to the children, "These are the things you are encouraged to do at Rosebud and these are the things you are not!" I tend to remain calm in a crisis, something my mother taught me as she was a theatre sister.

'The bias is towards a much softer approach. We don't smack the children ever, although some of the parents say they do at home. It isn't our place. My own personal stand is that if I had kids I might smack them if they were really playing up, but only after a sufficient warning.

'After my years of teaching I think I can pick trouble a mile off, you really get to know who or which group might begin to cause trouble. There is one little girl here who takes great delight in hitting others over the head with something hard! I do find it difficult not to use negative language when there are distraught children on the receiving end of her actions, but I endeavour to use positive language. I've often found that distracting or diversion is the best method!'

I asked Cathie if she had time to get to know all the children.

'We have 34 children at the centre and by now I know them all well. Personally, I find the little boys about age two the most difficult. They like to throw their weight around and cause some waves. The rest of the kids don't follow them though, they just ignore them. Past the age of three they become more manageable!

'When it gets a bit much for any one of us we'll all pitch in and help. Being with little children for eight hours a day can be very taxing, as you can imagine. We all need some respite. Taking turns with the cooking is good because it's time out. I do find it harder work than teaching because it is so intensive. It can get very stressful.

'I can really depend on the girls to do a good job when I'm not here. Sue is the director and is formally trained in child care. She is very committed and I respect the way she works with the children.

'I find that the parents want to know who the owner is and they like to interact with me. Children, of course, are very special to their parents and they want to know that their children are getting the best possible care. I think the parents are pleased that the owner is also involved in the day-to-day running of the business, it makes it more intimate. It also adds to my credibility that I've had a background in teaching.'

Cathie plans her day so that she can have some time to herself. 'I generally come in for the morning and then go off to do things like the banking in the afternoon. I have a good, easy-going relationship with the girls. We chat about anything and everything. It makes being a boss easy when you have genuinely nice people working for you. The girls are encouraged to ring me at home if needs be.

'In one of the private schools I worked in there was a headmistress I worked with called Dot Kellet who has since become my inspiration. She was a great example for me to follow because of her sense of fairness and she treated us all as individual people rather than teaching machines. Dot Kellet was a caring boss and every teacher had the utmost respect for her. She made even the "yuk" jobs seem interesting. I try to emulate the values she taught me.'

While we were speaking the children were eating the muffins they had just made for morning tea. Sue said they especially loved joining in with the preparation of the food.

'With the discovery of food allergies lots of children were diagnosed as being intolerant to certain substances in foods,' explains Cathie. 'We have to keep that in mind when we are cooking. The same goes for vegetarians. We don't have sweet drinks or cordial for the kids, those days are long gone! We try to vary the food to keep the kids interested and include a diversity of ethnic foods as well, although not too spicy. With us all taking turns it is good because the ideas don't get stale, there is a lot of variety.'

I was surprised to learn that one of the stipulations made of the centre was that there had to be a hot meal served in the middle of the day. I thought it was quite an old-fashioned notion and wondered why it was considered to be so important.

'Some of the kids going to child care don't always get a hot meal at home. Often parents are too busy or tired, and in some cases they can't afford to. It is a good policy because it ensures that their nutritional needs are met. The new accreditation laws will be quite strict about things like providing foods from the five food groups on a daily basis.

'We serve five meals a day, to cover the kids that come very early for breakfast, and for those who aren't picked up until late we provide a late afternoon tea. We sit at tables with them and encourage good manners and eating correctly. It's fun. On Mondays Sue will go shopping for the week's groceries. We spend about $250 a week, which also includes all the necessary things for cleaning.'

I asked Cathie if there was any formal structure to the children's day.

'It is mostly dictated by mealtimes and during the middle of the day they have a sleep. Of course there are those who won't or don't want to sleep and after trying for a little while we'll take them up to the other end of the centre and they'll mostly play quietly. They seem to understand about the need for quiet time.'

We were watching from the office as one of the staff members got the children to draw around her shape onto some paper. It was a wet day so some other children were watching a video down the other end of the room. I wondered how the staff kept coming up with new and imaginative ways of entertaining the children.

'It is important to vary the activities for both the children's and our sakes. Sometimes the girls will really have to try hard to think of new things to do. Occasionally the kids will say they don't want to draw today because they drew yesterday. Their attention spans can be limited and so it's necessary to change track often to keep up their interests.

'We have a good reputation here and it's growing. That's largely due to the girls. They have to be immensely patient and caring, which they are. Their work ethic is great and they are very honest and communicate well with the kids. It is important to show parents that there is an empathy there for the kids. We treat it more like a preschool in the way that we try to teach them things like counting and learning to recognise their names. We make sure there's lots of arts and craft activities. Kids are happier when they are stimulated. Parents don't want their children to watch a lot of television when they're here. We might let them watch half an hour of "Playschool".'

Cathie takes full responsibility for managing the centre's finances and says that it is very similar to budgeting the household bills.

'I take care of the business side and Sue organises the fee relief. We both are fairly messy with the paperwork, this office is normally impenetrable! At the centre we charge $38 a day. I'd like to be able to do it more cheaply, but I can't afford to because we are limited to the number of children we are allowed to have. Some of the government centres can afford to be as low as $26 a day. They are subsidised to cover the fees of the teachers. Private owners must also cover the cost of the loan or rent on top of teachers' wages.

'Although I enjoy this business immensely I don't think

it's a forever thing. Having accomplished my Diploma in Remedial Massage, I think I'll be quite happy to practise it eventually. At the moment I practise it when I can. I also am interested in the Tarot and counsel my friends, but only in a small way. John, my husband, thinks it's hocus-pocus but doesn't discourage me. I don't need his endorsement anyway. He will occasionally get me to look at his cards though, which for him is a pretty big step!

'I think it's great to treat kids with natural therapies. I think they can gain a lot by having massage. They learn about relaxation and touch. It is a very caring and giving thing and it's good to share that with kids. Children don't have quite the attention span of adults, so you don't tend to massage them as long. On the occasional weekend I hope to hold a small massage class for parents to practise on their children. It is especially good for children experiencing emotional disturbances or for unsettling times in their lives because it can be very calming.'

This discussion led us to talk about child abuse and I wondered if Cathie had ever come across any and if so, how did she deal with it.

'I've only come across it once, years ago. It's not that easy to identify because children are always getting into scrapes. If you suspect it there are strict codes of how you approach the problem. You have to be very careful because it can be a legal minefield.'

I asked Cathie how she saw the future unfolding for her.

'I believe that the next nine years are going to be full-on business years for me. I also have an interest in real estate and could see myself buying and selling businesses perhaps. My interest in alternative medicine is always growing and perhaps will win through.

'What guides me through life is an underlying spiritual belief that fate will make itself known. I was the supervisor of a Sunday school at one stage, although now I don't adhere to any particular religious ideology or belief system. I think it's quite good for children to have a scripture class once a week, I feel it doesn't harm them. I've always had a sense of a greater power guiding me and think I might possess a psychic ability that I've had since I was a child.'

Although Cathie tires easily and sometimes needs to manage pain she is in much better shape now than she has been for years. Being in charge of her own business has brought her immeasurable satisfaction and reward. Through setbacks she has found the courage to go on and find new ways to challenge herself and create an interesting and varied life.

'My friends tell me that when I broke off my first engagement, before I went out with John, they felt that was the pivotal and most challenging thing for me to go through in my life. They tell me this is not the case now, that taking on the challenges of life's setbacks and to finally buy my business has made me grow from being a child into a woman.'

S.R.

# Kim O'Donnell

## Namaku Bush Creations

*'I am walking on my dream.'*

Paddy Rose, *Reading the Country*, 1984

Kim O'Donnell's Aboriginal culture has played a crucial role in the development and direction of her bush jewellery enterprise. She has been running the business for two and a half years now and is still as enthusiastic about it as she was when it began. The distinctive pieces she makes are both inspired by and a tribute to her heritage. Her people are of the Barkindji tribe, a small group living around the Darling River, near Wilcannia, east of Broken Hill.

'That's where our stories come from and many are based on our relationship to the river. As a result I prefer being near streams and rivers, rather than open sea. It has definitely made an impact on me and it's where I feel most at home. I try to get back to our land every year.'

Kim grew up in Wilcannia and attended a mission school there.

'We were taught subjects within the curriculum but on coming to Sydney my sisters and I found that in Wilcannia we weren't taught enough. I was nine and a half years old then. We didn't know the basics like our times tables and we couldn't speak English properly. We came to Sydney after my parents separated. I have good and bad memories of my childhood. The bad was my mother being beaten by my dad. The good was growing up in the bush by the river with none of the comforts we take for granted today, such as electricity. My good memories have overridden the bad which I feel have made me a stronger person today.

'My mum was only 27 and now I wonder how on earth she did it. I'm 31 this year and I still think I'm a kid! If ever I think I've got it hard I have only to think of her struggle to get my own in perspective.

'I think she wanted to get as far away from Wilcannia as possible. We had absolutely no money other than the bus fare. I have extremely vivid memories of getting off the bus at Pitt Street and setting my eyes on the Darrell-Lea shop, I'll never forget it! I'd never seen so much chocolate in my life! I didn't know at that stage that it wasn't real, so I couldn't believe that people would put all that chocolate in the window and have it go to waste!'

Fortunately for Kim and her family, a doctor who visited Wilcannia with the Royal Flying Doctor Service was living in Sydney and he had kindly told them they were welcome to stay with him and his family if they decided to move to the city.

'It was our saving grace! We stayed there for a week. We were lucky to come across Mum Shirl, whom we ended up living down the road from. St Vincent De Paul and the Salvo's offered great support by bringing food and clothes parcels until we were on our feet. We had a lot of good people looking out for us. Mum eventually got some work at the Redfern Aboriginal Medical Service as the community bus driver. She then met my step-father and wanted to have another child, so they had a son and eventually married in Dubbo, New South Wales.'

Coming to Sydney was a real eye-opener in many ways for Kim. 'It was my first experience of racism and it was disheartening! I went to a Catholic school in a multicultural area and there were all sorts of kids from different non-English speaking backgrounds. The Greeks, Lebanese and Italians discriminated against us as they were discriminated against.'

On one fateful rainy day soon after they moved to Sydney, Kim's mother picked up her children from school and they all got terribly lost on the way home.

'It was our first day of school and we just cried and cried, huddled in a phone box. I think it was all such a big change for my mother that she got sick.'

Kim's mother was hospitalised with pneumonia six weeks after they arrived. They got through this battle with the kindness of friends.

'Our Aunty Elaine came down from Wilcannia to look

after us. In the end, it became a huge household of women. There were Mum and us, her three daughters, and Elaine and her daughter. We banded together to look after each other. My mother and Elaine were independent and very supportive, and picked each other up when one was feeling down.'

It's obvious when speaking to Kim that she was very influenced by these women. Seeing them cope despite often considerable set backs has given her a sense that she can do anything.

'Yes, I'm pro equal opportunities and I know it has given me a lot of strength.'

Kim's mother was extremely influential in Kim's ability to overcome odds and take on whatever she wanted to.

'My mum's values are great. She always encouraged us to do what we wanted to. She left school at fifteen and wanted us to achieve. Although she worked hard to make ends meet she always had time for us. She's a very strong person and she has always put herself out for others. She currently works for the Western Aboriginal Legal Service in Dubbo and has been invited to attend the Women's Conference in Beijing this year on behalf of women in the western region of New South Wales.'

During Kim's first year of high school the family moved to Dubbo.

'Mum didn't really want us to be raised in the city, so she was glad to pack up and go. Dubbo is halfway between Wilcannia and Sydney so we had the best of both worlds—holidays in Sydney with friends and holidays in Wilcannia with relatives.'

Kim stayed on in Dubbo until she left to go to university in Bathurst. After attending an orientation week for Aboriginal students at Charles Sturt University, Kim looked at the possibilities open to her. She had originally set her sights on nursing, but didn't get quite enough marks to pursue that. She believes that the stress during the HSC affected her badly. Once at Charles Sturt, she enrolled in a Social Welfare course, but after sitting in for a few lectures found that she wasn't particularly drawn to it. 'They got inside people's heads with all the psychology and that didn't appeal to me.

According to my way of thinking, some things that go on in our minds should be kept private.'

Kim also attended some lectures on teaching and found it more stimulating.

'Because my marks were poor from school, although I'd worked incredibly hard, I was put into uni on a trial basis. I ended up doing primary school teaching and I majored in Special Education, which trains you to teach those with special needs or with disabilities. The first six months were very hard and I worked hard too. I'm pleased to say that I came out with flying colours—A's and A plusses. By the end of third year I was ready to get out and do something, see the world.'

After her graduation Kim accepted a job offer teaching in the Northern Territory.

'The Northern Territory Education Department interviewed prospective teachers for various positions in remote areas in the Territory and asked if I'd be interested in teaching at Tennant Creek. My heart was set on Peppimenarti because my father was living near Darwin at the time. I hadn't seen him in years, so they sent me to the "top end".'

Kim was also interested in teaching in the Northern Territory because she felt a desire and obligation to work towards bettering conditions for Aboriginal children's education.

'One of Bob Hawke's promises, even before he was elected, was that there'd be 2000 qualified Aboriginal teachers teaching in public schools by 1990. Needless to say, that didn't happen!'

She had only one week to get ready for her initiation into teaching and was both nervous and excited by the prospect.

'It was the most amazing experience. I spent three years at Peppi and I kept a diary the whole time. The people in Peppi are now like a second family to me. The assistant I had, Noonook, is like a sister.'

While working in the Territory, Kim laid the foundations for her future business.

'Having a leaning towards making things and creativity, I became involved in basket-making afternoons with some of the women, once a week. We'd make coil baskets using native palm leaves. We'd jump in the truck which had a big cage on the back and "go bush" for a few hours. There are heaps of things to find: bush tomatoes, potatoes and onions, which we'd cook up. It was great! I'd also gather up any interesting bits and pieces I'd find on these expeditions including seed pods and leaves, just because I liked them and thought they were beautiful.'

In late 1989, after three years at Peppi and a year training to teach English as a second language in Darwin, Kim got itchy feet and was ready to travel overseas. She felt she'd accomplished what she'd wanted to and that it was time to move on.

'There was an ad in the paper asking for people to teach English in Japan. I went for three interviews and got the position. I didn't know anything about Japan, the language or the people, but I was interested in the challenge and the prospect of living in a foreign country.

'My friend's father was the Australian Ambassador based in Tokyo, and he asked his parents to make enquiries about the school's credentials. They informed me that, yes, it was a good school, so I felt a little more relaxed about my planned adventure to the land of the rising sun! Nakatsu is a rural area in Kyushū, southern Japan. There weren't many foreigners in the area at the time so we caused people to stare wherever we went.

'It was a great experience and I kept another diary. I was really interested in the culture and their ways. I'd venture out to cooking classes and endeavoured to find out about them through getting involved.'

After a year's teaching, Kim came home for her mother's 45th birthday. In 1991 she moved to Sydney and got a job teaching in Redfern, at a Skillshare centre called Namaroo.

'It was a seven-month project designed to bring mature-age students' skills up to scratch in areas like maths and writing. I really enjoyed it. The students, because of their age and the fact that they wanted to be there, had no behavioural problems like some children have. Wanting to learn is different to having to.'

This statement, I thought, summed up Kim's eager attitude to learning and approaching new things.

At this time Kim was able to study Japanese at Sydney University during her lunch hour.

'The project I was working on was nearly finished, so I had my eye out for something else. I saw an ad for someone to work as a shop assistant in an Aboriginal craft shop at the airport. I thought it would be good because I could combine studying Japanese and earn a bit of money. Because it was a tourist shop I thought I'd also be able to practise my Japanese on some of the customers. The "arty" aspect of the gallery appealed too, because of my interest in that area.'

Kim worked in the Rainbow Serpent for three years. As she observed the type of goods that were on sale in the shop, she became inspired to start making her own creations. She wore some of the jewellery she had made from gumnuts and seeds to the shop one day and her boss was impressed.

'He asked me where I got the lovely earrings I was wearing. I told him I'd made them myself from things I'd collected on my travels. He then asked me to bring in some more to see if they would sell through the shop. From the beginning he was very supportive.'

The jewellery was well received and this encouraged Kim to keep up production. At first she was quite happy to just see how it went as it had not been a particularly big dream for her to run her own business.

'Because I use mostly raw materials that my family and I gather ourselves, there wasn't much outlay apart from my time. My initial set-up costs were about $250, for a drill and a stand, some brushes, paints and jewellery connections. I knew roughly what the going rate was for jewellery, so we priced them accordingly. It was turning out to be quite profitable.

'I'd go out and buy the things I needed as I could afford to, like storage containers, a bookcase, a workbench and a drill. I started from home, on the lounge-room floor.'

Kim finds the work meditative.

'I can lose myself in the creative side of it. In the beginning I worked by myself, but later I had to employ my sister to help. In the early days I'd tend to work on my jewellery in the mornings or on weekends. The business still fitted in around my work in the shop.'

Seeing how other people presented their goods in the shop made her realise the need for marketing and helped her make informed decisions about the presentation of her own work.

'I knew that marketing was very important. I designed my own cards to attach to the jewellery. I also recognised that people like to know about the story behind the goods, who made it, what it's made of, where the artist is from. It was primarily a tourist outlet and people, particularly the Japanese, wanted to take home a unique souvenir from Australia. I needed to find and register a business name, so I called my business Namaku Bush Creations. Namaku means "mother earth" in our language. The logo is of a mother holding a baby in her arms. I like that image because I get raw materials for the jewellery from the earth. I use packaging with the logo on it.'

Initially Kim made earrings and then added necklaces to her range.

'Each piece is individual and that's part of its charm. The raw materials can be dependent on the seasons and climate. We keep up a store of goods for future use, but sometimes we'll run out of a particular seed or pod. We'll then substitute something else. It adds to the individual look in any case.'

Kim began painting on gumnuts and pods, but with a modern interpretation. I wondered what her views were on non-Aboriginal people making use of Aboriginal designs.

'I think as long as people are honest about it then the consumer can decide if it's valid to buy them. I certainly don't think it's good if advertising material is misleading and people think they are getting the genuine article when they're not. There is a fine line sometimes. For example, there is a white guy in Darwin who uses traditional techniques, but he grew up amongst Aborigines in Arnhem Land and although some Aborigines I know have their back up about it, I think it's okay. He doesn't make out that he's black and nor does his advertising.

'It's also complicated by the fact that a lot of people now modernise and modify those traditional techniques, look at Sally Morgan for example. I do think, though, that if it's a purely Aboriginal shop and it's advertised as such, then it should have work only by Aboriginals.'

Some of the materials Kim uses in her jewellery are quite unusual, like echidna quills and emu feathers.

'I started by just collecting seeds, pods and gumnuts. Part of our culture is our bush food, as you'd know. We eat kangaroos, emus and echidnas as a matter of course. My relatives cook the echidnas and keep the quills for me.'

Bush tucker is an intrinsic part of the Aboriginal culture. Using the quills in the jewellery could be seen as being very resourceful and a way to cut down on waste. Kim also gets her mother, who lives in Dubbo, to send her bags of emu feathers that she collects from other family members.

'Different parts of the bird have different kinds and colours of feathers that are good for particular pieces of jewellery. My mum will ring me and say, "Kim, I've got you a bag of feathers" and by hook or by crook she will get them to me!

'I love scavenging in the bush for things. The bush is just full of the most amazing pieces. If you're aware of what's available and at various times, there's so much you can use.

'When I went to visit my brother at school in Sydney, I parked in the local carpark. I noticed there was this great tree just laden with gumnuts and many of them had fallen on the ground. My brother looked rather oddly at me, knowing what I was going to do, so we just got down together and gathered up bags full of them! I think people must have thought we were mad! It was a great carpark for gumnuts.'

Kim decided to extend her merchandise into other areas and she has since added leather chokers, which can be quite elaborate, to the range. When the business grew to need more than just her own part-time hands Kim asked her sister to join her.

'At first, she'd watch me threading all the bits and pieces together and wonder how I managed it, patience-wise. Then she realised it was actually fun and so she helped me to keep up with the demand. Between us we worked out a wage for her and then I also employed another friend to actually thread the earrings together.'

At this stage Kim was keeping up with the demand from the Rainbow Serpent for her jewellery. She knew that in order to expand she would need to produce a stockpile of goods, so she gradually cut back her time in the shop from three to two days. Like many women starting a business have found, Kim knew that by working part-time and having the security of an assured income, she was less pressured. While working two days in the shop, she had the others free to make the jewellery.

Kim was beginning to realise the necessity of gaining some more knowledge about the actual running of the business.

'I enrolled in the Office of Small Business course run at Parramatta. I knew I had to learn how to keep my books and accounts properly. It was for four weeks, on Monday nights. The teacher there was a great influence on me and was keen to give us any advice we needed.'

Although things were ticking over quite nicely at the Rainbow Serpent, Kim wanted to expand. 'I wanted to get more outlets and so I just looked up the appropriate people, those who were selling similar ranges to the same sort of markets. On the first day of doing this I went to the Tribal Arts Gallery in The Rocks. I took some pieces and the rest were just photographs. They took my goods on straightaway and wrote me a cheque immediately for $500! I was amazed! I went home feeling elated. The next day I went out again and sold another $1200 worth of goods. By the end of the week I'd sold a total of $3000. After a month they wanted more.

'With the smaller shops, I'd ring up to see what was moving and what wasn't and I'd go in and replace or swap a piece if it had been sitting on the shelf too long.'

This service was not necessary, but Kim explains that it was beneficial to do business this way because it kept the customer happy. She was taking responsibility for the sales all the way down the line.

'It was good market research for me too, so I'd know better what was popular and what wasn't. If necessary, I'd go into the shop and talk about why the piece wasn't moving, perhaps we could look at the display? With my experience in the Rainbow Serpent I was able to identify pretty quickly why something might not be displayed appealingly.'

Over time, Kim built up fourteen outlets that she regularly supplied; many were small shops where she had pieces on consignment.

'At first I thought it was good for exposure but then I realised it was actually a bad thing because the reality is that you have to pay wages and costs upfront.'

Kim's eventual decision to take items off consignment and have buyers pay for them outright lost her some of the smaller outlets. Now her main customers are the early ones, the Rainbow Serpent and a few others.

She has now made a decision about her lifestyle that will obviously have some ramifications for her business.

'I decided to leave Sydney six months ago because I just wanted to get back to the environment. Although I learned a lot, I was never really happy living in the city. I had to get out again, back to Darwin to freedom and a better lifestyle.'

'I sent letters to all my customers telling them of my plans and they seem to understand. When you gotta go, you gotta go!

'I still wanted to maintain the business because it has become a part of me. I knew it'd be a bit more difficult, but I've bought a fax and an answering machine to make it easier for people to contact me and place orders. My sister has decided to go back and live in Broken Hill, so she won't continue on with the business. The owners of Rainbow Serpent are opening another shop in Brisbane Airport, so that will be another outlet. I'd like to get into a shop I've come across in Darwin, so I'm also working on that.'

In order to pay moving and living costs, Kim had to put the business on hold for a while. 'The reality is I had to make some money when I arrived. "You have to spend money to make money", was my boss' motto. I looked into borrowing money, but I really didn't want to go into debt.'

Kim is now employed by National Jet Systems, a small aviation company. She is a flight attendant based in Darwin, with Namaku still operating from home.

'I've set up a workshop but I am limited in terms of time by my work. Next month, for example, I am only in Darwin for twelve days! There is no point in expanding if I can't keep up. I am never going to be interested in mass-producing, I always want to keep it special and small.'

Kim strives to make her business fit into and reflect her philosophies about life. The care of the environment is a particularly important issue for her and she runs her enterprise in a way that shows her concern for the earth and adds to its protection.

Kim is interested in teaching the skills of jewellery-making. At the end of 1993 she was asked to teach at a Coonabarabran high school for a week on behalf of National Aborigines Week, which she really enjoyed. Combining teaching and creative pursuits is an attractive way for her to make full use of her skills.

Kim's teacher from the small business course has a particular interest in indigenous peoples' businesses and told her about an Indigenous Business Women's Conference organised by the Department of Employment, Education and Training.

'The conference was attended by women from all over the South Pacific Islands and around Australia. There was one condition that I attend, though, and that was only if I spoke. I was guest speaker! My biggest highlight was meeting Anita Roddick, founder of the Worldwide Body Shop chain. What an inspirational woman!'

A few months after that conference, Kim was asked to attend another for South Pacific Islanders, this time as a paid speaker. She clearly enjoys the teaching aspect of these forums and is always willing to attend them if she can.

Living in Darwin, Kim has now found her husband-to-be, Jason, and she is pregnant with her first child.

'My mother always said to me, "Life is what you make it".'

S.R.

# Maria Laspina and Rosalinda Tasca

## Rosemary's Kitchen

The name 'Rosemary's Kitchen' nicely sums up the team effort Rosalinda Tasca and her mother, Maria Laspina, have put into their business. What came naturally to Maria and Ros was something other people appreciated and were willing to pay for, so a business was born. They currently produce a changing selection of about a dozen gourmet treats including *pesto* (made with their own walnuts), marinated eggplant and olives, sun-dried tomatoes and paté, quince paste, apricots in brandy, plums in port and *pepperonata.* They use as much of their own produce in the range as possible. Always willing to improve or expand their range of merchandise, the women's natural curiosity about creating new products and their continuing hard work have paid off.

A decision made by the men of the family to change their farms' produce provided Maria and Rosalinda with the opportunity to start their own gourmet food business. Ros explains, 'About six or eight years ago my brother Joe made a decision that it was time to get out of farming tobacco. He was sick of it and thought it was time for a change. The industry has been on a downturn in any case. The boys decided to buy some hybrid vegetable seeds. We now have 100 acres of vegies and about 15 acres of kiwi fruit.'

In fact, they had to buy more land to accommodate all the new crops they were growing.

The farm is in a traditional tobacco-growing region and many of Maria and Ros' relatives live in the area. The land that the family now farm belonged to the parents of Maria's husband Sam, who first cultivated it 35 years ago. It has been necessary for the property to be used as productively as possible and to keep up-to-date with what the market requires. The family are all happy that the tobacco monoculture has gone, because this way it keeps them all interested. Also, planting different trees reminded them of home.

'With all the leftovers, or seconds, my mother and I would make things. One year the plum crop wasn't selling too well for the boys in the usual outlets, so we dried them and put them in port. Before that we'd been buying prunes and realised that our own were better!'

Ros explains that her mother provides the motivation for the business as well as putting in hours of hard work.

'Mum is not interested in idleness. She would do all this, although perhaps not at quite the volume, for herself and the extended family anyway. In the beginning we did it for ourselves and then concentrated on selling mostly sun-dried tomatoes. If there was a capsicum with a tiny blemish the boys couldn't sell it. We thought it was a terrible waste and so decided to do something about it.'

Maria met Sam here in Australia but ironically they found out that they were from not only the same area and town, but from the same street in Sicily! Maria is from a traditional Sicilian family. Her parents migrated with their children when she was ten years old. Maria was brought up around food, its preparation and its potential. Nothing was ever wasted if there was a way to pickle, preserve or bottle it.

'When we were kids in Sicily there were racks and racks of tomatoes drying in the sun.'

Maria and Ros have worked as a team for many years, originally in a coffee shop they owned and ran in Beechworth in north-east Victoria. Ros explains, 'We ran the coffee shop for six years. We used to have what we thought the locals wanted, all good home-baked stuff like quiches and home-made pies. Mum would come up with new and interesting recipes, like hot pork pies and vegetable pies made with *ratatouille* and *bechamel*. We'd use our home-grown vegies for those.'

In honour of their Italian heritage they served *lasagne* in the shop and held a pasta evening every Friday night.

'We bought a pasta-making machine so that we could make our own. We'd make *tricolore*, *tagliatelle* and *ravioli*. People loved it and we would get requests from delis to supply them with fresh pasta because they were impressed. We used to make *gnocchi* as well to wholesale, but phased that out because we couldn't charge appropriately for it. We still make single-serve *lasagnes* and we supply about sixty a week to a few shops.

'Well before sun-dried tomatoes were considered trendy we would bring the ones we'd make for ourselves into the shop and people responded really well! They thought they were great.'

The women realised there was a market to supply fresh pasta, amongst other things and now they supply half-a-dozen local restaurants and delicatessens on a weekly basis. One well-known eatery in local Beechworth is happy to take on anything the pair make and often buys sun-dried tomatoes and marinated olives from them literally by the bucket-load!

'We were wanting to move on from the shop, although there are times now when we miss it. In those years we never had time out or weekends off. We'd hire a waitress Friday and Saturday nights, but it was exhausting despite that. I was wanting to have a baby and my husband complained that I wasn't home enough.'

By the time they did eventually sell, Ros had had her first baby, Anthony, who is now six. The women wondered what else they could make besides the tomatoes and pasta.

'We were home and I was raising a child and I thought Mum and I could get together and use our skills. I can have my children around while I make the preserves, for example.

'There were acres of capsicum, so we decided to make *pepporanata* as well. They were all things Mum had recipes in her head for and things she had grown up with. To us it seemed natural.

'When we had the shop we would gauge what people wanted by their requests. If they'd say, "Oh, don't you have Twinings tea?" or "Leaves instead of bags?" we'd realise that we needed to supply those things. It was very much trial and error.'

Maria and Rosalinda are still using this method to find out what people want and then experimenting to see what they can come up with.

'Sun-dried tomato paté is currently our best-seller. Mum is a very good cook! She is the force behind the recipes, she develops them herself from her extensive background knowledge.'

As the women come across different fruits and vegetables they try out new recipes for them.

They realised that they had to look at the presentation and marketing of their product and they began by buying hand-printed labels, 50 at a time.

'Mum designed the label we now have. It took some adjusting though, because initially it was too big and covered too much of the jar. People like to see what they're getting!'

The women jazzed up the packaging further by adding raffia to the neck of the jars, and are happy with the result. They recognised that if they were going to be catering to different markets they'd need to present their goods appropriately.

'We've also designed pasta boxes to send our pasta off in. My brother had to organise boxes for his vegetable produce, so I asked him about getting some for our pasta. It cost a lot to get them printed up, but I think it was necessary.'

They also needed to find jars as the volume of products began to increase.

'We were put onto the "jar" people but it was quite an expensive outlay for us. We had to save the money for $1500 worth of jars at a time. We then had to have them freighted up on the train. We got 150 ml, 250 and 500 ml jars, with metal lids.'

Maria and Ros are a good example of those women who struggle to put their earnings back into their business. If they did not have enough savings for every capital outlay, they approached the bank which was willing to give them a loan because the bank manager knew the farmers and had known of the women's good track record in the shop.

The business is growing in increments. They have bought two major pieces of equipment: a dehydrator for the tomatoes and an industrial tomato cutter. The dehydrator is still being paid off but it is something they could not do without.

'We have put every bit of money into the printing, the freight costs, business cards and equipment. It has been a big commitment.'

The women were fortunate to come across a carrier whom

they had met through the shop who could deliver their goods on a regular basis. Getting the distribution right is an important consideration for a business such as theirs.

We went for a walk around part of the property and I was impressed by the variety and quantity of trees and bushes that were laden with goodies. The work on the farm is seasonal which sometimes limits the women's access to certain produce. Summer is very busy as many of the fruits and vegetables are harvested then. Ros told me that while it isn't always hectic, it can get very busy when the picking and preserving, marinating or pickling need to be done at the same time.

'All of January I have to admit that I didn't do a thing! Usually, from February to April we are extremely busy. There can be 400 kilos of tomatoes to wash, cut and dry in any one day in summer! Dad and the boys all pitch in and help.'

There were a few young helpers about and I wondered if they were hired.

'No. They are all relatives. If people are silly enough to come and visit, then they'll get roped into helping us! All the in-laws come and sit around and chat to us while we work.'

This was something that the women took delight in, the fact that they were around their families was a bonus.

Ros is grateful that she can leave home and go to work at her mother's house each day. This makes it easier for her to separate home and work but she still finds that people presume because she is at her mother's house she is not actually working. Maria adds, 'People still ask me, "What do you do? Do you like it?" They think that working means leaving home. It is definitely not the case here! They are slowly starting to take us seriously when they see our things in the shops and when they drop in and see that we really do work!'

Maria, being a traditional Italian wife and mother, feels it is necessary to still do all the other work herself. I thought this must make hers a very busy life! She admits, 'The one big drawback is that there isn't enough time for me.'

Ros assures me that she doesn't think her mother should do all that extra work and that she, personally, is more relaxed about it. Even so, she still has to do the shopping and on her return home in the evening there are chores to attend to. Ros keeps her family's food simple and relies on the home-made pasta for many of the dinners. They tend to stick with Italian food because they prefer it.

'Mum still makes the boys' beds and prepares a hot meal at lunchtime for them. Old habits die hard!'

Maria adds, 'I always have cooked for lots of people. Even if it's just my husband and myself, I'll cook enough for a family! I can't help myself!'

We sat down to a lovely al-fresco lunch with a variety of foods ranging from marinated eggplant, *pepperonata*, balsamic vinegar, salami and a wonderful iced tea, stewed with orange rind. I assumed the vinegar and salami to be bought, but Ros informed me that they were made by her male relatives.

'It is now an established tradition that on the Queen's Birthday weekend the men get together and make the salami. It is very much a male thing traditionally but the women are allowed to help with taking the meat off the bone. They do the whole process themselves, from slaughtering the pig to hanging and mixing it with the other "secret" ingredients. It's shrouded in a bit of mystery!

'The same goes for making the balsamic vinegar. My father-in-law makes it and there is then enough for the extended family for a year.'

The Italian women in the area also put aside their Labour Day weekends for the making of the tomato sauce that accompanies many an Italian meal. These traditions are kept alive by the large local Italian families.

The climate in north-east Victoria is very similar to where the family comes from in Sicily, so the trees and crops from their home are compatible with Australian conditions. Over the years, the family have planted all the same things that they grew up with in Sicily. When Ros was born 33 years ago, her parents planted an olive grove in her honour. They also thought it might be a good crop to sell but soon realised that tobacco would be more profitable. One year there was a disease that swept through the tobacco plants, so for insurance the next year they planted kiwi fruit.

We went to look at the kiwi fruit which covered a vast area. The vines had knotted and formed their own arbor. Maria informed me that to really see how much fruit the vines were bearing, it was essential to put your head between your legs and look up at them that way. It certainly made a difference! There were hundreds of fruit that I hadn't even noticed!

On the property were 30-year-old walnut trees, from which we stole some not-quite ready nuts, a fence of hazelnut trees (I suggested hazelnut spread as the women hadn't come up with a suitable use for them yet), persimmons, kiwi fruit, bay trees, plum and peach trees, olives, eggplant, capsicums, herbs and, of course, tomatoes. I thought the tomatoes were unusual because they were on the ground rather than growing upwards, on stakes. Ros explained that they were a different variety and easier to pick this way. We looked at all sorts of things growing or drying in the hothouses, like cabbages (they haven't quite found a good bottled recipe for that one yet!), and lovely plump prunes.

'We were the first to put in vegies. Other people in the district only know tobacco, so they feel safe going with that. It's all trial and error! We didn't know much about vegies when we began.'

The farm employs seasonal workers to pick the crops. They generally attract backpackers or locals who enjoy the social aspect of it. Maria says, 'It is chat, chat, chat all day out there. They work short hours to miss the heat of the day and we provide them with morning and afternoon tea in one of the sheds. There is a real shortage of workers at the moment.' She laments that, 'I think people don't want to work anymore, perhaps it is too easy on the dole not to. This year we have really noticed it.'

I realised that Maria and Ros were fortunate to have access to such fresh and abundant produce, but also recognised that many people wouldn't have the resourcefulness and commitment to follow that through into creating a business out of it. After talking to Maria I learned that here was a woman who was not going to let anything go to waste if she could help it! Perhaps more importantly, though, she was extremely hard working and active and she wasn't going to sit on the sidelines after her coffee shop closed.

'Mum's always been busy doing things. She and I would help pick the vegetable and fruit crops. After a while we thought we'd rather be inside cooking!'

Ros has the honour of being the primary tomato cutter. While walking around we visited some of the hothouses that were full of drying tomatoes. The smell was delicious. The tomatoes go through a few different processes, mainly to dry them out. Before the women bought the dehydrator there was considerably more wastage.

The drying of the tomatoes sounded to me like a rather nerve-racking procedure. The women would anxiously await the weather report each day of the five-day drying process. If it happened to rain, the tomatoes were ruined and couldn't be used. The humidity also played a part and it would take only a bit of humid weather to produce mould on them. The sorting process was all-important in this regard, because one mouldy tomato would ruin a whole jar full! Maria says, 'I know it sounds like a very labour-intensive process, don't get me wrong, it is. It doesn't worry me though because it is the way things were done back home. It's traditional. My husband Sam recalls his grandmother doing it in Sicily when he was a child, too.' The difference being perhaps in the quantity.

The women are now trying to develop a way to pack their 'half-dries'. As the name suggests, these are tomatoes which haven't been dried out thoroughly and have a full and soft texture.

'We supply them to a shop in Beechworth in buckets, swished around with some garlic, basil and oil. We'd like to work out ways of supplying them. We have yet to find out if they'll ferment when we bottle them. It's all a learning process!'

In terms of expansion, the women might consider setting up a small retail outlet of their own but they would leave this for a few years until Ros' two children are a little older, then they would probably run it from the property itself. Maria says, 'In order to expand on the number of stores we supply to, we would have to hire more people. My problem is that I don't think people will do the work to my standards.

We don't want to get too big because I want to be sure I can continue to supply people well.'

Ros adds, 'I'd like to see Mum slow down a bit, she works too hard, although she baulks at the idea of retiring. However, we want to keep the feeling we've got in the business and maybe that would be lost if we expanded too much.'

This is a common desire of many of the women we interviewed. They wanted their business to remain manageable and familiar. Increasing output for a primarily financial reward, if it meant sacrificing other important things, was not a big priority.

Ros finds that she spends an inordinate amount of time in the car, running around for the business and fitting that in with the demands of her boys. 'I have trouble some days getting the actual work I'm supposed to get done, finished. It can be a real juggling act. My ten-year plan is to pay off some debts and then possibly travel. Eventually I might take over from Mum, I think she'd like that. The really restricting thing is not being able to get away from it and you can't afford to get sick. Last year we all flew up to the Gold Coast for a holiday for ten days. October is not a bad time to go, the farm is less busy then. That was the first big holiday we'd had in years. It means getting a back-up of stock and getting our orders prepared beforehand. That takes time too.

'At the moment, because we are so busy there just isn't time to do many things. I don't bother with a garden at home because it's all here.'

The flower garden surrounding the house was full of bright annuals. I thought it was very impressive that someone in this busy family had taken the time to tend it.

'My grandmother comes over and dead-heads the roses and weeds it. Someone else will mow the lawn. Somehow it all gets done and everyone pitches in.'

When we sat down at lunchtime it was clear that the boys, husbands included, were very proud of what the women were doing. The family were used to dining on the riches of their own labour and were pleased to admit that there was hardly ever a necessity to buy food from the supermarket.

This year Maria and Sam plan to visit Italy, for the first

time since they arrived, 40-odd years ago. Maria was clearly delighted about going back to see her country again. Most of the extended family has now moved to Australia, so there would not be too many relatives to visit. I imagined that the street they grew up in would be very different now. I wondered if that was what Maria was most interested in seeing. Sam had a wry smile on his face when Maria said, 'Everyone thinks I am mad because what I'm really interested in seeing are the farms! I'd like to see what and how they produce things now. I believe it has changed a lot. Who knows, maybe I can pick up a tip or two!'

S.R.

# Marieke Brugman and Sarah Stegley

## Howqua Dale Gourmet Retreat

Marieke and Sarah are in the enviable position of being the proprietors of a rural gourmet retreat in north-east Victoria. They have had a long partnership and feel 'that what we've really done is "drop in", rather than drop out'.

I arrived at Howqua Dale Gourmet Retreat as the sun was setting behind the hills that hugged the property. It had been a rare weekend off for the proprietors, Sarah and Marieke and they had indulged themselves in what sounded to me like a rather arduous weekend of hiking through the bush. We sat down to a fresh, informal meal and despite the fact that we were all very tired, the conversation flowed until we were ready to drop!

The women have lived in this little piece of heaven for eighteen years now. Tucked into a valley just outside of Mansfield, the retreat comprises 16 hectares that are bordered by hills and the Howqua River. The property was one of the primary drawcards for the women, it has been in Sarah's family for a long time and she has always had a special affinity with it. Whenever she visited this land she left with a distinct sense of place and increasingly felt the desire to stay. Sarah says, 'I quite simply didn't want to be without it.'

The guest house and the women's own house are surrounded by spacious gardens which are lovingly tended by the two. The house where the women live is quite an impressive structure built by the women themselves out of a variety of woods. Sarah says, 'It was really one of the highlights building this. It took eleven months to complete and was just such a wonderful experience.'

They designed it especially to meet Marieke's specifications for the kitchen. The main room, where the kitchen is, is like a goldfish-bowl looking out onto the gardens. Marieke says, 'I love gardening and here we do it all organically. I make my living though from cooking, so I have to remain realistic about that.'

The women run the retreat primarily as a luxurious weekend 'country house'. The guests stay in the six double bedrooms in a guest house which is separate from the women's own living quarters. However, they eat in the main house in the evening and at lunchtime. It is unusual in that the approach is more akin to having been invited to stay at a friend's plush country manor. The atmosphere is very intimate and convivial.

Sarah told me that the property had previously been a farm of approximately 1400 hectares. She had managed it part-time before they both decided to move there permanently.

'It had been a pol hereford stud in those days and I really wanted to make something of it. I'd had the idea, we both had, that people might like to go to the country and have a "country hotel" experience. We thought that sounded like the perfect solution to earning a living from the property and enjoying ourselves as well. It's close to Mt Buller, which is a big skiing attraction in the winter, and Lake Eildon, where people go trout fishing. It was a plus that it wasn't too far off the beaten track. So, we endeavoured to fashion a business. It started as a somewhat naive and romantic idea and it has, I'm happy to say, become a reality.'

Sarah has a degree in agricultural science from a University in New Zealand and Marieke trained as an art historian and had been following a career in academia. They had actually known each other at high school and met up again years later, when, according to Marieke, they decided to 'nut out this mad concept'.

'Sarah came back from her travels overseas to manage, hands-on, her family's cattle farm and when we met up we were both looking for another direction. I knew I didn't want to be a perpetual student and I'd had a lifelong interest in food. We began to form this idea.'

Sarah adds, 'It was just a coincidence really, fate. If I hadn't met up again with Marieke and if she hadn't been a good cook . . . well, it's just lucky that it happened.'

Marieke insists that, 'you don't go into the people business if you don't like people. Sarah has consummate tact and discretion and is able to meet people on all levels, even if they are not particularly her cup-of-tea.

'She has always been a natural at front-of-house. She is just brilliant and has enormous diplomacy. In something like this it is essential to have someone who can make everyone feel immediately comfortable, safe and welcome. I think she has a skill that not many have. She will remember twelve people's names in half an hour and will then graciously introduce everyone as they arrive. This is not my own particular forte. I'm happier dealing with the behind-the-scenes.'

The women believe that the emphasis on good food, matched with Sarah's choice of wines from the extensive cellar and the beautiful setting, make it a special treat for those with weary palates and tired souls.

Marieke continues, 'We are really on about people enjoying every aspect of the weekend when they're here. We allow them the time to recover and give them the space to be themselves. They can sleep in or fish, ride horses or just laze about. They arrive on a Friday night and can be very stressed. We hand them a glass of champagne as soon as they arrive, prepare an informal meal and the weekend begins! Giving people the opportunity to give themselves back to themselves is very important. We treat people with equanimity. It really is very nourishing.'

Marieke and Sarah find that in order to give their full attention to their guests it is imperative that they keep their health in top condition. For Sarah, cycling 20 kilometres every day keeps her feeling vital and Marieke walks at least 8 kilometres every morning, 'straight up the hill'.

'I find that by doing this every day, regardless of the ensuing pressures, I gather a better perspective on the potential problems of the day ahead. It's my time for my mental housekeeping. By the time I return, no matter what the problem might have been when I set out, I feel much more relaxed about it. About seven years ago I found that I'd get extremely tired and I just wasn't keeping pace. Walking has helped enormously, it oxygenates my brain.'

She continues, 'It is ridiculous to blame a working life for your misery. I said to myself, "everyone has the right to one hour to themselves every day, no matter what the crisis".'

Sarah adds, 'Marieke has a very disciplined mind and body. Fitness is integral to her continued sense of well-being.'

Marieke feels that some of the tendencies women have towards overdoing it are very much conditioned into them. 'The culture of being a woman means that we are inclined to give, give, give. We have to stop doing that. To give ourselves permission without guilt is so important. You can't be attending to others all the time if you are going to retain any sense of yourself. When women design their lives they not only have to design the breaks "in", but also the breaks "out". Sarah and I are not saints, but we're good at what we do. I admire people who can go, go, go all the time, but I'm not one of them!'

'We work eighteen-hour days when we are working. We sleep four or five hours on those days. We have learned, over time, how to pace ourselves. We realised early on that we wouldn't be able to keep this up seven days a week. With the sort of input we give, I think it would be too much to ask.

'Cooking is extremely labour-intensive. In all our years here we've never had a day off sick. We used to sit up all night with the guests and chat away until the early hours, but we paid such a terrible price for it the next day that we gave that up.'

Howqua Dale seems to be unlike any other guest house I had heard of. The reason for this is that the experience people have there is very much part and parcel of who Marieke and Sarah are. It is not just their skills and the setting people come for, it is to be part of this life the women have created for themselves, which they extend to others. It is as if the women have invited people in to join an exclusive and intimate dinner party that continues over the whole weekend.

'We find that people like to make a special occasion of it. Although there are certainly no rules, we encourage people to dress up on the Saturday night to dine in the formal dining room. Breakfast, of course is more relaxed and Sarah prepares that in the guest house. Lunch is served late on Sunday and people will get ready to go home by Sunday evening. It is quite indulgent.'

Marieke continues, 'The philosophy here usually wins out. People are inclined to leave the power at the door. We get a lot of companies booking corporate weekends exclusively. They might want to entertain visitors from overseas or VIPs. It's the sort of place where top executive teams can have privacy and confidentiality. In the corporate sector they often come to workshop ideas. It's the right psychic space to get things done.'

The retreat indulges the women's desires to cook, eat and drink well, have stimulating company and live in the country. Marieke adds, 'We have created a life that incorporates broad value systems. It is intentionally small because there is only so much of ourselves that we can give. Our health, our attitude, are all important in the retreat's success. After eighteen years we have come to realise that it is in fact a viable business. We've survived through thick and thin.'

Sarah's agricultural background and her keen interest in things agricultural is satisfied by living at Howqua Dale.

'There isn't a day that goes past that I don't use my skills on the property. I use my training all the time in looking after things like the pumps and the watering systems, the garden . . . I must admit though, that after milking cows for eighteen months, it put me off early mornings! We have horses and cattle here, which I love.'

Surrounded by nature, happily aware of the changing seasons, Marieke and Sarah live inspired lives. However, this description alone may belie the hard work and dedication that it has taken to create a balance that most city dwellers only dream of. Redefining the retreat to better suit their own and their guests' needs is a continuing process. One of the ideas the women came up with was to hold live-in gourmet cooking classes. It was perhaps an obvious way to develop the retreat because of Marieke's cooking skills. They began holding the cooking schools in 1984 with the encouragement of the Council of Adult Education in Victoria.

'About half of the time is taken up with the cooking schools that I give. The agenda, theoretically, is obvious. We try to create the best possible environment for that to happen. It's set up so that people will learn, regardless of their skill or ability. They will absorb things at their own rate. Besides my own cooking weekends we also invite guest chefs in to give weekend schools. This year will be our busiest one so far.'

I looked at the list of forthcoming chefs and was impressed by the range. All the top names in food in Australia had, at some time, been invited to Howqua Dale. Marieke tells me, 'It is a total hands-on, residential situation. People don't get the access to that elsewhere. There's a whole market across a broad spectrum that want to learn and that want to be in there doing it. We choose chefs that are genuine, generous and good communicators. If people are interested and open about food they can learn a lot.'

Marieke explained that it was something the chefs also enjoyed very much. 'The chefs all say it is the best. We are not pompous about what we do here. The purpose of cooking is primarily a social one. One of the buzzes for me is to create love and get praise. It's a very nurturing thing, creating food for people. And it's fun, of course.'

The women also hold four-day schools, run by Marieke rather than guest chefs, which are very intensive and not for the faint-hearted!

Recently Marieke has targeted men specifically in her cooking classes. 'We decided to do a "men only" class once a year because we thought we weren't attracting men in sufficient numbers. It is a great hoot! Half the attendants are sent by a woman; a friend, a lover, a mother . . . by someone who knows that they would really enjoy it. Then there are the men who just love cooking and come on their own initiative. The dynamics change in every group.' Marieke finds that men often prefer to learn amongst other men because then it is less threatening to them.

Last year the women ran a fundraiser for a local environment project. Marieke said of it, 'I thought about fundraising and it occurred to me that it's always women who do it. I thought, how can we involve men in it more? So I came up with an idea to choose twelve local blokes to whom I would give five free cooking lessons. They would become volunteer chefs for a banquet for 70 people, to be held in Mansfield.

The stipulations were that I would give over the use of my kitchen for the first lesson and henceforth we would use each of theirs. They had to sell five tickets at $100 a head, which isn't an insignificant amount of money. Rural people are generally not used to paying good money for good food, so it was a new thing for them. Half of the men had never cooked before and I knew that they hadn't socialised before, so it was a rather ambitious experiment!

'On the night they created the most beautiful seven-course banquet. It was great because they came together as a team and emerged with a lot more experience and confidence. Cooking is a good vehicle with which men can develop camaraderie and companionship.'

Marieke and Sarah have diversified during the last three years into gourmet bicycle tours. They are fortunate that what pleases and interests them seems to attract other people also. This year they are planning tours of the Hunter Valley in New South Wales, Margaret River in Western Australia, along the Great Ocean Road, another in South Australia and yet another in Victoria, as yet to be decided. The *pièce de résistance* this year is a cycle tour they are planning to Portugal. Each tour takes a lot of organisation and they are designed to fit in with the best season and time for each of the destinations. The emphasis is on great food, good wine, some exercise and lots of fun.

The women are united in their view that in having an enterprise such as theirs, they have to be careful not to confuse their image. They think it is a relevant point for anyone in small business to take on board.

'Although we are quite happy and willing to expand into other related areas, it is essential that we maintain a particular and specific profile. For example, we hold what we call a "Spa" weekend once a year that invites those interested in rejuvenating themselves to come. It still involves good food, but far less of it. We also get an aerobics expert in and a masseuse. We love it! Our existing clients will tend to come to these and quite a lot of Sydneysiders. We are somewhat discreet about these special weekends though, because we don't want people to think we are a health farm, that isn't our aim. For one week though, we think it's great!'

The formula they began with is still a good one and the essence of it remains intact.

'When we began, the idea was very unusual here in Australia. An upmarket, gourmet hideaway retreat is still not your run-of-the-mill holiday experience. Howqua Dale was the first of its kind and we believe still the best of its kind. What makes it particularly special is the intimate exchange that goes on.'

When the women were thinking of opening Howqua Dale eighteen years ago they came up against resistance in some quarters.

'There is a lobby group well-known for their standard rejection of anyone applying for a liquor licence. They got on their high-horse and made some objections. It didn't stop us getting the licence though.

'Some people thought it was an odd proposal and said things like, "You're not seriously going to let those women go into business are you?" It was pioneering then. In 1977 you just didn't get good food and wine in the country. The two seemed mutually exclusive. Years later others followed our example. The journalists and press have been good to us, which certainly helps. We got support from high-profile magazines and that contributes to our profile. They support us because they feel we have a good product.'

Another thing the women cite as being invaluable is their long-kept mailing list. Sarah was busy putting well-designed pamphlets together into envelopes as we talked. It seemed that the attention to details was an integral part of the retreat.

'We have about 2000 people that we mail out to about forthcoming projects. We should probably rationalise this list more often, but at the moment we go back over it every six years. We have a 40 per cent return rate.'

Because of their diverse clientele the women have found themselves on the receiving end of much free advice. Sarah says, 'We often get high-powered businessmen coming for the weekend. When they are suitably impressed they want to give us all sorts of advice about expanding and what we could do to make it even more successful. What they seem to miss is that for us, this is success! What more could we want? We intentionally haven't overcapitalised because we want to stay here! We don't want to be bought out or merge with anyone.'

The women hire a shopper who goes to Melbourne and picks up orders they have placed during the week. They also hire help on Friday and Saturday nights and have someone clean on Mondays. Marieke says, 'We used to do it all ourselves, but now it is ridiculous to take on all that extra work. I don't want to do it anymore. I couldn't do it without my staff. I've trained so many in the past that now I've got a great team and I wouldn't want to lose them. It takes a great deal of effort to get your staff working as you want and need them to. Whatever we ask them to do we have done ourselves many times over. We don't make excessive requests.'

The stimulation city people often feel they will miss out on by living in the country is more than made up for in many ways for Marieke and Sarah. They visit Melbourne occasionally and have lively and interesting friends. The nature of their work often brings them in contact with an interesting cross-section of people and they have become good friends with many of the other locals.

'By Sunday night we are exhausted and are pleased to see our guests return home, although they are certainly not pushed out the door in any way. Some people will stay until Monday morning. We find we are still fairly revved up on Sunday night, so we'll often invite friends or family over to share the leftovers with us. We are both close to our families and we see them fairly often. In no way are we cut off.'

Sarah adds, 'Our clients have quite often become good friends. I am totally rewarded by the friends I have made, it's a very significant benefit. Many of our female friends tell us of the problems they encounter with the glass ceiling syndrome. There's no chance of me hitting a glass ceiling.'

They are both avid readers and Marieke's interest in politics keeps her views current. She is also active in women's issues through her participation in the Victorian Women's Trust. She has volunteered at least 24 hours of her time each week, for seven years.

'It is one of the only philanthropic women's organisations that I know of. They endeavour to support anything that will allow women their economic independence. They have an annual granting body which helps women to get started in business. It really is very courageous. They go guarantor for half of a loan, up to a set amount of money, in partnership with the State Bank. Unfortunately, their ability to do this has diminished somewhat because of interest rate rises.

'What we learned through the Victorian Women's Trust was that women's access to finance was the tip of the iceberg. We realised that women need not only to have access to information, they have to own their own information. Women must learn that they vote with their money, what are they going to do with their money? They need to use their economic independence to make a difference, to help change and redefine the mainstream. They are becoming shareholders for the first time in their own right. This has considerable political power.'

This was a subject the women felt passionately about and Marieke continued, 'Women currently are not suited to the mainstream, they are leaving and getting away from it. They have to take responsibility if they're going to say "it doesn't suit me", to leave behind some sort of legacy for their daughters and other women. Younger women coming up through the ranks now may not have come across the sexism of hitting a level in a company where they just can't go any further, but they will! What will they do then?

'We have many female friends in executive positions who are not taking up further opportunities for advancement within the company structures because they just don't like it. Their value systems don't match. They don't want to hold up the glass ceiling anymore. We found that women still have to toe the line in business. In order to effect change they need to have access to opportunity and training.'

Marieke and Sarah share a broad definition of success, one that includes being personally centred, having a sufficient income, and an awareness of what lies outside their own personal realm. They are keen to maintain their philosophies about life and work which have proved so beneficial over the past eighteen years.

S.R.

# Getting Down to Business

In writing *Jobs For the Girls* we had two goals in mind. One was to inspire those who always wanted to run a business of their own to go out and do it. The other was to shine a light on the realities of self-employment for women. We felt we needed to show that it isn't always easy; it is demanding and there are many pitfalls. This second objective was intended to give women a better understanding of what it is really like to run a business of their own; to put them in a position from which they can make informed decisions about whether being self-employed really suits their needs, goals and aspirations.

If, after reading about the highs and lows of these self-employed women's lives, you feel it is something you would like to try, then there is one final test of a more concrete nature that will help you assess the viability of your idea—creating a business plan.

## Leave no stone unturned

Find out as much as you can about the industry in which your business will operate. You can get information from the Bureau of Statistics, Austrade, the Office of Small Business, and many other private and government-run information services.

Collect current information about your market. Ask yourself who is your market, where are they situated, what do they buy or want, and why do they want it? The more you understand your market, the better you will be able to predict, attract and cater to its needs.

## The big picture

Once you have absorbed all the information, pinpoint exactly what you want your business to be and how you see it operating. In your plan include detailed information about your long-term goals and objectives, as well as articulating the ethics or ideals you want to uphold in the day-to-day running of the business. Project your business objectives and how you ultimately see the business and yourself.

Define the nature of your business, what you are offering and why. Write down the opportunties you see arising. Why is your business best placed to seize them?

## Who you're up against

After defining your business you must determine who your main competitors are. Who else is operating in the market and how is their product similar or different to the one you propose? Once you have studied your competition you can work out ways to distinguish yourself from them and attract your own clients.

One way people do this is by undercutting their competitors but this is an option to consider carefully. Will you sell yourself short? Remember, people will pay for good service, a great product or a fresh approach. Avoid tying yourself to a pricing structure that won't service your long-term needs or objectives.

## Hey look at me!

You can have the best product or service, but if no-one knows about it, then it's not of much use to anyone! Devise a promotional strategy that sets you apart from the rest. Consider how you want to position your product or service in the market, and use your promotion to differentiate your business idea from your competitors. Effective publicity doesn't have to be costly. Create new and exciting ways to generate awareness of your business. Look closely at some campaigns that have impressed you and think laterally about getting the word out about your business.

Setting yourself apart from others in your industry may mean doing something different in the packaging or delivery of your goods. It might also mean offering a service with a difference—friendlier, more responsive to the clients' needs, and a wider or more encompassing approach to service.

You are your business and how you come across is important too. Consider how you can best reflect the nature of your enterprise in your office set-up and in your manner and appearance.

## Dollars and cents

All the determination and best intentions will come to nothing in the business world unless you are able to finance them. It's the stumbling block of many businesses and another area that needs very careful attention. Estimate and project all your costs—leases, equipment, legal costs, production costs, staff, insurance, etc. Be generous in your estimates. How will you finance these needs? Your set-up costs and the capital needed to see you through the initial period of low cash flow must be accounted for. Can you sustain the inbalance of your financial scales through this period? Realistic projections and accurate financial assessments of your business throughout its life are essential. If you always know where the business is at financially, you will be able to respond quickly to changes in your market.

## Structures and procedures

Determine exactly the way you want your business to run. The first question involves the structure you want to adopt. Do you want to establish yourself as a sole trader, a partnership or a Limited Partnership, operate as a co-operative, or as a Proprietary Limited Company? Whichever structure you chose, the necessary applications need to be made with the appropriate bodies (Consumer Affairs, for example) and relevant documentation will have to be completed. The Office of Small Business has a thorough breakdown of the pros and cons of each of these. Investigate your options and ensure that if you are working with others, you all have similar goals.

Take time to establish office procedures and structures so that your business runs smoothly and efficiently from the very beginning. They are harder to initiate once the ball is rolling.

Ensure that you are protected in the event of a dispute. Keep a comprehensive diary that you can refer to in case of any misunderstandings. Always confirm orders, purchases or client directions in writing. It may seem a very formal way to operate, but it is perhaps the most fundamental and important aspect of running a business. You must protect yourself. Business can get nasty and not everyone remains true to their word.

## Time out

Running your own business can be all-consuming. It will take as much as you have to give and still demand more. It is very important to continually assess the true cost of running your own show. If you are constantly exhausted you will not be good for your own business and it will soon suffer. It's important to take time out to sit and think. Business is not static, it is constantly evolving. You will find that it is a fluid thing that needs periodic reassessment and re-evaluation. To do that effectively you need to stand back from your business and look at it with objective, rested eyes.

Remember your support systems and nurture and use them. Business does not have to be the focus of your whole life. As these interviews show, self-employment is important—it can give us economic independence, greater confidence and a whole lot more as well—but it can never give you everything. Nor should you expect yourself to be able to give it everything. Don't be scared to call in others if you need help with a specific problem or task—it's not a weakness, it's just smart.

*Gook luck!*

# Further Reading

Anna Borzi, *The Gender Finance Gap*, Sydney: Borzi Smythe Pty Ltd, 1994.

Lee Bryce, *The Influential Woman*, London: Piatkus, 1989.

Michael E. Gerber, *The 'E' Myth*, USA: HarperCollins, 1986.

Clive Hamilton, *The Mystic Economist*, ACT: Willow Pack Press, 1994.

Cyndi Kaplan, *There's a Lipstick in my Briefcase*, Sydney: Godiva Publishing Pty Ltd, 1993.

Amy Saltzman, *Down-shifting: Re-inventing Success on a Slower Track*, USA: HarperCollins, 1991.

Bob Sims, Sara Williams, *The Australian Small Business Guide*, Ringwood: Penguin, 1993.

Leonie V. Still, *Enterprising Women: Australian Women Managers and Entrepreneurs*, Sydney: Allen & Unwin, 1990.

Leonie V. Still, *Where To From Here?: The Managerial Woman in Transition*, Sydney: Business and Professional Publishing, 1993.

# Small Business Resource Guide

During our research we came across a vast number of courses and seminars offered by government agencies and community groups to assist people who want to establish their own businesses. Some programs were set up specifically to aid women in business or to offer advice to women who want to become self-employed.

## Aboriginal Economic Development

Offers Aboriginal family groups, individuals, groups and organisations in Western Australia support for business, community and product developments. It also offers a community stores program to assist point of sale store management and training. For Western Australian residents only.

**Aboriginal Economic Development Office**
Level 4, 220 Georges Terrace
Perth 6000
Ph: (09) 481 5033
Fax: (09) 481 7671

## AUSINDUSTRY

As part of the Commonwealth Government's Working Nation strategy, a national information hotline has been established, operating within the Department of Industry, Science and Technology. AUSINDUSTRY has a Freecall information service that aims to stay abreast of all state and Commonwealth schemes and advisory units. So if you have any specific queries or need information, this is often the best place to start. They can fax, send or give you information over the telephone about the relevant bodies to contact in your state. They also have industry specific information, for example, if you are in manufacturing they can send you information on that industry.

Freecall: 1800 026 121

## BizHelp

This is a computer-based guide to government programs that is designed to assist small businesses. It provides information about Commonwealth and state industry support bodies in particular, with some references to private sector programs. This software package is for sale and is updated quarterly.

National BIZHELP Distributor
Freecall: 1800 623 700

## Business Licence Centres

These centres offer information to intending and established business people. They provide information and application forms for all Commonwealth and state business licences.

**New South Wales**
Level 5, Stockland House
175 Castlereagh Street
Sydney 2000
Ph: (02) 286 0099
Country Freecall: 1800 463 976
Fax: (02) 261 4289

**Victoria**
100 Exhibition Street
Melbourne 3000
Ph: (03) 655 3300
Country Freecall: 1800 136 034
Fax: (03) 650 7728

**Queensland**
Level 12, 80 Albert Street
Brisbane 4000
Ph: (07) 221 1620
Country Freecall: 1800 177 885
Fax: (07) 221 3450

**Western Australia**
553 Hay Street
Perth 6000
Ph: (09) 220 0222
Country Freecall: 1800 199 125
Fax: (09) 221 1132

**Tasmania**
Level 5, ANZ Centre
22 Elizabeth Street
Hobart 7000
Ph: (002) 335 858
Tasmanian Freecall:
1800 005 262
Fax: (002) 335 800

**Northern Territory**
76 The Esplanade
Darwin 0800
Ph: (089) 89 7914
Country Freecall: 1800 193 111
Fax: (089) 89 7924

**South Australia**
74 South Terrace
Adelaide 5000

Ph: (08) 211 8599
Country Freecall: 1800 644 144
Fax: (08) 231 2742

**Australian Capital Territory**
Ground floor, North Building
London Circuit
Canberra 2601
Ph: (06) 205 0770
Fax: (06) 205 0755

## Commonwealth Government Bookshops

These provide a large range of booklets for small business owners, offering information on how to start a business, budgeting, management and growth. They are located in every capital city and also offer a mail-order service, which is particularly useful for those living in rural areas.

**New South Wales**
32 York Street
Sydney 2000
Ph: (02) 299 6737
Fax: (02) 262 1219

Shop 24
Horwood Place (off Macquarie Street)
Parramatta 2150
Ph: (02) 893 8466
Fax: (02) 893 8213

**Victoria**
347 Swanston Street
Melbourne 3000
Ph: (03) 663 3010
Fax: (03) 663 4840

**Queensland**
City Plaza
Cnr Adelaide and George Streets
Brisbane 4000
Ph: (07) 229 6822
Fax: (07) 229 1387

277 Flinders Mall
Townsville 4810
Ph: (077) 215 212
North Queensland country
Freecall: 1800 805 896
Fax: (077) 215 217

**Western Australia**
469 Wellington Street
Perth 6000
Ph: (09) 322 4737
Fax: (09) 481 4412

**Tasmania**
31 Criterion Street
Hobart 7000
Ph: (002) 341 403
Tasmanian country
Freecall: 1800 030 603
Fax: (002) 341 364

**Northern Territory**
AGPS Agent
NT Government Publications
13 Smith Street
Darwin 0800

Ph: (089) 897 152
Fax: (089) 897 972

**South Australia**
Level 3, Myer Centre
Rundle Mall
Adelaide 5000
Ph: (08) 231 0144
Fax: (08) 231 0135

**Australian Capital Territory**
70 Allinga Street
Canberra 2601
Ph: (06) 247 7211
Fax: (06) 257 1797

**Mail-order sales Australian Government Publishing Service**
GPO Box 84
Canberra 2601

**Australian Government Publishing Service phone shop**
Ph: (06) 295 4861
National Freecall: 1800 02 0049

## Koorie Women Mean Business

Offers culturally sensitive business assistance to Aboriginal and Torres Strait Islander women starting up, or already running their own businesses.

Victorian Women's Trust
2nd floor, 387 Little Bourke Street
Melbourne 3002
Ph: (03) 670 3460
Fax: (03) 642 0016

## New Enterprise Initiative Scheme (NEIS)

This is a program which helps eligible unemployed people to start their own businesses. The scheme offers training in management, business plan development, marketing and business skills. Places in these courses are limited and eligibility does not ensure acceptance to the program. There is a Formal Training Assistance allowance following completion of the course for up to 52 weeks. NEIS Allowance is equivalent to Jobsearch or Newstart income. Contact your local Department of Employment, Education and Training office or the Commonwealth Employment Service (CES) for details.

## Small Business Advisory Centres

These centres offer counselling and advice to small business owners with the aim of increasing the success rate of small businesses through management advice. They aim to provide impartial information on marketing, planning and financial management including applying for loans.

**New South Wales**
Office of Small Business
Level 3, Enterprise House
1 Fitzwilliam Street
Parramatta 2150
Ph: (02) 895 0555
Country Freecall: 1800 451 151
Fax: (02) 635 6859

**Victoria**
Small Business Victoria
Level 2, 100 Exhibition Street
Melbourne 3000
Ph: (03) 655 3300
Country Freecall: 1800 136 034
Fax: (03) 650 7728

**Queensland**
Small Business Development Corporation
Level 5, STC House
545 Queen Street
Brisbane 4000
Ph: (07) 834 6789
Country callers
Freecall: 1800 177 324
Fax: (07) 832 3827

**Western Australia**
Small Business Development Corporation
553 Hay Street
Perth 6000
Ph: (09) 220 0222
Country callers
Freecall: 1800 199 125
Fax: (09) 221 1132

**Tasmania**
Small Business Services
Level 5, ANZ Centre
22 Elizabeth Street
Hobart 7000
Ph: (002) 335 712
Tasmanian Freecall:
1800 030 688
Fax: (002) 335 800

**Northern Territory**
Territory Business Centre
Ground floor, Development House
76 The Esplanade
Darwin 0800
Ph: (089) 89 7916
Country callers
Freecall: 1800 193 111
Fax: (089) 89 7924

**Australian Capital Territory**
Business Services Centre
Ground floor, North Building
London Circuit
Canberra City 2600
Ph: (06) 205 0770
Fax: (06) 205 0755

**South Australia**
The Business Centre
145 South Terrace
Adelaide 5000
Ph: (08) 233 4600
South Australian
Freecall: 1800 188 018
Fax: (08) 231 1199

## Victorian Women's Trust

The Trust aims to support any measures—political, personal or legislative—which aid women in the pursuit of economic independence.

2nd floor, 387 Little Bourke Street
Melbourne 3002
Ph: (03) 670 3460
Fax: (03) 642 0016

## Women's Enterprise Connection

Provides practical training and assistance through the New Enterprise Initiative Scheme, to help women starting out or already established, in small business.

Women's Enterprise Connection
2nd floor, 387 Little Bourke Street
Melbourne 3000
Ph: (03) 670 3674
Fax: (03) 642 0016

## Women in Business Mentor Program

Many states offer schemes specifically for women. The Women in Business Mentor Program offers a linking service for those new to small business with women who have more experience. The Mentor Program links women in non-competing industries to enable them to share knowledge and experiences. The program hopes to establish a network of women in business with the idea that they will provide role models for other female entrepreneurs. Check with your local Small Business Advisory Office to find out if this program is available in your state.

## Women's Information and Referral Service (WIRC)

This service provides free information on a range of issues affecting women.

Ground floor, North Building
London Circuit
Canberra ACT 2061
Ph: (06) 205 1076 /75

## Working Women's Centre

In the 1993/94 Federal budget, the Commonwealth Government announced that it would establish Working Women's Centres nationally. The centres now assist women on work related issues, with a particular emphasis on the needs of women from non-English speaking backgrounds, Aboriginal and Torres Strait Islander women and those living in remote or rural areas.

The centres are available to all women, but each has a different emphasis according to their particular geographical and socio-economic situations.

**NSW Working Women's Centre**
Suites 1–4, 1 Barrack Lane
Parramatta 2150
Ph: (02) 689 2233
Fax: (02) 689 2841
Freecall: 1800 082 166

**Queensland Working Women's Centre**
Level 1, Mary Street
Brisbane 4000
Ph: (07) 224 6117
Fax: (07) 224 6111
Freecall: 1800 621 458

**Tasmanian Working Women's Centre**
160 Harrington Street
Hobart 7000
Ph: (002) 34 7007
Fax: (002) 34 3219
Freecall: 1800 644 589

**Northern Territory Working Women's Centre**
Shop 5, Anthony Plaza
Smith Street Mall
Darwin 0800
Ph: (089) 810 655
Fax: (089) 810 433
Freecall: 1800 817 055

**South Australian Working Women's Centre**
Norwich Centre
Ground floor, 55 King William Road
North Adelaide 5006
Ph: (08) 267 4000
Fax: (08) 267 4111
Freecall: 1800 652 697

## Youth Business Initiative Schemes

These schemes are offered in some states and offer advice and assistance to young people wanting to start a small business. Ask at your local CES or Business Advice Centre for details.

# The Westpac/Random House
# Best Business Plan
# Competition

*Enter the Westpac/Random House Best Business Plan Competition and win $10 000 towards starting your very own business!*

To win this fabulous prize, you will need to compile a comprehensive and detailed business plan based on your own idea for a small business. Your idea must be original.

In your submission you will need to consider all facets of running a business, including the planning, financing, production and marketing of your product or service. The winning business plan will be innovative, economically viable and practicable. Information on putting together a business plan is contained in *Jobs for the Girls*, written by Caro Llewellyn and Skye Rogers.

Entries will be judged by a panel which will include the authors of *Jobs for the Girls*, representatives of Westpac and Random House and a member of the business community.

Send your entry together with contact details to *The Westpac/Random House Best Business Plan Competition*, Random House Australia, 20 Alfred Street, Milsons Point, NSW 2061.

## Conditions of Entry

1. Information on prizes and how to enter forms part of these conditions of entry.
2. Employees of Random House Australia and their immediate families are ineligible to enter.
3. Employees of Westpac Banking Corporation ARBN 007 457 141, its subsidiaries and related companies, and their immediate families are ineligible to enter.
4. The first and only prize is $10 000 cash.
5. The promoter is Random House Australia Pty. Ltd., A.C.N. 004 721 797, 20 Alfred St., Milsons Point, NSW, 2061. All decisions made by the promoter concerning the competition including the determination of the winner shall be binding and final and no correspondence will be entered into.
6. Entries to be sent to Random House(address given) by midnight February 1, 1996 (closure date).
7. The winner will be announced on Friday, March 1, 1996.
8. The winner will be notified in writing and result published in *The Australian* newspaper on Friday, March 8, 1996.